Writings of
Daniel DeLeon

A Collection of Essays by One of the Founders
of American Revolutionary Socialism

Daniel DeLeon

Red and Black Publishers, St Petersburg, Florida

Library of Congress Cataloging-in-Publication Data

De Leon, Daniel, 1852-1914.
  [Essays. Selections]
  Writings of Daniel DeLeon : a collection of essays by one of the founders of
American revolutionary socialism / Daniel DeLeon.
      p. cm.
   ISBN 978-1-934941-38-6
1. Socialism--United States. 2. Labor unions and communism--United States. I. Title.
   HX86.D455 2008
   335.0092--dc22

                                                                        2008026408

Red and Black Publishers, PO Box 7542, St Petersburg, Florida, 33734

Contact us at: info@RedandBlackPublishers.com

      Printed and manufactured in the United States of America

Contents

Reform Or Revolution?

An address delivered at Wells' Memorial Hall, Boston, January 26, 1896

Mr. Chairman and Workingmen of Boston:

I have got into the habit of putting two and two together, and drawing my conclusions. When I was invited to come to Boston, the invitation reached me at about the same time as an official information that a reorganization of the party was contemplated in the city of Boston. I put the two together and I drew the conclusion that part of the purpose of the invitation was for me to come here to tell you upon what lines we in New York organized, and upon what lines we "wicked" Socialists of New York and Brooklyn gave the capitalist class last November the 16,000-vote black eye.

Organization

It has become an axiom that, to accomplish results, organization is requisite. Nevertheless, there is "organization" and "organization." That this is so appears clearly from the fact that the "pure-and-simplers" have been going about saying to the workers: "Organize! Organize!" and after they have been saying that, and have been "organizing" and "organizing" for the past thirty or forty years, we find that they are virtually where they started, if not worse off; that their "organization" partakes of the nature of the lizard, whose tail destroys what his foreparts build up.

I think the best thing I can do to aid you in organizing is to give you the principles upon which the Socialist sections of New York and Brooklyn are organized. To do that I shall go back to basic principles, and in explaining to you the difference there is between reform and revolution, I shall be able, step by step, to point out how it is we are organized, and how you ought to be.

I shall assume—it is a wise course for a speaker to adopt—that none in this audience knows what is "reform" and what is "revolution." Those who are posted will understand me all the better; those who are not will follow me all the easier.

We hear people talk about the "reform forces," about "evolution" and about "revolution" in ways that are highly mixed. Let us clear up our terms. Reform means a change of externals; revolution—peaceful or bloody, the peacefulness or the bloodiness of it cuts no figure whatever in the essence of the question—means a change from within.

Reform

Take, for instance, a poodle. You can reform him in a lot of ways. You can shave his whole body and leave a tassel at the tip of his tail; you may bore a hole through each ear, and tie a blue bow on one and a red bow on the other; you may put a brass collar around his neck with your initials on, and a trim little blanket on his back; yet, throughout, a poodle he was and a poodle he remains. Each of these changes probably wrought a corresponding change in the poodle's life. When shorn of all his hair except a tassel at the tail's tip he was owned by a wag who probably cared only for the fun he could get out of his pet; when he appears gaily decked in bows, probably his young mistress' attachment is of tenderer sort; when later we see him in the fancier's outfit, the treatment he receives and the uses he is put to may be yet again and probably are, different. Each of these transformations or stages may mark a veritable epoch in the poodle's existence. And yet, essentially, a poodle he was, a poodle he is and a poodle he will remain.

That is reform.

Revolution

But when we look back myriads of years, or project ourselves into far—future physical cataclysms, and trace the development of animal life from the invertebrate to the vertebrate, from the lizard to the bird, from the quadruped and mammal till we come to the prototype of the poodle, and finally reach the poodle himself, and so forward—then do we find radical changes at each step, changes from within that alter the very essence of his being, and that put, or will put, upon him each time a stamp that alters the very system of his existence.

That is revolution.

So with society. Whenever a change leaves the internal mechanism untouched, we have reform; whenever the internal mechanism is changed, we have revolution.

Of course, no internal change is possible without external manifestations. The internal changes denoted by the revolution or evolution of the lizard into the eagle go accompanied with external marks. So with society. And therein lies one of the pitfalls into which dilettantism or "reforms" invariably tumble. They have noticed that externals change with internals; and they rest satisfied with mere external changes, without looking behind the curtain. But of this more presently.

We Socialists are not reformers; we are revolutionists. We Socialists do not propose to change forms. We care nothing for forms. We want a change of the inside of the mechanism of society, let the form take care of itself. We see in England a crowned monarch; we see in Germany a sceptered emperor; we see in this country an uncrowned president, and we fail to see the essential difference between Germany, England or America. That being the case, we are skeptics as to forms. We are like grown children, in the sense that we like to look at the inside of things and find out what is there.

One more preliminary explanation. Socialism is lauded by some as an angelic movement, by others it is decried as a devilish scheme. Hence you find the Gomperses blowing hot and cold on the subject; and Harry Lloyd, with whose capers, to your sorrow, you are more familiar than I, pronouncing himself a Socialist in one place, and in another running Socialism down. Socialism is neither an aspiration of angels nor a plot of devils. Socialism moves with its feet firmly planted in the ground and its head not lost in the clouds; it takes science by the hand, asks her to lead and goes whithersoever she points. It does not take science by the hand, saying: "I shall follow you to the end of the road if it please me." No! It takes her by the hand and says: "Whithersoever thou leadest, thither am I bound to go." The Socialists, consequently, move as intelligent men; we do not mutiny because, instead of having wings, we have arms, and cannot fly as we would wish.

What then, with an eye single upon the differences between reform and revolution, does Socialism mean? To point out that, I shall take up two or three of what I may style the principal nerve centers of the movement.

Government — The State

One of these principal nerve centers is the question of "government" or the question of the "State." How many of you have not seen upon the shelves of our libraries books that treat upon the "History of the State"; upon the "Limitations of the State"; upon "What the State Should do and What It Should Not Do"; upon the "Legitimate Functions of the State," and so on into infinity? Nevertheless, there is not one among all of these, the products, as they all are, of the vulgar and superficial character of capitalist thought, that fathoms the question or actually defines the "State." Not until we reach the great works of the American Morgan, of Marx and Engels, and of other Socialist philosophers, is the matter handled with that scientific lucidity that proceeds from facts, leads to sound conclusions and breaks the way to practical work. Not until you know and understand the history of the "State" and of "government" will you understand one of the cardinal principles upon which Socialist organization rests, and will you be in a condition to organize successfully.

We are told that "government" has always been as it is today and always will be. This is the first fundamental error of what Karl Marx justly calls capitalistic vulgarity of thought.

When man started on his career, after having got beyond the state of the savage, he realized that cooperation was a necessity to him. He understood that together with others he could face his enemies in a better way than alone; he could hunt, fish, fight more successfully. Following the instructions of the great writer Morgan — the only great and original American writer upon this question — we look to the

Indian communities, the Indian settlements, as a type of the social system that our ancestors, all of them, without exception, went through at some time.

The Indian lived in the community condition. The Indian lived under a system of common property. As Franklin described it, in a sketch of the history and alleged sacredness of private property, there was no such thing as private property among the Indians. They cooperated, worked together, and they had a central directing authority among them. In the Indian communities we find that central directing authority consisting of the "sachems." It makes no difference how that central directing authority was elected; there it was. But note this: its function was to direct the cooperative or collective efforts of the communities and, in so doing, it shared actively in the productive work of the communities. Without its work, the work of the communities would not have been done.

When, in the further development of society, the tools of production grew and developed — grew and developed beyond the point reached by the Indian; when the art of smelting iron ore was discovered; when thereby that leading social cataclysm, wrapped in the mists of ages, yet discernible, took place that rent former communal society in twain along the line of sex, the males being able, the females unable, to wield the tool of production — then society was cast into a new mold; the former community, with its democratic equality of rights and duties, vanishes and a new social system turns up, divided into two sections, the one able, the other unable, to work at production. The line that separated these two sections, being at first the line of sex, could, in the very nature of things, not yet be sharp or deep. Yet, notwithstanding, in the very shaping of these two sections — one able, the other unable, to feed itself — we have the first premonition of the classes, of class distinctions, of the division of society into the independent and the dependent, into master and slaves, ruler and ruled.

Simultaneously, with this revolution we find the first changes in the nature of the central directing authority, of that body whose original function was to share in, by directing, production.

Just as soon as economic equality is destroyed and the economic classes crop up in society, the functions of the central directing authority gradually begin to change, until finally, when, after a long range of years, moving slowly at first and then with the present hurricane velocity under capitalism proper, the tool has developed further, and further, and still further, and has reached its present fabulous perfection and magnitude;

When, through its private ownership, the tool has wrought a revolution within a revolution by dividing society, no longer along the line of sex, but strictly along the line of ownership or non-ownership of the land on and the tool with which to work;

When the privately owned, mammoth tool of today has reduced more than fifty-two percent of our population to the state of being utterly unable to feed without first selling themselves into wage slavery, while it at the same time saps the ground from under about thirty-nine percent of our people, the middle class, whose puny tools, small capital, render them certain victims of competition with the large capitalist, and makes them desperate;

When the economic law that asserts itself under the system of private ownership of the tool has concentrated these private owners into about eight percent of the nation's inhabitants, has thereby enabled this small capitalist class to live without toil, and to compel the majority, the class of the proletariat, to toil without living;

When, finally, it has come to the pass in which our country now finds itself, that, as was stated in Congress, ninety-four percent of the taxes are spent in "protecting property" — the property of the trivially small capitalist class — and not in protecting life;

When, in short, the privately owned tool has wrought this work, and the classes — the idle rich and the working poor — are in full bloom, then the central directing authority of old stands transformed; its pristine functions of aiding in, by directing, production have been supplanted by the functions of holding down the dependent, the slave, the ruled, i.e., the working class.

Then, and not before, lo, the State, the modern State, the capitalist State! Then, lo, the government, the modern government, the capitalist government — equipped mainly, if not solely, with the means of suppression, of oppression, of tyranny!

In sight of these manifestations of the modern State, the anarchist — the rose-water and the dirty-water variety alike — shouts: "Away with all central directing authority; see what it does; it can only do mischief; it always did mischief!" But Socialism is not anarchy. Socialism does not, like the chicken in the fable, just out of the shell, start with the knowledge of that day. Socialism rejects the premises and the conclusions of anarchy upon the State and upon government. What Socialism says is: "Away with the economic system that alters the beneficent functions of the central directing authority from an aid to production into a means of oppression." And it proceeds to show that, when the instruments of production shall be owned no longer by the minority, but shall be restored to the Commonwealth; that when, as a result of this, no longer the minority or any portion of the people shall be in poverty and classes, class distinctions and class rule shall, as they necessarily must, have vanished, that then the central directing authority will lose all its repressive functions and is bound to reassume the functions it had in the old communities of our ancestors, become again a necessary aid, and assist in production.

The Socialist, in the brilliant simile of Karl Marx, sees that a lone fiddler in his room needs no director; he can rap himself to order, with his fiddle to his shoulder, and start his dancing tune, and stop whenever he likes. But just as soon as you have an orchestra, you must also have an orchestra director — a central directing authority. If you don't, you may have a Salvation Army powwow, you may have a Louisiana Negro breakdown; you may have an orthodox Jewish synagogue, where every man sings in whatever key he likes, but you won't have harmony — impossible.

It needs this central directing authority of the orchestra master to rap all the players to order at a given moment; to point out when they shall begin; when to have these play louder, when to have those play softer; when to put in this instrument, when to silence that; to regulate the time of all and preserve the accord. The orchestra director is not an oppressor, nor is his baton an insignia of tyranny; he is not there to bully anybody; he is as necessary or important as any or all of the members of the orchestra.

Our system of production is in the nature of an orchestra. No one man, no one town, no one state, can be said any longer to be independent of the other; the whole people of the United States, every individual therein, is dependent and interdependent upon all the others. The nature of the machinery of production; the subdivision of labor, which aids cooperation and which cooperation fosters, and which is necessary to the plentifulness of production that civilization requires, compel a harmonious working together of all departments of labor, and thence compel the establishment of a central directing authority, of an orchestral director, so to speak, of the orchestra of the cooperative commonwealth.

Such is the State or government that the Socialist revolution carries in its womb. Today, production is left to anarchy, and only tyranny, the twin sister of anarchy, is organized.

Socialism, accordingly, implies organization; organization implies directing authority; and the one and the other are strict reflections of the revolutions undergone by the tool of production. Reform, on the other hand, skims the surface, and with "referendums" and similar devices limits itself to external tinkerings.

Materialism — Morality

The second nerve center of Socialism that will serve to illustrate the difference between reform and revolution is its materialistic groundwork.

Take, for instance, the history of slavery. All of our ancestors - this may shock some of you, but it is a fact all the same — all of our ancestors were cannibals at one time. The human race, in its necessity to seek for food, often found it easier to make a raid and take from others the food they had gathered. In those olden, olden days of the barbarism of our ancestors, when they conquered a people and took away its property, they had no further use for the conquered; they killed them, spitted them over a good fire, roasted and ate them up. It was a simple and the only profitable way known of disposing of prisoners of war. They did with their captives very much what bees do yet; when they have raided and conquered a hive they ruthlessly kill every single denizen of the captured hive.

Our ancestors continued cannibals until their social system had developed sufficiently to enable them to keep their prisoners under control. From that moment they found it more profitable to keep their prisoners of war alive and turn them into slaves to work for them, than it was to kill them off and eat them. With that stage of material development, cannibalism was dropped. From the higher material plane on which our ancestors then stood, their moral vision enlarged and they presently realized that it was immoral to eat up a human being.

Cannibalism disappeared to make room for chattel slavery. And what do we see? Watch the process of "moral development" in this country — the classic ground in many ways to study history in, for the reason that the whole development of mankind can be seen here, portrayed in a few years, so to speak. You know how, today, the Northern people put on airs of morality on the score of having "abolished chattel slavery," the "traffic in human flesh," "gone down South and fought, and bled, to free the Negro," etc., etc. Yet we know that just as soon as manufacturing was introduced in the North, the North found that it was too expensive to own the Negro and take care of him; that it was much cheaper not to own the worker; and, consequently, that they "religiously," "humanely" and "morally" sold their slaves to the South, while they transformed the white people of the North, who had no means of production in their own hands, into wage slaves, and mercilessly ground them down. In the North, chattel slavery disappeared just as soon as the development of machinery rendered the institution unprofitable. The immorality of chattel slavery became clear to the North just as soon as, standing upon that higher plane that its higher material development raised it to, it acquired a better vision. The benighted South, on the contrary, that had no machinery, remained with eyes shut, and she stuck to slavery till the slave was knocked out of her fists.

Guided by the light of this and many similar lessons of history, Socialism builds upon the principle that the "moral sentiment," as illustrated by the fate of the slave, is not the cause, but a powerful aid to revolutions. The moral sentiment is to a movement as important as the sails are to a ship. Nevertheless, important though sails are, unless a ship is well laden, unless she is soundly, properly and scientifically constructed, the more sails you pile on and spread out, the surer she is to capsize. So with the organizations that are to carry out a revolution. Unless your Socialist organizations are as sound as a bell; unless they are as intolerant as science; unless they will plant themselves squarely on the principle that two and two make four and under no circumstances allow that they make five, the more feeling you put into them, the surer they are to capsize and go down. On the contrary, load your revolutionary ship with the proper lading of science; hold her strictly to the lodestar; try no monkeyshines and no dillyings and dallyings with anything that is not strictly scientific, or with any man who does not stand on our uncompromisingly scientific platform; do that, and then unfurl freely the sails of morality; then the more your sails, the better off your ship; but not unless you do that, will you be safe, or can you prevail.

Socialism knows that revolutionary upheavals and transformations proceed from the rock bed of material needs. With a full appreciation of and veneration for moral impulses that are balanced with scientific knowledge, it eschews, looks with just suspicion upon and gives a wide berth to balloon morality, or be it those malarial fevers that reformers love to dignify with the name of "moral feelings."

The Class Struggle

A third nerve center of Socialism by which to distinguish reform from revolution is its manly, aggressive posture.

The laws that rule sociology run upon lines parallel with and are the exact counterparts of those that natural science has established in biology.

In the first place, the central figure in biology is the species, not the individual specimen. In sociology, the economic classes take the place of the species in biology. Consequently, that is the central figure on the field of sociology that corresponds to and represents the species on the field of biology.

In the second place, struggle, and not piping peace; assimilation by the ruthless process of the expulsion of all elements that are not fit for assimilation, and not external coalition—such are the laws of growth in biology, and such are and needs must be the laws of growth in sociology.

Hence, Socialism recognizes in modern society the existence of a struggle of classes, and the line that divides the combatants to be the economic line that separates the interests of the property-holding capitalist class from the interests of the propertiless class of the proletariat. As a final result of this, Socialism, with the Nazarene, spurns as futile, if not wicked, the method of cajolery and seduction, or the crying of "Peace, peace, where there is no peace," and cuts a clean swath, while reform is eternally entangled in its course of charming, luring, decoying.

Illustrations

Let me now give you a few specific illustrations — based upon this general sketch — that may help to point out more clearly the sharp differences there are between reform and revolution, and the grave danger there lurks behind confounding the two.

You remember I referred to the fact that internal, i.e., revolutionary changes, are always accompanied with external changes of some sort, and that therein lay a pitfall into which reform invariably tumbled, inasmuch as reform habitually rests satisfied with externals, allows itself to be deceived with appearances. For instance:

The Socialist revolution demands, among other things, the public ownership of all the means of transportation. But, in itself, the question of ownership affects only external forms: The Post Office is the common property of the people, and yet the real workers in that department are mere wage slaves. In the mouth of the Socialist, of the revolutionist, the internal fact, the cardinal truth, that for which alone we fight, and which alone is entitled to all we can give to it - that is the abolition of the system of wage slavery under which the proletariat is working. Now, up step the Populists — the dupers, not the duped among them with a plan to nationalize the railroads. The standpoint from which they proceed is that of middle class interests as against the interests of the upper capitalists or monopolists. The railroad monopolists are now fleecing the middle class; these want to turn the tables upon their exploiters; they want to abolish them, wipe them out, and appropriate unto themselves the fleecings of the working class which the railroad monopolists now monopolize. With this reactionary class interest in mind, the duper-Populist steps forward and holds this plausible language:

"We, too, want the nationalization of the roads; we are going your way; join us!"

The reform straws are regularly taken in by this seeming truth; they are carried off their feet; and they are drawn heels over head into the vortex of capitalist conflicts. Not so the revolutionist. His answer follows sharp and clear:

"Excuse me! Yes you do want to nationalize the railroads, but only as a reform; we want nationalization as a revolution. You do not propose, while we are fixedly determined, to relieve the railroad workers of the yoke of wage slavery under which they now grunt and sweat. By your scheme of nationalization, you do not propose, on the contrary, you oppose all relief to the workers, and you have set dogs at the heels of our propagandists in Chautauqua County, N.Y., whenever it was proposed to reduce the hours of work of the employees."

While we, the revolutionists, seek the emancipation of the working class and the abolition of all exploitation, duper-Populism seeks to rivet the chains of wage slavery more firmly upon the proletariat. There is no exploiter like the middle class exploiter. Carnegie may fleece his workers—he has 20,000 of them—of only fifty cents a day and yet net, from sunrise to sunset, $10,000 profits; the banker with plenty of money to lend can thrive with a trifling shaving of each individual note; but the apple woman on the street corner must make a hundred and five hundred percent profit to exist. For the same reason, the middle class, the employer of few hands, is the worst, the bitterest, the most inveterate, the most relentless exploiter of the wage slave.

You may now realize what a grave error that man will incur who will rest satisfied with external appearance. Reform is invariably a cat's paw for dupers; revolution never.

Take now an illustration of the revolutionary principle that the material plane on which man stands determines his perception of morality. One man writes to *The People* office: "You speak about the immorality of capitalism, don't you know that it was immoral to demonetize silver?" Another writes: "How queer to hear you talk about immorality; don't you know it is a type of immorality to have a protective tariff?" He wants free trade. A third one writes: "Oh, sir, I admire the moral sentiment that inspires you, but how can you make fun of prohibition? Don't you know that if a man is drunk, he will beat his wife and kill his children?" And so forth. Each of these looks at morality from the standpoint of his individual or class interests. The man who owns a silver mine considers it the height of immorality to demonetize silver. The importer who can be benefited by free trade thinks it a heinous crime against good morals to set up a high tariff. The man whose wage slaves come on Monday somewhat boozy, so that he cannot squeeze, pilfer out of them as much wealth as he would like to, becomes a pietistic prohibitionist.

One of our great men, a really great man, a man whom I consider a glory to the United States—Artemus Ward—with that genuine, not bogus, keen Yankee eye of his saw, and with that master pen of his excellently illustrated this scientific truth, with one of his yarns. He claimed, you know, that he traveled through the country with a collection of wax figures representing the great men and criminals of the time. On one occasion he was in Maine. At about that time a little boy, Wilkins, had killed his uncle. Of course, the occurrence created a good deal of a sensation, and Artemus Ward tells us that, having an eye to the main chance, he got up a wax figure which he exhibited as Wilkins, the boy murderer. A few years later, happening again in the same Maine village, it occurred to him that the boy Wilkins had proved a great attraction in the place. He hunted around among his figures, found none small enough to represent a boy, and he took the wax figure that he used to represent Captain Kidd with, labeled that "Wilkins, the Boy Murderer," and opened his booth. The people flocked in, paid their fifteen cents admission, and Artemus started to explain his figures. When he reached the "Boy Murderer," and was expatiating upon the lad's wickedness, a man in the audience rose, and in a rasping, nasal voice, remarked: "How is that? Three years ago you showed us the boy, Wilkins, he was a boy then, and died since; how can he now be a big man?" Thereupon Artemus says: "I was angry at the rascal, and I should have informed against him, and have him locked up for treason to the flag."

With the master hand of genius Artemus here exposed the material bases of capitalist "patriotism," and pointed to the connection between the two. The material plane, on which the fraudulent showman stood, determined his moral impulse on patriotism.

The higher the economic plane on which a class stands, and the sounder its understanding of material conditions, all the broader will its horizon be, and, consequently, all the purer and truer its morality. Hence it is that, today, the highest moral vision, and the truest withal, is found in the camp of the revolutionary proletariat. Hence, also, you will perceive the danger of the moral cry that goes not hand in hand with sound knowledge. The morality of reform is the corruscation of the *ignis fatuus*; the morality of revolution is lighted by the steady light of science.

Take another illustration, this time on the belligerent poise of Socialism, to distinguish reform from revolution.

The struggles that mark the movements of man have ever proceeded from the material interests, not of individuals, but of classes. The class interests on top, when rotten—ripe for overthrow, succumbed, when they did succumb, to nothing short of the class interests below. Individuals from the former class frequently took leading and invaluable part on the side of the latter, and individuals of the latter regularly played the role of traitors to civilization by siding with the former, as did, for instance, the son of the venerable Franklin when he sided with the British. Yet in both sets of instances, the combatants stood arrayed upon platforms that represented opposite class interests. Revolutions triumphed, whenever they did triumph, by asserting themselves and marching straight upon their goal. On the other hand, the fate of Wat Tyler ever is the fate of reform. The rebels, in this instance, were weak enough to allow themselves to be wheedled into placing their movement into the hands of Richard II, who promised "relief"—and brought it by marching the men to the gallows.

You will perceive the danger run by movements that—instead of accepting no leadership except such as stands squarely upon their own demands—rest content with and entrust themselves to "promises of relief." Revolution, accordingly, stands on its own bottom, hence it cannot be overthrown; reform leans upon others, hence its downfall is certain.

Of all revolutionary epochs, the present draws sharpest the line between the conflicting class interests. Hence, the organizations of the revolution of our generation must be the most uncompromising of any that yet appeared on the stage of history. The program of this revolution consists not in any one detail. It demands the unconditional surrender of the capitalist system and its system of wage slavery; the total extinction of class rule is its object. Nothing short of that—whether as a first, a temporary, or any other sort of step can at this late date receive recognition in the camp of the modern revolution.

Upon these lines we organized in New York and Brooklyn, and prospered; upon these lines we have compelled the respect of the foe. And I say unto you, go ye, and do likewise.

The Reformer—The Revolutionist

And now to come to, in a sense, the most important, surely the most delicate, of any of the various subdivisions of this address.

We know that movements make men, but men make movements. Movements cannot exist unless they are carried on by men; in the last analysis it is the human hand and the human brain that serve as the instruments of revolutions.

How shall the revolutionist be known? Which are the marks of the reformer? In New York a reformer cannot come within smelling distance of us but we can tell him. We know him; we have experienced him; we know what mischief he can do; and he cannot get within our ranks if we can help it. He must organize an opposition organization, and thus fulfill the only good mission he has in the scheme of nature—pull out from among us whatever reformers may be hiding there.

But you may not yet be familiar with the cut of the reformer's jib. You may not know the external marks of the revolutionist. Let me mention them.

The modern revolutionist, i.e., the Socialist, must, in the first place, by reason of the sketch I presented to you upon the development of the State, necessarily work in organization, with all that that implies. In this you have the first characteristic that distinguishes the revolutionist from the reformer; the reformer spurns organization; his symbol is "Five Sore Fingers on a Hand"—far apart from one another.

The modern revolutionist knows full well that man is not superior to principle, that principle is superior to man, but he does not fly off the handle with the maxim and thus turn the maxim into absurdity. He firmly couples the maxim with this other; that no principle is superior to the movement or organization that puts it and upholds it in the field.

The engineer knows that steam is a powerful thing, but he also knows that unless the steam is in the boiler, and unless there is a knowing hand at the throttle, the steam will either evaporate or the boiler will burst. Hence, you will never hear an engineer say: "Steam is the thing," and then kick the locomotive off the track. Similarly, the revolutionist recognizes that the organization that is propelled by correct principles is as the boiler that must hold the steam, or the steam will amount to nothing. He knows that in the revolution demanded by our age, organization must be the incarnation of principle. Just the reverse of the reformer, who will ever be seen mocking at science, the revolutionist will not make a distinction between the organization and the principle. He will say: "The principle and the organization are one."

A Western judge, on one occasion, had to do with a quibbling lawyer, who was defending a burglar — you know what a burglar is-- and rendered a decision that was supremely wise. The prisoner was charged with having stuck his hand and arm through a window and stolen something, whatever it was. The judge sentenced the man to the penitentiary. Said the lawyer: "I demur; the whole of the man did not break through the window; it was only his arm." "Well," said the judge, "I will sentence the arm; let him do with the body what he likes." As the man and his arm were certainly one, and as the man would not wrench his arm out of its socket and separate it from the body, he quietly went to the penitentiary, and I hope is there yet to serve as a permanent warning against "reform science."

Again, the modern revolutionist knows that in order to accomplish results or promote principle, there must be unity of action. He knows that, if we do not go in a body and hang together, we are bound to hang separate. Hence, you will ever see the revolutionist submit to the will of the majority; you will always see him readiest to obey; he recognizes that obedience is the badge of civilized man. The savage does not know the word. The word "obedience" does not exist in the vocabulary of any language until its people got beyond the stage of savagery. Hence, also, you will never find the revolutionist putting himself above the organization. The opposite conduct is an unmistakable earmark of reformers.

The revolutionist recognizes that the present machinery and methods of production render impossible — and well it is they do — the individual freedom of man such as our savage ancestors knew the thing; that today, the highest individual freedom must go hand in hand with collective freedom; and none such is possible without a central directing authority. Standing upon this vigor — imparting high plane of civilization, the revolutionist is virile and self-reliant, in striking contrast with the mentally sickly and, therefore, suspicious reformer. Hence the cry of "Bossism!" is as absent from the revolutionist's lips as it is a feature on those of the reformer.

Another leading mark of the revolutionist, which is paralleled with the opposite mark on the reformer, is the consistency, hence morality, of the former, and the inconsistency, hence immorality, of the latter. As the revolutionist proceeds upon facts, he is truthful and his course is steady; on the other hand, the reformer will ever be found prevaricating and in perpetual contradiction of himself. The reformer, for instance, is ever vaporing against "tyranny," and yet watch him; give him rope enough and you will always see him straining to be the top man in the shebang, the man on horseback, the autocrat, whose whim shall be law. The reformer is ever prating about "morality," but just give him a chance, and you will catch him every time committing the most immoral acts, as, for instance, sitting in judgment on cases in which he himself is a *particeps criminis*, or countenancing and profiting by such acts. The reformer's mouth is ever full with the words "individual freedom," yet in the whole catalogue of defiers of individual freedom, the reformer vies with the frontmost.

Finally, you will find the reformer ever flying off at a tangent, while the revolutionist sticks to the point. The scatterbrained reformer is ruled by a centrifugal, the revolutionist by a centripetal force.

Somebody has aptly said that in social movements an evil principle is like a scorpion; it carries the poison that will kill it. So with the reformers; they carry the poison of disintegration that breaks them up into twos and ones and thus deprives them in the end of all power for mischief; while the power of the revolutionist to accomplish results grows with the gathering strength that its posture insures to him.

The lines upon which we organize in New York and Brooklyn are, accordingly, directly opposed to those of reformers. We recognize the need of organization with all that that implies—of organization, whose scientific basis and uncompromising posture inspire respect in the foe, and confidence in those who belong with us. This is the *sine qua non* for success.

Right here allow me to digress for a moment. Keep in mind where I break off that we may hitch on again all the easier.

Did you ever stop to consider why it is that in this country where opportunities are so infinitely superior, the working class movement is so far behind, whereas in Europe, despite the disadvantages there, it is so far ahead of us? Let me tell you.

In the first place, the tablets of the minds of our working class are scribbled all over by every charlatan who has let himself loose. In Europe, somehow or other, the men who were able to speak respected and respect themselves a good deal more than most of our public speakers do here. They studied first; they first drank deep at the fountain of science; and not until they felt their feet firmly planted on the rock bed of fact and reason, did they go before the masses. So it happens that the tablets of the minds of the European, especially the Continental working classes, have lines traced upon them by the master hands of the ages. Hence every succeeding new movement brought forward by the tides of time found its work paved for and easier. But here, one charlatan after another who could speak glibly, and who could get money from this, that, or the other political party, would go among the people and upon the tablets of the minds of the working classes he scribbled his crude text. So it happens that today, when the apostle of Socialism goes before our people, he cannot do what his compeers in Europe do, take a pencil and draw upon the minds of his hearers the letters of science; no, he must first clutch a sponge, a stout one, and wipe clean the pot-hooks that the charlatans have left there. Not until he has done that can he begin to preach and teach successfully.

Then, again, with this evil of mis-education, the working class of this country suffers from another. The charlatans, one after the other, set up movements that proceeded upon lines of ignorance; movements that were denials of scientific facts; movements that bred hopes in the hearts of the people; yet movements that had to collapse. A movement must be perfectly sound, and scientifically based or it cannot stand. A falsely based movement is like a lie, and a lie cannot survive. All these false movements came to grief, and what was the result? - disappointment, stagnation, diffidence, hopelessness in the masses.

The Knights of Labor, meant by Uriah Stephens, as he himself admitted, to be reared upon the scientific principles of Socialism — principles found today in no central or national organization of labor outside of the Socialist Trade & Labor Alliance — sank into the mire. Uriah Stephens was swept aside; ignoramuses took hold of the organization; a million and a half men went into it, hoping for salvation; but, instead of salvation, there came from the veils of the K. of L. Local, District and General Assemblies the developed ignoramuses, that is to say, the labor fakers, riding the workingman and selling him out to the exploiter. Disappointed, the masses fell off.

Thereupon bubbled up another wondrous concern, another idiosyncrasy — the American Federation of Labor, appropriately called by its numerous English organizers the American Federation of Hell. Ignoramuses again took hold and the lead. They failed to seek below the surface for the cause of the failure of the K. of L.; like genuine ignoramuses, they fluttered over the surface. They saw on the surface excessive concentration of power in the K. of L., and they swung to the other extreme — they built a tapeworm. I call it a tapeworm, because a tapeworm is no organism; it is an aggregation of links with no cohesive powers worth mentioning. The fate of the K. of L. overtook the A.F. of L. Like causes brought on like results, false foundations brought on ruin and failure. Strike upon strike proved disastrous in all concentrated industries; wages and the standard of living of the working class at large went down; the unemployed multiplied; and again the ignorant leaders naturally and inevitably developed into approved labor fakers; the workers found themselves shot, clubbed, indicted, imprisoned by the identical Presidents, governors, mayors, judges, etc. — Republican and Democratic — whom their misleaders had corruptly induced them to support.

Today there is no A. F. of L. — not even the tapeworm — any more. If you reckon it up, you will find that if the 250,000 members which it claims paid dues regularly every quarter, it must have four times as large a fund as it reports. The fact is the dues are paid for the last quarter only; the fakers see to this to the end that they may attend the annual rowdidow called the "A. F. of L. Convention" — and advertise themselves to the politicians. That's all there is left of it. It is a ship, never seaworthy, but now stranded and captured by a handful of pirates; a tapeworm pulled to pieces, condemned by the rank and file of the American proletariat. Its career only filled still fuller the workers' measure of disappointment, diffidence, helplessness.

The Henry George movement was another of these charlatan booms that only helped still more to dispirit people in the end. The "single tax," with its half-antiquated, half-idiotic reasoning, took the field. Again great expectations were raised all over the country — for a while. Again a semi-economic lie proved a broken reed to lean on.

Down came Humpty Dumpty, and all the king's horses and all the king's men could not now put Humpty Dumpty together again. Thus the volume of popular disappointment and diffidence received a further contribution.

Most recently there came along the People's Party movement. Oh, how fine it talked! It was going to emancipate the workers. Did it not say so in its preamble, however reactionary its platform? If bluff and blarney could save a movement, the People's Party would have been imperishable. But it went up like a rocket, and is now fast coming down a stick. In New York State it set itself up against us when we already had 14,000 votes, and had an official standing. It was going to teach us "dreamers" a lesson in "practical American politics." Well, its vote never reached ours, and last November when we rose to 21,000 votes, it dropped to barely 5,000, lost its official standing as a party in the state, and as far as New York and Brooklyn are concerned, we simply mopped the floor with it.

These false movements, and many more kindred circumstances that I could mention, have confused the judgment of our people, weakened the spring of their hope, and abashed their courage. Hence the existing popular apathy in the midst of popular misery; hence despondency despite unequaled opportunities for redress; hence the backwardness of the movement here when compared with that of Europe.

To return now where I broke off. The Socialist Labor Party cannot, in our country, fulfill its mission—here less than anywhere else—without it takes a stand, the scientific soundness of whose position renders growth certain, failure impossible, and without its disciplinary firmness earns for it the unqualified confidence of the now eagerly onlooking masses both in its integrity of purpose and its capacity to enforce order. It is only thus that we can hope to rekindle the now low-burning spark of manhood and womanhood in our American working class, and re-conjure up the Spirit of '76.

We know full well that the race or class that is not virile enough to strike an intelligent blow for itself, is not fit for emancipation. If emancipated by others, it will need constant propping, or will collapse like a dish-clout. While that is true, this other is true also: In all revolutionary movements, as in the storming of fortresses, the thing depends upon the head of the column—upon that minority that is so intense in its convictions, so soundly based on its principles, so determined in its action, that it carries the masses with it, storms the breastworks and captures the fort. Such a head of the column must be our Socialist organization to the whole column of the American proletariat.

Again our American history furnishes a striking illustration. When Pizarro landed on the western slope of the Andes, he had with him about 115 men. Beyond the mountains was an empire — the best organized empire of the aborigines that had been found in America. It had its departments; it had its classes; it was managed as one body numbering hundreds of thousands to the Spaniards' hundred. That body the small army of determined men were to capture. What did Pizzaro do? Did he say, "Let us wait till we get some more?" Or did he say, "Now, boys, I need every one of you 115 men"? No, he said to them: "Brave men of Spain, yonder lies an empire that is a delight to live in, full of gold, full of wealth, full of heathens that we ought to convert. They are as the sands of the sea, compared with us, and they are entrenched behind their mountain fastnesses. It needs the staunchest among you to undertake the conquest. If any, through the hardships of travel, feel unequal to the hardships of the enterprise, I shall not consider him a coward; let him stand back to protect our ships. Let only those stay with me who are determined to fight, and who are determined to conquer." About twenty men stood aside, about ninety-five remained; with ninety-five determined men he scaled those mountains and conquered that empire.

That empire of the Incas is today capitalism, both in point of its own inherent weakness and the strength of its position. The army that is to conquer it is the army of the proletariat, the head of whose column must consist of the intrepid Socialist organization that has earned their love, their respect, their confidence.

What do we see today? At every recent election, the country puts me in mind of a jar of water — turn the jar and all the water comes out. One election, all the Democratic vote drops out and goes over to the Republicans; the next year all the Republican vote drops out and goes over to the Democrats. The workers are moving backward and forward; they are dissatisfied; they have lost confidence in the existing parties they know of, and they are seeking desperately for the party of their class. At such a season, it is the duty of us revolutionists to conduct ourselves in such manner as to cause our organization to be better and better known, its principles more and more clearly understood, its integrity and firmness more and more respected and trusted — then, when we shall have stood that ground well and grown steadily, the masses will in due time flock over to us. In the crash that is sure to come and is now just ahead of us, our steadfast Socialist organization will alone stand out intact above the ruins; there will then be a stampede to our party — but only upon revolutionary lines can it achieve this; upon lines of reform it can never be victorious.

As the chairman said that time would be allowed for questions, I shall close at this point, but not before — you will pardon the assumption — not before I call upon you, in the name of the 6,000 "wicked," revolutionary Socialists of New York and Brooklyn, to organize, here in Boston, upon the genuinely revolutionary plan. Your state is a large manufacturing state; there can be no reason why your vote should not grow, except that, somehow or other, you have not acted as revolutionists. Every year that goes by in this way is a year wasted.

Never forget that every incident that takes place within your, within our, ranks is noted by a large number of workers on the outside. Tamper with discipline, allow this member to do as he likes, that member to slap the Party constitution in the face, yonder member to fuse with reformers, this other to forget the nature of the class struggle and to act up to his forgetfulness — allow that, keep such "reformers" in your ranks and you have stabbed your movement at its vitals. With malice toward none, with charity to all, you must enforce discipline if you mean to reorganize to a purpose. We know that in struggles of this kind, personal feelings, unfortunately, play a part; you cannot prevent that; let the other side, the reformer, fill the role of malice that its weak intellect drives it to; do you fill the role of the square-jointed revolutionist — and if there must be amputation, do it nobly, but firmly. Remember the adage that the tenderhanded surgeon makes stinging wounds, and lengthens the period of suffering and pain. The surgeon that has a firm hand to push the knife as deep as it ought to go, and pulls it out, and lets the pus flow out, that surgeon makes clean wounds, shortens pain, brings cure quickly about.

No organization will inspire the outside masses with respect that will not insist upon and enforce discipline within its own ranks. If you allow your own members to play monkeyshines with the party, the lookers-on, who belong in this camp, will justly believe that you will at some critical moment allow capitalism to play monkeyshines with you; they will not respect you, and their accession to your ranks will be delayed.

There is, indeed, no social or economic reason why the vote of Boston should not be one of the pillars of our movement. And yet that vote is weak and virtually stationary, while in New York and Brooklyn it has on the whole been leaping forward. If you realize the importance of the revolutionary construction of our army; if you comprehend the situation of the country — that there is a popular tidal wave coming; that, in order to bring it our way and render it effective, we must be deserving thereof, whereas, if we are not, the wave will recede with disastrous results; if you properly appreciate the fact that every year that passes over our heads brings to our lives greater danger, throws a heavier load upon the shoulders of our wives, makes darker the prospects of our sons, exposes still more the honor of our daughters — if you understand that, then for their sakes, for our country's sake, for the sake of the proletarians of Boston, organize upon the New York and Brooklyn plan.

Questions

Mr. Dooling: I would like to inquire what it is proposed shall replace wages? How are men to be supported when wages are done away with? Upon the answer to that question will depend largely whether the middle class will support Socialism.

The Speaker: I must disagree with the gentleman that the middle class is going to be brought into this movement by any information upon what is going to be substituted for wages. The middle class will have to be sold at auction by the sheriff. That alone will enlighten it as a class. When it has lost its property, whereby it is now skinning some unhappy devils, and its members have themselves become wage slaves, then it will see what this whole question of wages amounts to, and what should "substitute wages."

Individuals among the middle class may, however, be intelligent enough to study the question and, in that way, to learn, before they become wage slaves, the secret of the wages question.

Now, what are wages?

Wages are that part of the product of labor which the capitalist pays to the workingman out of the proceeds of the workingman's own products. Say that a workingman produces $4 a day, and that $1 is paid him for his labor. That $1 is taken out of the wealth that he himself produces, and it is kindly given back to him by the capitalist, who pockets the other $3. That is one feature of wages.

Another is that wages are the price of labor in the labor market, and that in the labor market, labor stands on the same footing as any other commodity. It is governed by the law of supply and demand, its price, the same as that of anything else—hairpins, shoes or cast-off clothing, is determined by the law of supply and demand—the more there is of these, the cheaper their price. Likewise with labor. Under the capitalist system, labor is a commodity in the market. The workingman must sell his labor, which he gets paid for with the thing called wages, at the market price. If the supply of labor is so much larger than the demand, then, instead of getting his one dollar out of the four that he produces in the illustration above given, he may get only ninety-five cents; if the demand for labor goes down further, he may get ninety cents as the price of his labor; and if it goes still further below the supply, still further down would go the price of labor, i.e., wages. The price of labor may sink to I don't know how low a level.

Some of you may say that the workingman has to live, and there is a limit. No, there is no limit. The only limit that there is, is a limit to the rapidity of the decline. Wages cannot fall from a hundred cents to ten cents, but they can fall by easy gradations even below ten cents.

We have, for instance, this story about the Chinese that in some places they live only upon the rats they catch; that in other places, their stomachs having been squeezed still more, they live upon the tails of rats that others ate; and that in still other places there are Chinamen who live upon the smell of the tail of the rats. This may sound like a joke, and yet there is more truth than poetry about it.

In the history of France we have it reported that large masses of the population lived, in the eighteenth century, during the ancient regime, upon herbs, the price of which for the whole year would not have been five francs. The human stomach is like an India rubber ball; you can squeeze it, and squeeze it, and squeeze it, and you can shave off and pare off the wants of the workingman till his wants are merely those of the beast.

Wages, then, are the part of the product of labor which the capitalist allows the workingman to keep, and which the capitalist does not steal, along with the other three parts.

Now, then, for the same reason that wages are what I have said, there can be, under Socialism, no "wages," because sticking to my previous illustration, under Socialism that workingman must get all the four dollars which he produces.

What are the things which compel the workingman today to receive wages?

First—the capitalist class owns all the things necessary to produce with; it holds the land, the railroads and the machinery with which to labor. The working class owns none of these necessities, all of which it needs to labor with; hence it must sell itself.

Second—The reason why the wageworker must put up with so small a return is that under this system he is not treated as a human being, Christianity to the contrary notwithstanding. The capitalists are refined cannibals; they look at the workingman in no other light than a horse; in fact, in a worse light; they will take care of a horse, but let the workingmen die. Labor is cheap, and is treated that way under capitalism. Under Socialism, standing upon that high scientific plane, we see a higher morality. We see that labor should not be treated as a chattel; it should not be treated as a commodity; it should not be treated as shoes, and potatoes and hairpins and cast-off clothing, but as a human being capable of the highest intellectual development. So treating him, the wageworker of today becomes a part owner in the machinery of production, and being part owner in the machinery of production he then gets the full return of his labor; he is then free from the shackles that compel him to accept wages; he becomes the boss of the machine, whereas today he is its appendage.

Under Socialism, we don't need potato bugs, as a friend puts it, to raise potatoes. Some people think that the wageworker class must carry the capitalist on its back. As well say that you must have potato bugs, or you won't have any potatoes. If you remove the potato bugs, you will have all the more potatoes; remove the capitalist class and you will have the whole of your product; there will not then be any potato bug, i.e., capitalist, to sponge up the bulk of your product.

John F. O'Sullivan: I should like to ask the speaker if the four dollars, as per the illustration, given to the worker — in other words, if he gets the full product of his labor or work — wouldn't that be wages all the same?

The Speaker: If you choose to call water Paris green, that's your business. Suppose I came to you and said: "Paris green is not poisonous, it is an excellent thing for the human system"; and suppose I went on saying: "See here, I am taking Paris green, look at me. You see, it refreshes and does not kill me!" What would you think of that? You would be justified to say I was juggling with words. And that is what I tell you. You have no right to call water Paris green; it is known all the world over as water, and Paris green is known as Paris green, a poison.

Now in the same way "wages" is a technical term. The term means in political economy that portion of the product of labor that the workingman is allowed to keep, and that is not stolen from him by the capitalist.

Now you may say, "Well, granted; but suppose we call the revenue of a man his wages, and I mean by that the full proceeds of his labor — wouldn't that be the same?"

Yes, it would be the same if you mean the right thing, but here I would warn you — and in that consists one of the "wickednesses" of us New York and Brooklyn Socialists — we insist upon strict, technical terms, because if you juggle with terms in that way you will have a Tower of Babel confusion.

The Bible, which I recommend to you to read carefully, furnishes in its Tower of Babel story a warning worth taking to heart. When the Lord wanted to confuse the Jews so that they shouldn't build that tower and get into heaven by that route, he introduced the confusion of language among them. Thereupon, when a man said, "Bring me a brick," they brought him a chair, and when a man said, "Bring me a chair," they struck him over the head with a crowbar; and so, not being able to understand one another, the building of the tower was given up, and the people scattered to the four winds.

Now, we Socialists brace ourselves against all Tower of Babel confusion. When we say "wages," we mean the thing that is so styled by scientific political economy, and we won't allow its well marked and sharply drawn character to be blurred. Wages are what they are understood to be technically, and we call them by no other name.

The four dollars your workingmen would get would not be "wages." Those four dollars would be the proceeds of labor. Today he gets wages, and wages mean only that part of his product, as I said before, which capital does not steal away from him.

Unless you define wages in that way, you will not be able to have a clear, scientific understanding of what profits are, namely, that portion of the product of labor which the capitalist does steal from the worker. The worker produces a certain amount of wealth, and that is divided into two parts. One small part is called wages; the big part is called profits. Now, by sticking to scientific definitions, we are aided in the understanding of the nature of capitalism, and the relations that exist between the capitalist class and the workmen's class. We are aided in understanding that capital, i.e., the capitalist class, and labor are enemies born.

Since wages are a part of the product of labor, and profits are another part, it follows that you cannot increase profits without reducing wages, and you cannot increase wages without reducing profits. It follows that the interests of the man who gets profits are dead against the interests of the working class. In other words, the two are enemies born, and the fight between them cannot be patched up; it must be fought to a finish.

You will now understand the danger of a loose use of the word "wages"; it simply aids the labor fakers —

[Applause, during which the speaker is informed that the questioner is the president of the Boston Central Labor Union.]

It seems that I hit the nail more squarely on the head than I knew. Well, as I was saying:

Such loose use of the term "wages" positively aids the labor faker in his work of bunko — steering you into the political shambles of the capitalists.

The Democratic and Republican capitalists, at election time, seem to be enemies; but, after they get into their offices, shake hands and have a good laugh. Now, in order that these gentlemen should laugh, the political agents of their class must have been kept in office, and the representatives of the working class must have been kept out. To have that, the workingmen must have voted for the capitalist candidates—it matters not whether Democratic or Republican, that is all one—and to induce the workers to cut their own throats in that way. They must be made to believe that "Capital and labor are brothers." This is the important work for which the labor faker is commissioned by the capitalists. He must make it plausible to the workers that they and their skinners are brothers.

So long as a workingman imagines capital is his brother, he will expect something from his "brother." When the Irish worker first arrived in this country, they thought an Irishman all the world over was his brother, and united with him against the "iron heel of England," and thus he trusted the Irishman capitalist. But his "brother," the Irishman capitalist, while patting him on the back, skinned and bled and used him in the approved capitalist way. It was the same with the Jewish workingmen. They came to this country, and imagined that the Jewish capitalist was their brother—all of the seed of Abraham. The Jewish capitalist fostered the profitable delusion and rode on the backs of his Abrahamic brothers. And so with the American capitalist and the American workingman, down to the end of the list of nationalities.

By insisting upon a strict use of the terms "wages," "profits," etc., we enable the working class to understand and proceed from the fundamental truth that the interests of the workingmen bind these together, and are opposed to those of the capitalist—whether Jew or Gentile, Irishman or American, Democrat or Republican, silver bug or gold bug or bed bug. And, by doing that, we lame the arm of the labor faker that is sent to tell the workingman: "The capitalist is your brother; and I am your brother; so come to your dear brother, and get skinned."

Question (no name): The social question is an economic question. Why should not an economic organization be enough?

The Speaker: The social question and all such questions are essentially political. If you have an economic organization alone, you have a duck flying with one wing. You must have a political organization or you are nowhere.

Watch the capitalist closely, and see whether the social question is exclusively an economic one, or whether the political wing is not a very necessary one. The capitalist rules in the shop. Is he satisfied with that? Watch him at election time, it is then he works; he has also another workshop, not an economic one — the legislatures and capitols in the nation. He buzzes around them and accomplishes political results. He gets the laws passed that will protect his economic class interests, and he pulls the wires when these interests are in danger, bringing down the strong arm of political power over the heads of the striking workingmen, who have the notion that the wages or social question is only an economic question.

Make no mistake: The organization of the working class must be both economic and political. The capitalist is organized upon both lines. You must attack him on both.

What Means This Strike?

An address delivered at the City Hall, New Bedford, Mass., February 11, 1898

Workingmen and workingwomen of New Bedford:

Ye striking textile workers; and all of you others, who, though not now on strike, have been on strike before this, and will be on strike some other time:

It has been the habit in this country and in England that, when a strike is on, "stars" in the labor movement are invited to appear on the scene, and entertain the strikers; entertain them and keep them in good spirits with rosy promises and prophesies, funny anecdotes, bombastic recitations in prose and poetry; stuff them full of rhetoric and wind — very much in the style that some generals do, who, by means of bad whiskey, seek to keep up the courage of the soldiers whom they are otherwise unable to beguile.

Such has been the habit in the past; to a great extent it continues to be the habit in the present; it was so during the late miners' strike; it has been so to some extent here in New Bedford; and it is so everywhere, to the extent that ignorance of the social question predominates.

To the extent, however, that Socialism gets a footing among the working class such false and puerile tactics are thrown aside.

The Socialist workingmen of New Bedford, on whose invitation I am here; all those of us who are members of that class conscious revolutionary international organization of the working class, that throughout the world stands out today as the leading and most promiseful feature of the age—all such would consider it a crime on the part of the men, whom our organization sends forth to preach the gospel of labor, if they were to spend their platform time in "tickling" the workers.

Our organization sends us out to teach the workers, to enlighten them on the great issue before them, and the great historic drama in which most of them are still unconscious actors.

Some of you, accustomed to a different diet, may find my speech dry. If there be any such here, let him leave. He has not yet graduated from that primary school reared by experience in which the question of wages is forced upon the workers as a serious question, and they are taught that it demands serious thought to grapple with, and solve it.

If, however, you have graduated from that primary department, and have come here with the requisite earnestness, then you will not leave this hall without having, so to speak, caught firm hold of the cable of the labor movement; then the last strike of this sort has been seen in New Bedford; then, the strikes that may follow will be as different from this as vigorous manhood is from toddling infancy; then you will have entered upon that safe and sure path along which eternal disaster will not, as heretofore, mark your tracks, but New Bedford, Massachusetts, and the nation herself, will successively fall into your hands, with freedom as the crowning fruit of your efforts.

Three years ago I was in your midst during another strike.

The superficial observer who looks back to your attitude during that strike, who looks back to your attitude during the strikes that preceded that one, who now turns his eyes to your attitude in the present strike, and who discovers substantially no difference between your attitude now and then, might say, "Why, it is a waste of time to speak to such men; they learn nothing from experience; they will eternally fight the same hopeless battle; the battle to establish 'safe relations' with the capitalist class, with the same hopeless weapon: the 'pure and simple' organization of labor!"

But the Socialist does not take that view. There is one thing about your conduct that enlists for and entitles you to the warm sympathy of the Socialist, and that is that, despite your persistent errors in fundamental principles, in aims and methods, despite the illusions that you are chasing after, despite the increasing poverty and cumulating failures that press upon you, despite all that, you preserve manhood enough not to submit to oppression, but rise in the rebellion that is implied in a strike.

The attitude of workingmen engaged in a bona fide strike is an inspiring one. It is an earnest that slavery will not prevail. The slave alone who will not rise against his master, who will meekly bend his back to the lash, and turn his cheek to him who plucks his beard - that slave alone is hopeless. But the slave, who, as you of New Bedford, persists, despite failures and poverty, in rebelling, there is always hope for.

This is the reason I have considered it worth my while to leave my home and interrupt my work in New York, and come here, and spend a few days with you. I bank my hopes wholly and build entirely upon this sentiment of rebellion within you.

Whence Do Wages Come, And Whence Profits?

What you now stand in need of, aye, more than of bread, is the knowledge of a few elemental principles of political economy and of sociology.

Be not frightened at the words. It is only the capitalist professors who try to make them so difficult of understanding that the very mentioning of them is expected to throw the workingman into a palpitation of the heart. The subjects are easy of understanding.

The first point that a workingman should be clear upon is this: What is the source of the wages he receives; what is the source of the profits his employer lives on? The following dialogue is not uncommon:

Workingman—"Do I understand you rightly, that you Socialists want to abolish the capitalist class?"

Socialist—"That is what we are after."

Workingman—"You are!? Then I don't want any of you. Why, even now my wages are small; even now I can barely get along. If you abolish the capitalist I'll have nothing; there will be nobody to support me."

Who knows how many workingmen in this hall are typified by the workingman in this dialogue!

When, on payday, you reach out your horny, "unwashed" hand it is empty. When you take it back again, your wages are on it. Hence the belief that the capitalist is the source of your living, that he is your bread-giver, your supporter. Now that is an error, an optic illusion.

If early in the morning you go on top of some house and look eastward, it will seem to you that the sun moves and that you are standing still. Indeed, that was at one time the general and accepted belief. But it was an error, based upon an optic illusion. So long as that error prevailed the sciences could hardly make any progress. Humanity virtually stood stock still. Not until the illusion was discovered, and the error overthrown, not until it was ascertained that things were just the other way, that the sun stood still, and that it was our planet that moved at a breakneck rate of speed, was any real progress possible.

So likewise with this illusion about the source of wages. You cannot budge, you cannot move one step forward unless you discover that, in this respect also, the fact is just the reverse of the appearance: that, not the capitalist, but the workingman, is the source of the worker's living; that it is not the capitalist who supports the workingman, but the workingman who supports the capitalist; that it is not the capitalist who gives bread to the workingman, but the workingman who gives himself a dry crust, and sumptuously stocks the table of the capitalist.

This is a cardinal point in political economy; and this is the point I wish first of all to establish in your minds. Now, to the proof.

Say that I own $100,000. Don't ask me where I got it. If you do, I would have to answer you in the language of all capitalists that such a question is un-American. You must not look into the source of this, my "original accumulation". It is un-American to pry into such secrets. Presently I shall take you into my confidence. For the present I shall draw down the blinds, and keep out your un-American curiosity. I have $100,000, and am a capitalist.

Now I may not know much; no capitalist does; but know a few things, and among them is a little plain arithmetic. I take a pencil and put down on a sheet of paper, "$100,000." Having determined that I shall need at least $5,000 a year to live with comfort, I divide the $100,000 by $5,000; the quotient is 20. My hair then begins to stand on end. The 20 tells me that, if I pull $5,000 annually out of $100,000, these are exhausted during that term. At the beginning of the 21st year I shall have nothing left.

"Heaven and earth, I would then have to go to work if I wanted to live!"

No capitalist relishes that thought. He will tell you, and pay his politicians, professors and political parsons, to tell you, that "labor is honorable." He is perfectly willing to let you have that undivided honor, and will do all he can that you may not be deprived of any part of it; but, as to himself, he has for work a constitutional aversion. The capitalist runs away from work like the man bitten by a mad dog runs away from water.

I want to live without work on my $100,000 and yet keep my capital untouched. If you ask any farmer, he will tell you that if he invests in a Durham cow she will yield him a supply of 16 quarts a day, but, after some years, the supply goes down; she will run dry; and then a new cow must be got. But I, the capitalist, aim at making my capital a sort of $100,000 cow, which I shall annually be able to milk $5,000 out of, without her ever running dry.

I want, in short, to perform the proverbially impossible feat of eating my cake, and yet having it. The capitalist system performs that feat for me. How?

I go to a broker. I say, Mr. Broker, I have $100,000. I want you to invest that for me. I don't tell him that I have a special liking for New Bedford mills' stock; I don't tell him I have a special fancy for railroad stock; I leave the choosing with him. The only direction I give him is to get the stock in such a corporation as will pay the highest dividend. Mr. Broker has a list of all of these corporations, your New Bedford corporations among them, to the extent that they may be listed. He makes the choice, say, of one of your mills right here in this town.

I hire a vault in a safe deposit company, and I put my stock into it. I lock it up, put the key in my pocket, and I go and have a good time. If it is too cold in the north I go down to Florida. If it is too hot there I go to the Adirondack Mountains. Occasionally I take a spin across the Atlantic and run the gauntlet of all the gambling dens in Europe. I spend my time with fast horses and faster women. I never put my foot inside the factory that I hold stock in; I don't even come to the town in which it is located, and yet, lo and behold, a miracle takes place!

Those of you versed in Bible lore surely have read or heard about the miracle that God performed when the Jews were in the desert and about to die of hunger. The Lord opened the skies and let manna come. But the Jews had to get up early in the morning, before the sun rose; if they overslept themselves the sun would melt the manna, and they would have nothing to eat. They had to get up early, and go out, and stoop down and pick up the manna and put it in baskets and take it to their tents and eat it.

With the appearance of the manna on earth the miracle ended. But the miracles that happen in this capitalist system of production are so wonderful that those recorded in the Bible don't hold a candle to them. The Jews had to do some work, but I, stock-holding capitalist, need do no work at all. I can turn night into day, and day into night. I can lie flat on my back all day and all night; and every three months my manna comes down to me in the shape of dividends. Where does it come from? What does the dividend represent?

In the factory of which my broker bought stock, workmen, thousands of them, were at work; they have woven cloth that has been put upon the market to the value of $7,000; out of the $7,000 that the cloth is worth my wage workers receive $2,000 in wages, and I receive the $5,000 as profits or dividends. Did I, who never put my foot inside of the mill; did I, who never put my foot inside of New Bedford; did I, who don't know how a loom looks; did I, who contributed nothing whatever toward the weaving of that cloth; did I do any work whatever toward producing those $5,000 that came to me? No man with brains in his head instead of sawdust can deny that those $7,000 are exclusively the product of the wage workers in that mill. Out of the wealth thus produced by them alone, they get $2,000 in wages, and I, who did nothing at all, I get the $5,000.

The wages these workers receive represent wealth that they have themselves produced; the profits that the capitalist pockets represent wealth that the wage workers produced, and that the capitalist, does what?—let us call things by their names—that the capitalist steals from them.

You may ask: But is that the rule, is not that illustration an exception? Yes, it is the rule; the exception is the other thing.

The leading industries of the United States are today stock concerns, and thither will all others worth mentioning move. An increasing volume of capital in money is held in stocks and shares. The individual capitalist holds stock in a score of concerns in different trades, located in different towns, too many and too varied for him even to attempt to run. By virtue of his stock, he draws his income from them; which is the same as saying that he lives on what the workingmen produce but are robbed of. Nor is the case at all essentially different with the concerns that have not yet developed into stock corporations.

Again, you may ask: The conclusion that what such stockholders live on is stolen wealth because they evidently perform no manner of work is irrefutable, but are all stockholders equally idle and superfluous? Are there not some who do perform some work? Are there not "directors"?

There are "directors," but these gentlemen bear a title much like those "generals" and "majors" and "colonels" who now go about, and whose generalship, majorship and colonelship consisted in securing substitutes during the war.

These "directors" are simply the largest stockholders, which is the same as to say that they are the largest sponges; their directorship consists only in directing conspiracies against rival "directors," in bribing legislatures, executives and judiciaries, in picking out and hiring men out of your midst to serve as bellwethers, that will lead you, like cattle, to the capitalist shambles, and tickle you into contentment and hopefulness while you are being fleeced. The court decisions removing responsibility from the "directors" are numerous and increasing; each such decision establishes, from the capitalist government's own mouth, the idleness and superfluousness of the capitalist class.

These "directors," and the capitalist class in general, may perform some "work," they do perform some "work," but that "work" is not of a sort that directly or indirectly aids production, any more than the intense mental strain and activity of the "work" done by the pickpocket is directly or indirectly productive.

Finally, you may ask: No doubt the stockholder does no work, and hence lives on the wealth we produce; no doubt these "directors" have a title that only emphasizes their idleness by a swindle, and, consequently, neither they are other than sponges on the working class; but did not your own illustration start with the supposition that the capitalist in question had $100,000, is not his original capital entitled to some returns?

This question opens an important one; and now I shall, as I promised you, take you into my confidence; I shall raise the curtain which I pulled down before the question, Where did I get it? I shall now let you pry into my secret.

Whence does this original capital, or "original accumulation," come? Does it grow on the capitalist like hair on his face, or nails on his fingers and toes? Does he secrete it as he secretes sweat from his body? Let me take one illustration of many.

Before our present Governor, the Governor of New York was Levi Parsons Morton. The gentleman must be known to all of you. Besides having been Governor of the Empire State, he was once Vice President of the nation, and also at one time our Minister to France. Mr. Morton is a leading "gentleman"; he wears the best of broadcloth; his shirt bosom is of spotless white; his nails are trimmed by manicurists; he uses the elitest language; he has front pews in a number of churches; he is a pattern of morality, law and order; and he is a multimillionaire capitalist. How did he get his start millionaire-ward? Mr. Morton being a Republican, I shall refer you to a Republican journal, the *New York Tribune,* for the answer of this interesting question. The *Tribune* of the day after Mr. Morton's nomination for Governor in 1894 gave his biography.

There we are informed that Mr. Morton was born in New Hampshire of poor parents; he was industrious, he was clever, he was pushing, and he settled, a poor young man, in New York City, where in 1860, mark the date, he started a clothing establishment; then, in rapid succession, we are informed that he failed, and started a bank!

A man may start almost any kind of a shop without a cent. If the landlord gave him credit for the rent, and the brewer, the shoe manufacturer, the cigar manufacturer, etc., etc., give him credit for the truck, he may start a saloon, a shoe shop, a cigar shop, etc., etc., without any cash, do business and pay off his debt with the proceeds of his sales. But there is one shop that he cannot start in that way. That shop is the banking shop. For that he must have cash on hand. He can no more shave notes without money than he can shave whiskers without razors.

Now, then, the man who just previously stood up before a notary public and swore "So help him, God," he had no money to pay his creditors, immediately after, without having in the meantime married an heiress, has money enough to start a bank on! Where did he get it?

Read the biographies of any of our founders of capitalist concerns by the torchlight of this biography, and you will find them all to be essentially the same, or suggestively silent upon the doings of our man during the period that he gathers his "original accumulation." You will find that "original capital" to be the child of fraudulent failures and fires, of high-handed crime of some sort or other, or of the sneaking crime of appropriating trust funds, etc. With such "original capital" - gotten by dint of such "cleverness," "push" and "industry" as a weapon, the "original" capitalist proceeds to fleece the working class that has been less "industrious," "pushing" and "clever" than he. If he consumes all his fleecings, his capital remains of its original size in his hands, unless some other gentleman of the road, gifted with greater "industry," "push" and "cleverness" than he, comes around and relieves him of it; if he consume not the whole of his fleecings, his capital moves upward, million-ward.

The case is proved. Labor alone produces all wealth. Wages are that part of labor's own product that the workingman is allowed to keep. Profits are the present and running stealings perpetrated by the capitalist upon the workingman from day to day, from week to week, from month to month, from year to year. Capital is the accumulated past stealings of the capitalist, cornerstoned upon his "original accumulation."

Who of you before me fails now to understand, or would still deny that, not the capitalist supports the workingman, but the workingman supports the capitalist; or still holds that the workingman could not exist without the capitalist? If any there be, let him raise his hand and speak up now. None? Then I may consider this point settled, and shall move on.

The Class Struggle

The second point, on which it is absolutely necessary that you be clear, is the nature of your relation, as working people, to the capitalist in this capitalist system of production. This point is an inevitable consequence of the first.

You have seen that the wages you live on and the profits the capitalist riots in are the two parts into which is divided the wealth that you produce. The workingman wants a larger and larger share. So does the capitalist. A thing cannot be divided into two shares so as to increase the share of each.

If the workingman produces, say, $4 worth of wealth a day, and the capitalist keeps 2, there are only 2 left for the workingman. If the capitalist keeps 3, there is only 1 left for the workingman. If the capitalist keeps 3 1/2, there is only 1/2 left for the workingman. Inversely, if the workingman pushes up his share from 1/2 to 1, there are only 3 left to the capitalist. If the workingman secures 2, the capitalist will be reduced to 2. If the workingman push still onward and keep 3, the capitalist will have to put up with 1.

And if the workingman makes up his mind to enjoy all that he produces, and keep all the 4, the capitalist will have to go to work.

These plain figures upset the theory about the workingman and the capitalist being brothers.

Capital—meaning the capitalist class—and labor have been portrayed by capitalist illustrated papers as Chang and Eng [the Siamese twins]. This, I remember, was done notably by *Harper's Weekly*, the property of one of the precious "Seeley Diners"—you remember that "dinner." The Siamese Twins were held together by a piece of flesh. Wherever Chang went, Eng was sure to go. If Chang was happy, Eng's pulse throbbed harder. If Chang caught cold, Eng sneezed in chorus with him. When Chang died, Eng followed suit within five minutes.

Do we find that to be the relation of the workingman and the capitalist? Do you find that the fatter the capitalist, the fatter also grows the workingmen? Is not your experience rather that the wealthier the capitalist, the poorer are the workingmen? That the more magnificent and prouder the residences of the capitalist, the dingier and humbler become those of the workingmen? That the happier the life of the capitalist's wife, the greater the opportunities of his children for enjoyment and education, the heavier becomes the cross borne by the workingmen's wives, while their children are crowded more and more from the schools and deprived of the pleasures of childhood? Is that your experience, or is it not?

The pregnant point that underlies these pregnant facts is that:

Between the working class and the capitalist class, there is an irrepressible conflict, a class struggle for life. No glib-tongued politician can vault over it, no capitalist professor or official statistician can argue it away; no capitalist parson can veil it; no labor faker can straddle it; no "reform" architect can bridge it over. It crops up in all manner of ways, like in this strike, in ways that disconcert all the plans and all the schemes of those who would deny or ignore it. It is a struggle that will not down, and must be ended, only by either the total subjugation of the working class, or the abolition of the capitalist class.

Thus you perceive that the theory on which your "pure and simple" trade organizations are grounded, and on which you went into this strike, is false. There being no "common interests," but only hostile interests, between the capitalist class and the working class, the battle you are waging to establish "safe relations" between the two is a hopeless one.

Put to the touchstone of these undeniable principles the theory upon which your "pure and simple" trade organizations are built, and you will find it to be false; examined by the light of these undeniable principles the road that your false theory makes you travel and the failures that have marked your career must strike you as its inevitable result. How are we to organize and proceed? you may ask. Before answering the question, let me take up another branch of the subject. Its presentation will sweep aside another series of illusions that beset the mind of the working class, and will, with what has been said, give us a sufficient sweep over the ground to lead us to the right answer.

The Development Of Capitalist Society

Let us take a condensed page of the country's history. For the sake of plainness, and forced to it by the exigency of condensation, I shall assume small figures.

Place yourselves back a sufficient number of years with but 10 competing weaving concerns in the community. How the individual 10 owners came by the "original accumulations" that enabled them to start as capitalists you now know. Say that each of the 10 capitalists employs 10 men; that each man receives $2 a day, and that the product of each of the 10 sets of men in each of the 10 establishments is worth $40 a day. You know now also that it is out of these $40 worth of wealth, produced by the men, that each of the 10 competing capitalists takes the $20 that he pays the 10 men in wages, and that out of that same $40 worth of wealth he takes the $20 that he pockets as profits. Each of these 10 capitalists makes, accordingly, $120 a week.

This amount of profits, one should think, should satisfy our 10 capitalists. It is a goodly sum to pocket without work. Indeed, it may satisfy some, say most of them. But if for any of many reasons it does not satisfy any one of them, the whole string of them is set in commotion.

"Individuality" is a deity at whose shrine the capitalist worships, or affects to worship. In point of fact, capitalism robs of individuality, not only the working class, but capitalists themselves. The action of any one of the lot compels action by all; like a row of bricks, the dropping of one makes all the others drop successively.

Let us take No. 1. He is not satisfied with $120 a week. Of the many reasons he may have for that, let's take this: He has a little daughter; eventually, she will be of marriageable age; whom is he planning to marry her to? Before the public, particularly before the workers, he will declaim on the "sovereignty" of our citizens, and declare the country is stocked with nothing but "peers." In his heart, though, he feels otherwise. He looks even upon his fellow capitalists as plebeians; he aspires at a prince, a duke, or at least a count for a son-in-law; and in visions truly reflecting the vulgarity of his mind he beholds himself the grandfather of prince, duke or count grandbrats. To realize this dream he must have money; princes, etc., are expensive luxuries. His present income, $120 a week, will not buy the luxury. He must have some more.

To his employees he will recommend reliance on heaven; he himself knows that if he wants more money it will not come from heaven, but must come from the sweat of his employees' brows.

As all the wealth produced in his shop is $40 a day, he knows that, if he increases his share of $20 to $30, there will be only $10 left for wages. He tries this. He announces a wage reduction of 50 percent.

His men spontaneously draw themselves together and refuse to work; they go on strike.

What is the situation? In those days it needed skill, acquired by long training, to do the work; there may have been corner loafers out of work, but not weavers; possibly at some great distance there may have been weavers actually obtainable, but in those days there was neither telegraph nor railroad to communicate with them; finally, the nine competitors of No. 1, having no strike on hand, continued to produce, and thus threatened to crowd No. 1 out of the market. Thus circumstanced, No. 1 caves in. He withdraws his order of wage reduction.

"Come in," he says to his striking workmen, "let's make up; labor and capital are brothers; the most loving of brothers sometimes fall out; we have had such a falling out; it was a slip; you have organized yourselves in a union with a $2 a day wage scale; I shall never fight the union; 1 love it, come back to work." And the men did. Thus ended the first strike.

The victory won by the men made many of them feel bold. At their first next meeting they argued: "The employer wanted to reduce our wages and got left; why may not we take the hint and reduce his profits by demanding higher wages; why should we not lick him in an attempt to resist our demand for more pay?"

But the labor movement is democratic. No one man can run things. At that union meeting the motion to demand higher pay is made by one member, another must second it; amendments, and amendments to the amendments, are put with the requisite seconders; debate follows; points of order are raised, ruled on, appealed from and settled; in the meantime it grows late, the men must be at work early the next morning, the hour to adjourn arrives, and the whole matter is left pending. Thus much for the men.

Now for the employer. He locks himself up in his closet. With clenched fists and scowl on brow, he gnashes his teeth at the victory of his "brother" labor, its union and its union regulations. And he ponders. More money he must have and is determined to have. This resolution is arrived at with the swiftness and directness which capitalists are capable of.

Differently from his men, he is not many, but one. He makes the motion, seconds it himself, puts it, and carries it unanimously. More profits he shall have. But how? Aid comes to him through the mail. The letter carrier brings him a circular from a machine shop. Such circulars are frequent even today. It reads like this:

"Mr. No. 1, you are employing 10 men. I have in my machine shop a beautiful machine with which you can produce, with five men, twice as much as now with 10. This machine does not chew tobacco. it does not smoke. Some of these circulars are cruel and add: This machine has no wife who gets sick and keeps it home to attend to her. It has no children who die, and whom to bury it must stay away from work. It never goes on strike. It works and grumbles not. Come and see it."

Invention

Right here let me lock a switch at which not a few people are apt to switch off and be banked. Some may think, "Well, at least that machine capitalist is entitled to his profits; he surely is an inventor."

A grave error. Look into the history of our inventors, and you will see that those who really profited by their genius are so few that you can count them on the fingers of your hands, and have fingers to spare.

The capitalists either take advantage of the inventor's stress and buy his invention for a song; the inventor believes he can make his haul with his next invention; but before that is perfected, he is as poor as before, and the same advantage is again taken of him; until finally, his brain power being exhausted, he sinks into a pauper's grave, leaving the fruit of his genius for private capitalists to grow rich on; or the capitalist simply steals the invention and gets his courts to decide against the inventor.

From Eli Whitney down, that is the treatment the inventor, as a rule, receives from the capitalist class.

Such a case, illustrative of the whole situation, happened recently. The Bonsack Machine Co. discovered that its employees made numerous inventions, and it decided to appropriate them wholesale.

To this end, it locked out its men, and demanded of all applicants for work that they sign a contract whereby, in "consideration of employment" they assign to the company all their rights in whatever invention they may make during the term of their employment.

One of these employees, who had signed such a contract, informed the company one day that he thought he could invent a machine by which cigarettes could be held closed by crimping at the ends, instead of pasting. This was a valuable idea; and he was told to go ahead. For six months he worked at this invention and perfected it; and, having during all that time received not a cent in wages or otherwise from the company, he patented his invention himself.

The company immediately brought suit against him in the federal courts, claiming that the invention was its property; and the federal court decided in favor of the company, thus robbing the inventor of his time, his money, of the fruit of his genius, and of his unquestionable rights.

"Shame?" Say not "Shame!" He who himself applies the torch to his own house has no cause to cry "Shame!" when the flames consume it. Say rather, "Natural!", and smiting your own breasts, say, "Ours the fault!" Having elected into power the Democratic, Republican, Free Trade, Protection, Silver or Gold platforms of the capitalist class, the working class has none but itself to blame if the official lackeys of that class turn against the working class the public powers put into their hands.

The capitalist owner of the machine shop that sends the circular did not make the invention.

The Screws Begin To Turn

To return to No. 1. He goes and sees the machine; finds it to be as represented; buys it; puts it up in his shop; picks out of his 10 men the five least active in the late strike; sets them to work at $2 a day as before; and full of bows and smirks, addresses the other five thus: "I am sorry I have no places for you; I believe in union principles and am paying the union scale to the five men I need; I don't need you now; good bye. I hope I'll see you again." And he means this last as you will presently perceive.

What is the situation now? No. 1 pays, as before, $2 a day, but to only five men; these, with the aid of the machine, now produce twice as much as the 10 did before; their product is now $80 worth of wealth; as only $10 of this goes in wages, the capitalist has a profit of $70 a day, or 250 percent more. He is moving fast toward his prince, duke or count son-in-law.

Now watch the men whom his machine displaced; their career throws quite some light on the whole question. Are they not "American citizens"? Is not this a "Republic with a Constitution"? Is anything else wanted to get a living? Watch them!

They go to No. 2 for a job; before they quite reach the place, the doors open and five of that concern are likewise thrown out upon the street. What happened there? The "individuality" of No. 2 yielded to the pressure of capitalist development. The purchase of the machine by No. 1 enabled him to produce so much more plentifully and cheaply; if No. 2 did not do likewise, he would be crowded out of the market by No. 1. No. 2, accordingly, also invested in a machine, with the result that five of his men are also thrown out.

These 10 unemployed proceed to No. 3, hoping for better luck there. But what sight is that that meets their astonished eyes? Not five men, as walked out of Nos. 1 and 2, but all No. 3's 10 have landed on the street; and, what is more surprising yet to them, No. 3 himself is on the street, now reduced to the condition of a workingman along with his former employees. What is it that happened there? In this instance the "individuality" of No. 3 was crushed by capitalist development. The same reason that drove No. 2 to procure the machine rendered the machine indispensable to No. 3. But having, differently from his competitors Nos. 1 and 2, spent all his stealings from the workingmen, instead of saving up some, he is now unable to make the purchase; is, consequently, unable to produce as cheaply as they; is, consequently, driven into bankruptcy, and lands in the class of the proletariat, whose ranks are thus increased.

The now 21 unemployed proceed in their hunt for work, and make the round of the other mills. The previous experiences are repeated. Not only are there no jobs to be had, but everywhere workers are thrown out, if the employer got the machine; and if he did not, workers with their former employers, now ruined, join the army of the unemployed.

What happened in that industry happened in all others. Thus the ranks of the capitalist class are thinned out, and the class is made more powerful, while the ranks of the working class are swelled, and the class is made weaker. This is the process that explains how, on the one hand, your New Bedford mills become the property of ever fewer men; how, according to the census, their aggregate capital runs up to over $14,000,000; how, despite "bad times," their profits run up to upwards of $1,300,000; how, on the other hand, your position becomes steadily more precarious.

No. 1's men return to where they started from. Scab they will not. Uninformed upon the mechanism of capitalism, they know not what struck them; and they expect "better times," just as so many equally uninformed workingmen are expecting today; in the meantime, thinking thereby to hasten the advent of the good times, No. 1's men turn out the Republican' party and turn in the Democratic, turn out the Democratic and turn in the Republican, just as our misled workingmen are now doing, not understanding that, whether they put in or out Republicans, Democrats, Protectionists or Free Traders, Goldbugs or Silverbugs, they are every time putting in the capitalist platform, upholding the social principle that throws them out of work or reduces their wages.

But endurance has its limits. The superintendent of the Pennsylvania Railroad for the Indiana Division, speaking, of course, from the capitalist standpoint, recently said: "Many solutions are being offered for the labor question; but there is just one and no more. It is this: Lay a silver dollar on the shelf, and at the end of a year you have a silver dollar left; lay a workingman on the shelf, and at the end of a month you have a skeleton left."

"This," said he, "is the solution of the labor problem." In short, starve out the workers.

No. 1's men finally reach that point. Finally that happens that few if any can resist. A man may stand starvation and resist the sight of starving wife and children; but if he has nor wherewith to buy medicine to save the life of a sick wife or child, he loses all control. On the heels of starvation, sickness follow, and No. 1's men throw to the wind all union principles. They are now ready to do anything to save their dear ones. Cap in hand, they appear before No. 1, the starch taken clean out of them during the period they "lay on the shelf." They ask for work. They themselves offer to work for $1 a day.

And No. 1, the brother of labor, who but recently expressed devotion to the union, what of him? His eyes sparkle at "seeing again" the men he had thrown out, at their offer to work for less than the men now employed. His chest expands, and, grabbing them by the hand in a delirium of patriotic ecstasy, he says: "Welcome, my noble American citizens. I am proud to see you ready to work and earn an honest penny for your dear wives and darling children. I am delighted to notice that you are not, like so many others, too lazy to work. Let the American eagle screech in honor of your emancipation from the slavery of a rascally union. Let the American eagle wag his tail an extra wag in honor of your freedom from a dictatorial walking delegate. You are my long lost brothers. Go in, my $1-a-day brothers!" — and he throws his former $2-a-day brothers heels-over-head upon the sidewalk.

When the late $2-a-day men have recovered from their surprise, they determine on war. But what sort of war? Watch them closely, and you may detect many a feature of your own in that mirror. "Have we not struck," argue they, "and beaten this employer once before? If we strike again, we shall again beat him." But the conditions have wholly changed.

In the first place, there were no unemployed skilled workers during that first strike; now there are; plenty of them, dumped upon the country, not out of the steerage of vessels from Europe, but by the native-born machine.

In the second place, that very machine has to such an extent eliminated skill that, while formerly only the unemployed in a certain trade could endanger the jobs of those at work in that trade, now the unemployed of all trades, virtually the whole army of the unemployed, bear down upon the employed in each. We know of former shoemakers taking the jobs of hatters, former hatters taking the jobs of weavers, former weavers taking the jobs of cigarmakers, former cigarmakers taking the jobs of machinists, former farmhands taking the jobs of factory hands, etc., etc., so easy has it become to learn what now needs to be known of a trade.

In the third place, telegraph and railroad have made all of the unemployed easily accessible to the employer.

Finally, different from former days, the competitors have to a great extent consolidated. Here in New Bedford, for instance, the false appearance of competition between the mill owners is punctured by the fact that to a great extent seemingly "independent" mills are owned by one family, as is the case with the Pierce family.

Not, as at the first strike, with their flanks protected, but now wholly exposed through the existence of a vast army of hungry unemployed; not, as before, facing a divided enemy, but now faced by a consolidated mass of capitalist concerns, how different is now the situation of the strikers! The changed conditions brought about changed results; instead of victory, there is defeat; and we have had a long series of them. Either hunger drove the men back to work; or the unemployed took their places; or, if the capitalist was in a hurry, he fetched in the help of the strong arm of the government, now his government.

Principles Of Sound Organization

We now have a sufficient survey of the field to enable us to answer the question, How shall we organize so as not to fight the same old hopeless battle?

Proceeding from the knowledge that labor alone produces all wealth; that less and less of this wealth comes to the working class. and more and more of it is plundered by the idle class or capitalist; that this is the result of the working class being stripped of the tool, machine, without which it cannot earn a living; and, finally, that the machine or tool has reached such a state of development that it can no longer be operated by the individual but needs the collective effort of many; proceeding from this knowledge, it is clear that the aim of all intelligent class-conscious workingmen must be the overthrow of the system of private ownership in the tools of production because that system keeps them in wage slavery.

Proceeding from the further knowledge of the use made of the government by the capitalist class, and of the necessity that class is under to own the government, so as to enable it to uphold and prop up the capitalist system; proceeding from that knowledge, it is clear that the aim of all intelligent, class-conscious workingmen must be to bring the government under the control of their own class, by joining and electing the American wing of the international Socialist party — the Socialist Labor Party of America, and thus establishing the Socialist Cooperative Republic.

But in the meantime, while moving toward that ideal, though necessary, goal, what to do? The thing cannot be accomplished in a day, nor does election come around every twenty-four hours. Is there nothing that we can do for ourselves between election and election? Yes—plenty.

When crowded, in argument, to the wall by us New Trade Unionists, by us of the Socialist Trade and Labor Alliance, your present, or old and "pure and simple" organizations, yield the point of ultimate aims; they grant the ultimate necessity of establishing Socialism; but they claim "the times are not yet ripe" for that; and, not yet being ripe, they lay emphasis upon the claim that the "pure and simple" union does the workers some good *now* by getting something *now* from the employers and from the capitalist parties. We are not "practical" they tell us; they are.

Let us test this theory on the spot. Here in New Bedford there is not yet a single New Trade Unionist organization in existence. The "pure and simple" trade union has had the field all to itself. All of you, whose wages are now *higher* than they were five years ago, kindly raise a hand. All of you whose wages are now *lower* than five years ago, please raise a hand. The proof of the pudding lies in the eating. Not only does "pure and simpledom" shut off your hope of emancipation by affecting to think such a state of things is unreachable now, but in the meantime and *right now*, the "good" it does to you, the "something" it secures for you "from the employers and from the politicians" is lower wages.

That is what their "practicalness" amounts to in point of fact. Presently I shall show you that they prove "practical" only to the labor fakers who run them, and whom they put up with. No, no; years ago, before capitalism had reached its present development, a trade organization of labor could and did afford protection to the workers, even if, as the "pure and simple" union, it was wholly in the dark on the issue. That time is no more.

The New Trade Unionist knows that no one or two, or even half a dozen elections will place in the hands of the working class the government of the land; and New Trade Unionism, not only wishes to do something now for the workers, but it knows that the thing can be done, and how to do it.

"Pure and simple" or British trade unionism has done a double mischief to the workers. Besides leaving them in their present pitiable plight, it has caused many to fly off the handle and lose all trust in the power of trade organization. The best of these, those who have not become pessimistic and have not been wholly demoralized, see nothing to be done but voting right on election day—casting their vote straight for the SLP. This is a serious error. By thus giving over all participation in the industrial movement, they wholly disconnect themselves from the class struggle that is going on every day; and by putting off their whole activity to a single day in the year, election day, they become floaters in the air. I know several such. Without exception they are dreamy and flighty and unbalanced in their methods.

The utter impotence of "pure and simple" unionism today is born of causes that may be divided under two main heads.

One is the contempt in which the capitalist and ruling class holds the working people. In 1886, when instinct was, unconsciously to myself, leading me to look into the social problem, when as yet it was to me a confused and blurred interrogation mark, I associated wholly with capitalists. Expressions of contempt for the workers were common. One day I asked a set of then why they treated their men so hard, and had so poor an opinion of them. "They are ignorant, stupid and corrupt," was the answer, almost in chorus.

"What makes you think so?" I asked. "Have you met them all?"

"No," was the reply, "we have not met them all individually, but we have had to deal with their leaders, and they are ignorant, stupid and corrupt. Surely these leaders must be the best among them, or they would not choose them."

Now, let me illustrate. I understand that two days ago, in this city, Mr. Gompers went off at a tangent and shot off his mouth about me. What he said was too ridiculous for me to answer. You will have noticed that he simply gave what he wishes you to consider as his opinion; he furnished you no facts from which he drew it, so that you could judge for yourselves. He expected you to take him on faith. I shall not insult you by treating you likewise. Here are the facts on which my conclusion is based:

In the State of New York we have a labor law forbidding the working of railroad men more than 10 hours. The railroad companies disregarded the law. In Buffalo, the switchmen struck in 1892 to enforce the law; thereupon the Democratic governor, Mr. Flower, who had himself signed the law, sent the whole militia of the state into Buffalo to help the railroad capitalists break the law, incidentally to commit assault and battery with intent to kill, as they actually did, upon the workingmen. Among our state Senators is one Jacob Cantor. This gentleman hastened to applaud Gov. Flower's brutal violation of his oath of office to uphold the Constitution and the laws. Cantor applauded the act as a patriotic one in the defense of "law and order."

At a subsequent campaign, this Cantor being a candidate for reelection, the New York *Daily News*, a capitalist paper of Cantor's political complexion, published an autograph letter addressed to him and intended to be an endorsement of him by labor. This letter contained this passage among others: "If any one says you are not a friend of labor, he says what is not true."

By whom was this letter written and by whom signed? By Mr. Samuel Gompers, "President of the American Federation of Labor."

Whom are you hissing, Gompers or me?

Do you imagine that the consideration for that letter was merely the "love and affection" of Senator Cantor?

Again: The Republican party, likewise the Democratic, is a party of the capitalist class; every man who is posted knows that; the conduct of its presidents, governors, judges, congresses and legislatures can leave no doubt upon the subject. Likewise the free coinage of silver, or Populist party, was, while it lived, well known to be a party of capital; the conduct of its runners, the silver mine barons, who skin and then shoot down their miners, leaves no doubt upon that subject. But the two were deadly opposed: one wanted gold, the other silver. Notwithstanding these facts, a "labor leader" in New York City appeared at a recent campaign standing, not upon the Republican capitalist party platform only, not upon the Free-Silver capitalist party platform only, but on both; he performed the acrobatic feat of being simultaneously for gold and against silver, for silver against gold.

Who was that "labor leader"? Mr. Samuel Gompers, "President of the American Federation of Labor."

Again: In Washington there is a son of a certain labor leader with a government job. He is truly "non-partisan."' Democrats may go and

Republicans may come, Republicans may go and Democrats may come, but he goeth not; the Democratic and the Republican capitalists may fight like cats and dogs, but on one thing they fraternize like cooing doves, to wit, to keep that son of a labor leader in office.

Who is the father of that son? Mr. Samuel Gompers, "President of the A.F. of L."

Again: You have here a "labor leader," named Ross.

[Applause]

Unhappy men! Unhappy men! As well might you applaud the name of your executioner.

When I was here about three years ago I met him. He was all aglow with the project of a bill that he was going to see through your legislature, of which he was and is now a member. It was the anti-fines bill; that, thought he, was going to put an end to an infamous practice of the mill owners. I argued with him that it does not matter what the law is; the all important thing was, which is the class charged with enforcing it? So long as the capitalist class held the government, all such labor laws as he was straining for, were a snare and a delusion. What I said seemed to be Greek to him. He went ahead and the bill passed. And what happened? You continued to be fined after, as before; and when one of you sought to enforce the law, was he not arrested and imprisoned? And when another brought the lawbreaking mill owner, who continued to fine him, into court, did not the capitalist court decide in favor of the capitalist, and thus virtually annulled the law? And where was Mr. Ross all this time? In the Massachusetts Legislature. Do you imagine that his ignorance of what a capitalist government means, and of what its "labor laws" amount to, did not throw its shadow upon and color you in the capitalist's estimation? Do you, furthermore, imagine that his sitting there in that legislature, a member of the majority party at that, and never once demanding the prompt impeachment of the court that rendered null that very law that he had worked to pass, do you imagine that while he plays such a complaisant role he is a credit to the working class?

No need of further illustrations. The ignorance, stupidity and corruption of the "pure and simple" labor leaders is such that the capitalist class despises you. The first prerequisite for success in a struggle is the respect of the enemy.

The other main cause of the present impotence of "pure and simple" unionism is that, through its ignoring the existing class distinctions, and its ignoring the close connection there is between wages and politics, it splits up at the ballot box among the parties of capital, and thus unites in upholding the system of capitalist exploitation.

Look at the recent miners' strike; the men were shot down and the strike was lost; this happened in the very midst of a political campaign; and these miners, who could at any election capture the government, or at least, by polling a big vote against capitalism, announce their advance toward freedom, are seen to turn right around and vote back into power the very class that had just trampled upon them.

What prospect is there, in sight of such conduct, of the capitalists becoming gentler? Or of the union gaining for the men anything *now* except more wage reductions, enforced by bullets? None! The prospect of the miners and other workers doing the same thing over again, a prospect that is made all the surer if they allow themselves to be further led by the labor fakers whom the capitalists keep in pay, renders sure that capitalist outrages will be repeated, and further capitalist encroachments will follow.

Otherwise were it if the union, identifying politics and wages, voted against capitalism; if it struck at the ballot box against the wage system with the same solidarity that it demands for the strike in the shop.

Protected once a year by the guns of an increasing class-conscious party of labor, the union could be a valuable fortification behind which to conduct the daily class struggle in the shops.

The increasing Socialist Labor Party vote alone would not quite give that temporary protection in the shop that such an increasing vote would afford if, in the shop also, the workers were intelligently organized, and honestly, because intelligently, led.

Without organization in the shop, the capitalist could outrage at least individuals.

Shop organization alone, unbacked by that political force that threatens the capitalist class with extinction, the working class, being the overwhelming majority, leaves the workers wholly unprotected.

But the shop organization that combines in its warfare the annually recurring class-conscious ballot can stem capitalist encroachment from day to day.

The trade organization is impotent if built and conducted upon the impotent lines of ignorance and corruption. The trade organization is *not* impotent if built and conducted upon the lines of knowledge and honesty; if it understands the issue and steps into the arena fully equipped, not with the shield of the trade union only, but also with the sword of the Socialist ballot.

The essential principles of sound organization are, accordingly, these:

1st — A trade organization must be clear upon the fact that, not until it has overthrown the capitalist system of private ownership in the machinery of production, and made this the joint property of the people, thereby compelling everyone to work if he wants to live, is it at all possible for the workers to be safe.

2nd — A labor organization must be perfectly clear upon the fact that it cannot reach safety until it has wrenched the government from the clutches of the capitalist class; and that it cannot do that unless it votes, not for men but for principles, unless it votes into power its own class platform and program: the abolition of the wages system of slavery.

3rd — A labor organization must be perfectly clear upon the fact that politics are not, like religion, a private concern, any more than the wages and the hours of a workingman are his private concern. For the same reason that his wages and hours are the concern of his class, so is his politics. Politics is not separable from wages. For the same reason that the organization of labor dictates wages, hours, etc:, in the interest of the working class, for that same reason must it dictate politics also; and for the same reason that it execrates the scab in the shop, it must execrate the scab at the hustings.

The Socialist Trade And Labor Alliance

Long did the Socialist Labor Party and New Trade Unionists seek to deliver this important message to the broad masses of the American proletariat, the rank and file of our working class. But we could not reach, we could not get at them. Between us and them there stood a solid wall of ignorant, stupid and corrupt labor fakers. Like men groping in a dark room for an exit, we moved along the wall, bumping our heads, feeling ever onwards for a door; we made the circuit and no passage was found. The wall was solid. This discovery once made, there was no way other than to batter a breach through that wall. With the battering ram of the Socialist Trade and Labor Alliance we effected a passage; the wall now crumbles; at last we stand face to face with the rank and file of the American proletariat; and we are delivering our message, as you may judge from the howl that goes up from that fakers' wall that we have broken through.

I shall not consider my time well spent with you if I see no fruit of my labors; if I leave not behind me in New Bedford Local Alliances of your trades organized in the Socialist Trade and Labor Alliance. That will be my best contribution toward your strike, as they will serve as centers of enlightenment to strengthen you in your conflict, to the extent that it may now be possible.

In conclusion, my best advice to you for immediate action, is to step out boldly upon the streets, as soon as you can; organize a monster parade of the strikers and of all the other working people in the town; and let the parade be headed by a banner bearing the announcement to your employers:

"We will fight you in this strike to the bitter end; your money bag may beat us now; but whether it does or not, that is not the end, it is only the beginning of the song; in November we will meet again at Philippi, and the strike shall not end until, with the falchion of the Socialist Labor Party ballot, we shall have laid you low for all time!"

This is the message that it has been my agreeable privilege to deliver to you in the name of the Socialist Labor Party, and of the New Trade Unionists or Alliance men of the land.

The Burning Question Of Trades Unionism

An address delivered at the New Auditorium Hall, Newark, N.J., April 21, 1904

Workingmen and Workingwomen of Newark:

That the Trades Union Question is a burning one is obvious from the space it fills in the public mind, the acrimony of the discussion and the wide divergence of opinion on the subject.

Obvious also is the conclusion that a subject that can draw upon itself so much attention, that can produce so much acrimony, and on which opinion takes so many shades—running from extreme and unqualified support through all manner of gradations across the gamut, to extreme and unqualified opposition—cannot choose but be a vital one, and certainly must have a latent something about it that will not down.

Finally, it is obvious that such a question deserves attention—close, serious and sober—and that the solution be grappled with and found. Nor is the task impossible. Despite the widely conflicting views, the solution is not only possible but easy—but possible and easy only by either rising high enough above, or penetrating deep enough below the squabble to enable the inquirer to detect the fact that, despite their being seemingly irreconcilable, the conflicting views have important points of contact. In other words, the solution of the problem depends upon the perception of the fact that there is no real conflict; that what there is is a failure to harmonize views that are supplemental to one another; and that the failure proceeds from the blindness of each side to perceive the element of soundness in the others—a perception without which none can understand the bearings of his own position, and consequently stands stock-fast, impotent—except for suicide.

Before entering upon the analysis of the subject, there is one thing I must request of my audience. It is this: To drop, for the present, all recollections of the corruption and dishonesty in the Trades Union Movement that surely will obtrude themselves upon your minds. Need I say that dishonesty plays an important role in the issue? It does. I shall come to that. But for the present I shall eliminate that factor. It can only confuse if taken up now. Leave it out for the present. The actual and important lines of the question being first established, the corruption element will then fall of itself into natural grooves and help to elucidate the principles. Taken now it can only becloud them.

Never forget this—dishonesty in argument is like a creeping plant that needs support; it would collapse and lie prone but for some solid truth around which to wind its tendrils for support. Let's first ascertain the truth.

Nothing so well illustrates the general situation on the fierce discussion that is going on about Trades Unionism as a certain choice poem of our genial New York poet, the late lamented John Godfrey Saxe. Many of you may have heard it, perhaps even learned it by heart on the school benches. All of you can hear it with profit once more.

The Blind Men And The Elephant

It was six men of Indostan
To learning much inclined,
Who went to see the Elephant
(Though all of them were blind),
That each by observation
Might satisfy his mind.

The First approached the Elephant,
And happening to fall
Against his broad and sturdy side,
At once began to bawl:
"God bless me! but the Elephant
Is very like a wall!"

The Second feeling of the tusk,
Cried, "Ho! what have we here
So very round and smooth and sharp?
To me 'tis mighty clear
This wonder of an Elephant
Is very like a spear!"

The Third approached the animal,
And happening to take
The squirming trunk within his hands,
Thus boldly up and spake:
"I see," quoth he, "the Elephant
Is very like a snake!"

The Fourth reached out his eager hand,
And felt about the knee.
"What most this wondrous beast is like
Is mighty plain," quoth he;
'Tis clear enough the Elephant
Is very like a tree!"

The Fifth who chanced to touch the ear,
Said: "E'en the blindest man
Can tell what this resembles most;
Deny that fact who can,
This marvel of an Elephant
Is very like a fan!"

The Sixth no sooner had begun
About the beast to grope,
Than, seizing on the swinging tail
That fell within his scope,
"I see," quoth he, "the Elephant
Is very like a rope!"

And so these men of Indostan
Disputed loud and long,
Each in his own opinion
Exceeding stiff and strong,
Though each was partly in the right,
And all were in the wrong!

Why? Why were they all in the wrong? Simply because none could see where the others were right, and, consequently, was unable to understand even himself.

Leaving general illustrations and stepping into the concrete, let us take two or three instances on the question itself.

Take this instance — President Eliot of Harvard says: "The scab is a hero!" President Gompers of the A. F. of L. says: "The scab is a scamp!" It may need a superhuman effort, but, I pray you exercise it. Repress the thoughts of dishonesty that the mention of these two names must inevitably conjure up to your minds. Let us examine the two utterances, regardless of who made them. They are made. That is enough for our purpose. They seem wholly irreconcilable. Are they, in fact? Let us see:

Here is a shop. What with fines, the intensity of the work demanded, and other impositions, the wages are inhumanly low. On top of that, a further reduction is inflicted upon the men, and they rebel. A strike is on. Presently men who are not starving, but who either occupy other positions in the employer's service and wish to ingratiate themselves with their masters, or who despise labor, step into the shop and help him out. Such instances occurred in the telegraphers' strike and a shoemakers' strike in New York, and recently when Yale students took the places of striking car drivers in New Haven. Who will deny that the man who does such a thing is a scab and a scamp?

But now, look at this other picture. A number of breweries in this neighborhood and New York had a contract with their employees; the contract expired and the breweries wanted a new contract less favorable to the men. In order to accomplish that they needed the help of the officers of the union. They obtained it. A contract, that tied the men's hands and left them at the employers' mercy, is drawn up and jammed through the union partly under false pretenses and partly by brute force. Members of the rank and file rebel, and their spokesman, Valentine Wagner, demands an explanation from the officers. He is fined for "insubordination," and fine is laid upon fine until the amount has risen to $80; as he still remains "insubordinate," and as the officers are in league with the brewery bosses, the man is expelled, thrown out of work as "not being a member of the union," and left to starve. These facts have all been made public and proved. Thereupon, to the threat that if he dared work in any brewery lie would be called a "scab," Valentine Wagner announced that not only would he dare, but that he would deem it an honor to be called a "scab"! Who would deny that Valentine Wagner is a hero?

Are the two utterances, "The scab is a scamp," and "The scab is a hero," utterly irreconcilable? Evidently not. Evidently they harmonize perfectly. And in perceiving the common ground for both, we are enlightened on what the "scab" is. The "scab" is he who by his voluntary conduct helps to lower the standard of the worker. He who for the pleasure of it, or out of currishness to the master, will help to break a strike for better conditions is a "scab" and "scamp," and a "scamp" and "scab" is the union officer who conspires with the master against the interests of the men. They are both scabs because, by helping to down the worker, they sap the nation and introduce disease, death and the pestilence of a degraded people. That is the test of the "scab." The scab may wear the union label as well as not.

Take this other instance—one set of people says: "The union must be a good thing because the capitalists hate it"; another set says: "The union is a bad thing because the capitalists love it." These two utterances seem wholly irreconcilable. Are they, in fact? Let us see:

Look at what is going on in Colorado. The right of habeas corpus, the dignity of the courts, the right of free assemblage and free speech—in short, all the great civic conquests of the past—are trampled on by the capitalist class in power in that state, and all for the purpose of smashing the Western Federation of Miners. If ever there was an instance of hatred this is one. The capitalists hate that union to the point of endangering even the privileges that their own class still stands in need of.

But now look at this other picture. Charles Corregan, a member of the Syracuse, N.Y., local of the International Typographical Union, speaking on the public stump for the Socialist Labor Party, gave facts and figures concerning an important factor in the labor movement, to wit, the manner in which the pure and simple trades union is run by its officers, and he illustrated the points with the officers of his own union. He is thereupon tried by these officers, convicted and fined in his absence without charges being presented to him; and as he refused to pay a fine imposed under such conditions, a strike was ordered in the shop against him and he was thrown out of work. The very fact that a strike could be called against him, that the employer virtually lined up with the officers, points to the point I am reaching.

Corregan sued the union for reinstatement and damages, the court threw the case out and, mark you, the capitalist press, particularly that of New York, announced the decision with flaming and jubilating headlines as a union victory.

Are the two utterances, "The capitalists hate the union" and "The capitalists love the union," as irreconcilable as they looked at first?

What is it that discloses their reconcilability? Why, the facts, which, taken together, point to the common ground of the utterances, and thereby clarify both. That common ground tells us that capitalism justly sees in Socialism, in the Socialist Labor Party, its unquestioned foe, while with equal accuracy it perceives in the union an organism of various possibilities—a possibility of injury to the capitalist class, and also a possibility of safety and protection; where the possibility of injury takes shape, as in Colorado, hatred is developed for the union; where the possibility of safety and protection takes shape, as in Corregan's case, love is developed for the union.

We are making progress out of the woods. But, before proceeding further in our march, let us establish a collateral point hinted at by these facts.

The country has in recent years been twice convulsed by two economic-political issues that may be called great when we consider the millions of votes that they shared among them. And both these issues may yet spring up again. The one is the tariff, the other the silver issue.

When the tariff was the issue, the Democratic free trader declared that protection was robbery; on the other hand, the Republican protectionist pronounced free trade unpatriotic. The free trader argued that the tariff was like an artificial mountain raised at the gates of the nation and, thereby, increasing the cost of goods. "Tear down these mountains," said he, "and prices will decline." That is all true, but we Socialists know that if the artificial mountains of the tariff are removed, prices will go down true enough, but seeing labor is a merchandise under the capitalist system of production, its own price, wages, must go down along with that of all other merchandise. The advantage, accordingly, of lower prices is lost to the working class.

The Republican protectionist argued that it was the duty of government to promote by protecting and protect by promoting the interests of the people. "A tariff," said the Republicans, "protects the country inasmuch as it enables it to differentiate its industries, unchecked by foreign competition." This also is all true, but we Socialists know that if government is to be at all justified it is upon the ground of the protection it affords to the people; and we also know that, under the capitalist system, the "people" who count are not the workers, but the capitalist shirkers, and, consequently, that the advantage to be derived from the theory of protection does not extend to the workers, to the majority of the people. They are left out in the cold. The tariffs protect the capitalists against foreign competition, but not the workers. The largest infloods of foreign labor have been instigated and taken place under Republican "protection" administrations.

Accordingly, while both "free trade" and protection have an element of truth in them, that element is in both cases lost to the people under capitalist rule. It takes Socialism, the Socialist Republic, to harmonize the two opposites. Under the dome of the Socialist Republic the discord between the two principles vanishes, and only the truth remains. Under Socialism the "mountains" of tariffs may be safely removed: the decline in prices will not then drag down labor's earnings because labor will have ceased to be merchandise and become a human factor—what it now is only in the speeches of capitalist politicians at election time, and in the sermons of the political parsons between election and election. Likewise with regard to protection. The principle of organized mutual protection through government becomes truthful and effective only under Socialism where, there being only one class, the working class, government is truly of, by, and for the people.

It is similarly with the silver question. The free coinagists denounced the gold standard men as robbers; the gold standard men denounced the free coinagists as bandits—and each was right and both were wrong. As to the free coinagists: their theory was that money is a good thing and that the more there is of a good thing the larger is the per capita thereof for the people. We know that right as the premises are, under capitalism the conclusions become wrong.

There are infinitely more hats, shoes, coats and other good things today than thirty years ago in the land; but everybody knows that the workingman's per capita of these good things has not increased. He has remained where he was, if not even below, while the increase has gone to the Anna Goulds, the Consuelo Vanderbilts, the international capitalists in short. And we understand the reason why.

Under capitalism, the workingman being a merchandise, his price (wages) does not depend upon the quantity of good things in existence, but upon the quantity of him in the labor market. The same as, regardless of the quantity of money there may be in the money market, pork chops will fetch a smaller price if the pork chop market is overstocked, so will the merchandise labor fetch a smaller price, however much money there may be, if the labor market is overstocked. And capitalism does that very thing. Privately-owned improved machinery, and concentration of plants, ruthlessly displace labor and overstock the labor market.

Thus, capitalism renders absurd the premises above mentioned of free coinagism. On the other hand, the gold standard men proceeded from the principle that money is a merchandise and must have value, from which they concluded that the workingman would be robbed unless he was paid with what they call a 100-cent dollar. Here again, right as the premises are, capitalism renders the conclusion false. As shown above, labor being a merchandise, it matters nothing what the counter is in which it is paid. Its price depends upon its market value; and it is all one to it whether it gets paid with one 100-cent gold dollar for its day's toil, or with two fifty-cent silver dollars.

Accordingly, while both the free coinage and the gold standard principle have an element of truth in them, under capitalism the truth is lost to the workers. It takes Socialism to harmonize the two. Under Socialism, labor no longer being a merchandise, the more good things it produces, the more it has, and the 100-cent dollar ceases to be its merchandise badge and, thereby, a fraud upon it.

These two sets of illustrations will suffice. They throw light upon what otherwise is puzzling in modern society, to wit, that correct principles work evil. Free trade and protection are both accompanied with increasing masses of pauperism; gold standard and silver standard leave nothing to choose between them for the masses. The sense in each is turned into nonsense by capitalist rule; it is Socialism that alone can redeem them.

And as the Socialist key alone can unlock the secret of this conflict of thought, it is the Socialist key alone that can unlock the secret of the conflict of thought with regard to the burning question of trades unionism. Equipped with this key, we shall be able to acquire a full grasp of the question at hand, and see the elephant in full with all his members coordinate, and not as a jumble of "rope," "spear," "snake," "wall," "tree" and what other things the blind men of the story took the animal to be.

Pro- And Anti-Unionist Arguments

Let us take two types on the question—both honest—but one holding that the trades union pure and simple is all-sufficient and useful, while the other holds that the trades union is worthless; in other words, one holding the trunk of the elephant and claiming he is a snake, the other holding his tail and claiming he is a rope; bring the two together, and, both being honest, this dialogue will take place between them:

Anti-unionist—"Drop your union, it is no good. Smash it!"

Pro-unionist—"What! my union no good? I am a member of the Housesmiths' and Bridgemen's Union. I know what I am talking about. Before we had a union we could barely make two dollars a day. Now that we have a union I make four and sometimes five dollars. Don't tell me the union is no good."

Anti-unionist—"You are hasty in your judgment. You are judging all the unions by one, and your own union by only one epoch of its existence. I grant that through your union you are now getting two dollars more. But that is only a temporary affair. Exceptional circumstances aided Sam Parks in bringing up your wages. But how long will that last? Look at the other unions, take the census of the men. Without exception, earnings are lower. The census itself admits that wages are now lower than they were ten years ago. What happened to the older unions will happen to yours. They were not able to raise earnings of the working class. Already the day is at hand when your union will be in the same fix. No, it is not true that the union can raise wages, speaking of the union in general."

Pro-unionist—"Well, that's so. Speaking with union men of other trades, they all say how hard it is for them to get along. Yes, the union cannot raise earnings. But it is a good thing all the same; it can keep wages from declining."

Anti-unionist—"You are mistaken again. Look over the field. Look below the surface. You will find that, despite the union, earnings go down as a whole. Look at the savage reductions inflicted upon the steel and iron workers. A numerically strong union. Despite the union, a savage reduction was made."

Pro-unionist—"Well, I can't deny that (after a pause), but you must admit that if we had no union the decline would be swifter. Will you deny that the union acts as a brake upon the decline? Would we not be down to the coolie stage today if it were not for the union?"

Anti-unionist—"You have admitted that the union cannot raise wages; you have admitted that it cannot keep wages where they are; and you have admitted that it cannot prevent their reduction. Your last ditch is that it keeps wages from going down as fast as they would otherwise go. I'll now drive you out of that ditch. If your theory means anything it means that the union will last, at least, as a brake. Now you know that periodically men are laid off by the thousands, and hundreds of thousands. These laid-off men want to live; they will offer themselves for a lower price. If your union strikes it goes to smash, if it does not strike it melts to smash, so that, even as a brake, the day is at hand when your unions will exist no more."

Pro-unionist—"You have hit me hard. Perhaps you think you have knocked me out. But you have not. As sure as a man will raise his hand by mere instinct, to shield himself against a blow, so surely will workingmen, instinctively, periodically gather into unions. The union is the arm that labor instinctively throws up to screen its head."

Unquestionably both the pure and simple pro-unionist and the anti-unionist are knocked out. They have knocked out each other.

The pro-unionist's last statement is a knockout blow to the man who imagines that the union is a smashable thing.

On the other hand, the anti-unionist's argumentation, whereby he brings out the fact that the union's claims of potential triumph are false, and that, driven from defeat to defeat, the union can gather for the next defeat only, knocks out the pro-unionist. That is to say, the pure and simple pro-unionist.

In their mutual trituration the materials are gathered with which Socialism can build the four-jointed truth. Let us now take the "tail" and "trunk" and "legs" and "ears" and "body" of the elephant as furnished us by these two typical disputants, and construct the animal. The disputants' positions will be found to be, not inherently irreconcilable, but fully reconcilable.

Starting from the principle, an undeniable one, that the spirit of union formation is an instinctive one, the question immediately presents itself: Is there no way by which the instinctive motion of self-defense can be rendered effective? Does it follow that because the man who raises his hand to protect his head from the threatened blow with a crowbar, has both his arm and his skull crushed, that therefore the instinctive motion of self-defense might as well be given up? The question suggests the immediate answer. The answer is no, it does not follow. And the question, furthermore, indicates what does follow. It follows that the arm which periodically is thrown up in self-defense, must arm itself with a weapon strong enough to resist—at least to break the blow.

Naval warfare did not end when guns of stronger power were contrived. What followed was that stronger armor plate was contrived for the battleships; nor did naval warfare end there; when battleships became so impregnable, contact mines were invented which sink these as if by magic. And so it can be done here.

Pro-unionists always talk about the union being a "natural condition." But they forget that so are hair and nails. No sensible man will pull hairs and nails out by the root; but neither would any sensible man say that because hair and nails are natural they must be allowed to grow untrimmed and untended. Pro-unionists always talk about the condition under which the union was born. So are babes born under puny condition. No sensible man would kill the babe because so born; but neither will any sensible man propose to keep the babe forever in the condition under which it was born. That it is a natural growth is an important fact to recognize, but how to improve it is equally important, and that can be done by bringing the above pro- and anti-unionist arguments together.

The last anti-unionist argument condenses in itself all the previous ones. It correctly points out that the large displacements of labor render the union futile. It implies unionism in general, but that is a mistake. It is true if applied to unionism as it is today, that is to say, in the babe form under which it was born.

My point will be made clear if we suggest to both the pro-unionist and the anti-unionist that all the members of a trade be enlisted in the union—those at work, those temporarily displaced, and those that may be considered permanently displaced. At the bare thought of such a proposition both the pro-unionist and the anti-unionist will throw up their hands; and both their gestures of hand and face indicate that neither of the two has of the union any but a babe condition notion.

Why will the pro-unionist look dismayed at the proposition? He will because he knows that his union is there to give jobs to its members; that none join it but for jobs; and, consequently, that if the applicants exceed the jobs the union would immediately go to pieces, if they are all inside. The notion of the anti-unionist is the exact reverse of the pro-unionist's notion. And both are right from their standpoint, but their standpoint is wrong; it is as wrong as that of the blind men at the several limbs of the elephant. The thought suggested by the pro-unionist's last argument, that the union is like the instinctive motion of the man who raises his arm to protect his head when assailed, gives us in hand the method to proceed by.

Instructed upon the nature of the weapon of assault, man will strengthen the arm that he throws up in defense of his head. But the effectiveness of that strengthening depends entirely upon the correctness of his idea on the nature of the instrument of assault.

In the babe condition under which the union is born naturally, it has no conception of the nature of the weapon that it instinctively raises up its arm in self-defense against.

In that natural and original babe condition the union does not realize that its members are merchandise in the present state of society; it does not realize the law that governs the value and price of merchandise; consequently, it does not realize the law that underlies its own value and price, that is, its wages; it does not realize the cause of its degraded merchandise status; it does not realize that its lack of the natural (land) and social (capital) opportunities keep it down; accordingly, it does not realize there is no improvement, let alone salvation, for it so long as it labors under the status of merchandise; finally, and most important of all, and as a result of all, it does not understand that it cannot improve faster than the rest of the working class.

In other words, it does not understand the import of the "solidarity of labor."

It matters not what phrases the pure and simple trades union may use, the fact that none of them would like today to see all the members of the trade in the union, the fact that the trades not directly concerned, aye, even those directly concerned, do not rise in indignation when such other trades as the railroaders are found willing to transport militias from one end of the country to the other in order to break a strike—these facts demonstrate that the meaning of the word solidarity is a closed book to the pro-unionist.

On the other hand, the anti-unionist is utterly mistaken when he proceeds from the theory that this closed book is to remain closed; in other words that the union can never rise above its babe state of natural birth; in other words, that the union is useless.

Leaving for later on the feature of the remoter utility of the union, in fact, its real revolutionary and historic mission, let us be first clear upon the fundamental error that, odd enough to say, both the pure and simple pro-unionist and the anti-unionist stand.

The honest pro-unionist frankly admits that the best he can expect of his union is to act as a brake on the decline. In other words, he admits that the union only serves as a rear guard to a retreating army. Obviously, from that standpoint the anti-unionist's position is impregnable when he holds that the rear guard of a retreating army, which can do nothing but retreat, is a futile thing. But equally obvious is the fact that the whole strength of the anti-unionist position lies in the babe original condition that the union has remained in.

The point need but be made and it will be accepted by every thinking man that all the reasons which the anti-unionist advances why the union is bound to go to smash through the displacement of labor will fall flat the moment the union gets out of its natural, original babe condition, realizes that it not only endangers the future but that it also loses the present by turning itself into a jobs-providing machine. Even if the union cannot grasp its great historic and revolutionary mission, it certainly must, for the sake of the immediate present, be supposed to be willing to adapt its methods, not to the babe, but the adult conditions of capitalism.

Capitalism displaces labor; capitalism needs a large army of idle and reserve labor for the periods of industrial expansion.

By constituting itself a jobs-furnishing institution, the union turns itself into a pint measure into which it is impossible for the gallon measure of labor to be received. And thus it is not only the capitalist, from in front, but labor, from behind, that triturates the union. In order to be able to contain the gallon measure of labor the union must expand to gallon size; in order to expand to gallon size it must drop its idle aspirations as a jobs-furnishing monopoly. And this can be done only if it rises to the elevation of its political mission. Then will it understand the solidarity of its class generally and of the members of its trade in particular.

Even if as many 50,000 out of a trade of 100,000 members cannot be provided for with jobs, the union could do better by taking them all in. But this sounds like a purely chimerical idea under the general babe condition notions that exist. The chimera, however, becomes possible if the members are all tutored to understand that the best the union can do for them today is to check the decline and prevent it from going as fast as it otherwise would.

Not only in the long run, but all along, would such a union fare at least as well as it fares today, besides being in a condition to actually fulfill its great revolutionary historic mission that I have all along been alluding to.

What is that great historic revolutionary mission?

It must be admitted that however philosophic, possibly even Socialist, the anti-unionist may pronounce himself, he is on this subject not a bit more enlightened than the pro-unionist.

It is to me surprising to find men who call themselves Socialists, and who reason socialistically up to a certain point, suddenly go to pieces when they touch the union question. They take certain facts into consideration, these facts correctly point to the eventual destruction of the union, and from these they conclude that the union might as well be smashed now as later. They fail to consider all the facts in the case. They are the real utopians of today who imagine the Socialist Commonwealth can be established like spring establishes itself through its balmy atmosphere, and without effort melts away the winter snows. These anti-union utopians only see the political feature of the labor movement. According to them, all that a lance would need is its iron head.

On the other hand, the pro-unionists have their noses so close to the ground that they fail to see the political aspect of the trades union movement, and can only see what they call its industrial aspect. In other words, they virtually hold that all that a lance would need is its shaft. It goes without saying that neither he who thinks a lance is all iron head, nor he who thinks that it is all shaft has a correct idea of what a lance is, or what its uses are.

Each may have a technical, theoretic, more or less practical knowledge of each particular part of a lance, but a lance neither of them will have, nor can wield.

I shall show you that unless the political aspect of the labor movement is grasped, Socialism will never triumph; and that unless its trades union aspect is grasped the day of its triumph will be the day of its defeat.

Who of you has not heard some workingman when told that some fellow workingman of his was nominated for Mayor, or for Governor, or for Congress, sneeringly say: "What's he? What could he do in Congress? What does he know about law? Why, he wouldn't know how to move!" The matter is serious; it is no laughing matter. The workingman who utters himself in that way is right and he is wrong. He is absolutely right when he considers that the workingman is not a fit man to handle the laws of the land; but he is wrong when he considers that that is a disqualification. In other words, he is wrong in supposing that the political mission of labor is to dabble with or tinker upon capitalist laws.

And mark you, his blunder proceeds direct, both from the pro-unionist industrial mental attitude and from the anti-unionist's political mental attitude. In this respect is realized into what errors the political anti-unionist drops in his own domain of politics, and into what error the industrial pro-unionist drops in his own industrial domain—due to the circumstance that both fail to realize that their various domains dovetail into each other.

Open any law book, whatever the subject be—contract, real estate, aye, even marital relations, husband and wife, father and son, guardian and ward—you will find that the picture they throw upon the mind's canvas is that of everyone's hands at everyone's throat. Capitalist law reflects the material substructure of capitalism. The theory of that substructure is war, conflict, struggle. It can be no otherwise. Given the private ownership of natural and social opportunities, society is turned into a jungle of wild beasts, in which the "fittest" wild beast terrorizes the less "fit," and these in turn imitate among themselves the "fit" qualities of the biggest brute. No nuptial veils of lace or silk can conceal this state of things on the matrimonial field; no rhetoric can hide it on any other field. The rawboned struggle is there. It is inevitable. It is a shadow cast by the angles of fact of the capitalist system.

Now, then, is it the mission of the labor or Socialist movement to continue or to uproot the material conditions that cast the shadow? Its mission is to uproot it. Consequently its mission cannot be to tinker at the laws that capitalism finds it necessary to enact. As well say that a housekeeper is unfit to clean a neglected house because she has no technical knowledge of the construction of the vermin that has been rioting in it, as to say that, because labor has no knowledge of the technique of the vermin of capitalist laws, it is unfit to take the broom handle and sweep the vermin into the ash barrel of oblivion.

Accordingly, the political aspect of the labor movement spells revolution. It points out exactly the duty of the Socialist or class-conscious workingmen elected to office — no tinkering, no compromise, unqualified overthrow of existing laws. That means the dethronement of the capitalist class.

And what does that, in turn, mean with regard to the subject in hand?

Did you notice, and did you realize, all that there was in the capitalist threat of closing down the shops and stopping production if Bryan was elected in 1896? We know that Bryan was a reactionary capitalist; nevertheless, the fact was brought out in his campaign by that upper-capitalist threat that the ruling capitalists have it in their power to create a panic any time the government slips from their hands. What places that power in their hands? Now watch close, think close — What places that power in their hands is the pure and simple trades union: it is the fact that the working class is not organized. And I have shown you that the pure and simple trades union is unable to organize the working class; that it keeps the working class hopelessly divided.

The majority of the voters are workingmen. But even if this majority were to sweep the political field on a class-conscious, that is, a bona fide labor or Socialist ticket, they would find the capitalist able to throw the country into the chaos of a panic and to famine unless they, the workingmen, were so well organized in the shops that they could laugh at all shut-down orders, and carry on production.

Such a complete organization is impossible under pure and simple trades union methods; being impossible on the industrial field, the seeming unity that swept the political field would be a flash in the pan.

Political organization must necessarily partake today of capitalist conditions; accordingly, the votes cast for a Congressman, for instance, are not the votes of any one trade, but of a mixture of scores of trades.

Civilized society will know no such ridiculous thing as geographic constituencies. It will only know industrial constituencies. The parliament of civilization in America will consist, not of Congressmen from geographic districts, but of representatives of trades throughout the land, and their legislative work will not be the complicated one which a society of conflicting interests, such as capitalism, requires but the easy one which can be summed up in the statistics of the wealth needed, the wealth producible, and the work required — and that any average set of workingmen's representatives are fully able to ascertain, infinitely better than our modern rhetoricians in Congress.

But we are not there yet, nor will we be there the day we shall have swept the political field. We shall not be there for the simple reason that in order to get there through that first political victory we shall have been compelled to travel along the lines of capitalist political demarcations; and these I have shown you are essentially non-unionist; that is to say, they ignore industrial bonds and recognize only geographic ones.

It follows that, today, the very best of political organization is wholly exclusive of industrial organization, and will have to continue so until the political victory has been won, and the trades organizations have been able to continue production in the teeth of capitalist revolt; until the nation shall have had time to reconstruct itself upon the labor — that is, the Socialist basis.

Thus we see that the head of the lance of the Socialist movement is worthless without the shaft. We see that they are not even parallel, but closely connected affairs; we see that the one needs the other, that while the head, the political movement, is essential in its way, the shaft of the lance, the industrial movement, is requisite to give it steadiness. The labor movement that has not a well-pointed political lance-head can never rise above the babe condition in which the union is originally born; on the other hand, unhappy the political movement of labor that has not the shaft of the trades union organization to steady it. It will inevitably become a freak affair. The head of the lance may "get there," but unless it drags in its wake the strong shaft of the trades union it will have "got there" to no purpose.

Accordingly, the trades union question is indeed a burning one. On it is pivoted the success of the Socialist movement. And for the reason I have indicated, the confusion on the subject is inevitable.

Seeing that a thing called a union may act as a drag upon the Socialist movement, the temptation is strong upon the part of anti-unionists to drop it. I have shown you how fatal such dropping would be. The political and the industrial movement are one; he who separates them dislocates the Socialist movement.

I should not close without some concreter advice. Should we join unions? Should we not join them? It seems to me these concrete questions stand answered by what I have said before. Nevertheless, he in whose mind such a question still arises is led thereto by the thought of the corrupt practices that exist in unions. I shall take up that point summarily. It now can be handled without giving it undue proportions. It now may even be handled to advantage and help to clinch previous points.

There is no difference between what is called the corruption in the unions and what is noticed in shipwrecks when men become cannibals. I cannot now think of any of the numerous corrupt labor leaders, whom we all know of, who did not start honest enough. But coupled to his honesty was ignorance. He knew not the kind of a weapon that labor instinctively raises its arm to ward off when it shapes itself into unions. He failed, of course. He then imputed the failure to inevitableness. The capitalist helped him along. He lost all hope in the working class. He then decided to feather his own nest. Friendly relations between him and capitalist thought followed inevitably, and he became what Mark Hanna so well called him—the labor lieutenant of the capitalist class.

In that capacity we have seen him engineer strikes in favor of one competing capitalist against another. In that capacity we have seen him act as an agent of the stock exchange, starting strikes to lower stock, or keeping up strikes to favor competing concerns.

Of course, he could not do this if the rank and file of the union were enlightened. For this reason it was in his interest, and in the interest of the class whose lieutenant he is, to keep enlightenment from the masses.

Frequently, also, his position enables him to compel the workingmen of his trade to accept his yoke before they can get work.

He who says remedy this evil by any one means holds silly language. The evil must be attacked by as many means as seem available.

Shall we then "join unions"? The Socialist Labor Party has answered the question by endorsing the Socialist Trade and Labor Alliance, and by waging unflagging war against the Gompers pack; and the answer that the party gave is justified by the light of the analysis that I have submitted to you.

That analysis shows you that trades organizations are essential; they are essential to break the force of the onslaught of the capitalist, but this advantage is fruitful of good only in the measure that the organization prepares itself for the day of final victory.

Accordingly, it must be every Socialist's endeavor to organize his trade. If there is an organization of his trade in existence that is not in the hand of a labor lieutenant of capital, he should join it and wheel it into line with the Socialist Trade and Labor Alliance.

If, however, the organization is entirely in the hands of such a labor lieutenant of capital; if its membership is grown so fast to him and he to them, that the one cannot be shaken from the other; if, accordingly, the organization, obedient to the spirit of capitalism, insists upon dividing the working class by barriers more or less high and chicanery against the admission of all the members of the trade who apply for admission; if his grip of mental corruption upon it is such as to cause a majority of its members to applaud and second his endeavors to keep that majority at work at the sacrifice of the minority within and of the large majority of the trade without—in that and in all such cases, such an organization is not a limb of the labor movement, it is a limb of capitalism; it is a guild; it is a degeneration back to the old starting point of the bourgeois or capitalist class; and though it decks itself with the name of "labor" it is but a caricature, because a belated reproduction, of the old guild system.

Such a bizarre resuscitation of pristine bourgeois organizations may mask itself all it likes with the mask of "labor," but it does so only to the injury of the working class, of the proletariat, and it deserves no quarter at the Socialist's hands.

Such an organization is no more a labor organization than is the army of the czar of Russia, which, though composed wholly of workingmen, is officered by the exploiting class. In such a case the Socialist must endeavor to set up a bona fide labor trades union and to do what he can to smash the fraud. The labor cannon that one day will surely decimate the czar's army, and defeat it, will bring redemption even to the workingmen in that army, although many of them may be killed by it.

Let me sum up, starting with where I closed.

In the first place, the trades union has a supreme mission. That mission is nothing short of organizing by uniting, and uniting by organizing, the whole working class industrially—not merely those for whom there are jobs, accordingly, not only those who can pay dues. This unification or organization is essential in order to save the eventual and possible victory from bankruptcy, by enabling the working class to assume and conduct production the moment the guns of the public powers fall into its hands—or before, if need be, if capitalist political chicanery pollutes the ballot box. The mission is important also in that the industrial organization forecasts the future constituencies of the parliaments of the Socialist Republic.

In the second place, the trades union has an immediate mission. The supreme mission of trades unionism is ultimate. That day is not yet. The road thither may be long or short, but it is arduous. At any rate, we are not yet there.

Steps in the right direction, so-called "immediate demands," are among the most precarious. They are precarious because they are subject and prone to the lure of the "sop" or the "palliative" that the foes of labor's redemption are ever ready to dangle before the eyes of the working class, and at which, aided by the labor lieutenants of the capitalist class, the unwary are apt to snap—and be hooked.

But there is a test by which the bait can be distinguished from the sound step, by which the trap can be detected and avoided, and yet the right step forward taken. That test is this: Does the contemplated step square with the ultimate aim? If it does, then the step is sound and safe; if it does not, then the step is a trap and disastrous.

The "immediate step" that acts like a brake on the decline of wages belongs to the former category, provided only the nature of the brake is not such that it inevitably invites a future decline, that requires a further brake and which brake only invites some later decline, and so on, towards a catastrophe or towards final cooliedom.

We have seen that the pure and simple trades union belongs to the latter category, the category of "traps," and we have seen the reason why—it is merely a jobs-securing machine; consequently, it inevitably rends the working class in twain and, on the whole, has the love and affection of the capitalist exploiter.

In the third place, and finally, the union formation, with its possibility for good, being a natural, an instinctive move, is bound to appear, and reappear, and keep on reappearing, forever offering to the intelligent, serious and honest men in the labor or Socialist movement the opportunity to utilize that instinctive move by equipping it with the proper knowledge, the proper weapon, that shall save it from switching off into the pure and simple quagmire so beloved, and develop into the new trades union so hated of capitalism.

This is the theoretical part of the burning question of trades unionism. Its practical part implies struggle, dauntless struggle against, and war to the knife with that combination of ignoramuses, ripened into reprobates—the labor faker who seeks to coin the helplessness of the proletariat into cash for himself, and the "intellectual" (God save the mark!) who has so superficial a knowledge of things that the mission of unionism is a closed book to him; who believes the union will "fritter out of existence"; who, consequently, is actually against the union, all his pretenses of love for it notwithstanding; and who meantime imagines he can promote Socialism by howling with pure and simple wolves that keep the working class divided and, consequently, bar the path for the triumph of Socialism, or, as the capitalist Wall Street Journal well expressed it, "constitute the bulwark of modern society against Socialism."

The trades union question is, accordingly, not only a burning one, it presents the most trying aspect of the Socialist movement. It brings home to us the fact that not theory only is needed but manly fortitude — that fortitude which the Socialist Labor Party gathers, builds and tests, and without which the Socialist or labor movement becomes ridiculous or infamous.

Questions

William Walker: I desire to ask the speaker whether he considers it wise for a political party to identify itself with a trades union organization if such identification causes the political party to be kept back?

Answer: This question is a begging of the question. It proceeds from assuming as settled the very premises that are under discussion. It proceeds from the assumption which I denied, that a party of Socialism can ignore the trades union. I shall nevertheless answer it. It enables me to take up the question by entering through another gate.

Some eight months ago, when I last delivered an address here in Newark, a gentleman who is now associated with the questioner in setting up here in Newark a so-called Essex County Independent Socialist Club, Mr. Harry Carless, spoke after me and said in substance — the gentleman who just asked the question was present, he will admit that I quote my critic of that day correctly. My critic said: "The Socialist Labor Party should have nothing to do with the trades unions. Affiliation with trades unions keeps the party back. A political party wants to take in as many people as possible. It wants to be as large as possible. A union does not. I am a member of a union, the Silver Polishers', and I am also a Socialist. My union had a meeting this afternoon; all that they want is to get higher wages and to keep all others of the trade out. They adopted a resolution along this line, and I voted with them in the interest of the organization. Now, their position, like that of all unions, is purely selfish. What has the Socialist Labor Party to do with such things? It should keep its hands off. If it does not it will suffer."

My answer was this: "The gentleman furnishes me with the very facts that overthrow him. He is a member of a trades union that wishes to keep out applicants. What would be his fix in a Socialist party? Say his Socialist organization is in session in the evening, and the men whom he, along with the other members of his trades union, refused admission in the afternoon, knock at the door applying for membership. What will he do? He correctly stated that a political party needs numbers. He will have to admit them into his Socialist party organization. And what will happen when those men come in and hear him making a grandiloquent speech on the 'solidarity of labor,' on the 'necessity of workingmen to unite,' on the 'brotherhood of the wage slave,' and on all those things that a Socialist, a good Socialist, as the gentleman says he is, is bound to emphasize? What do you think will happen, when the men whom he has just voted to keep out of his union hear him thus glibly declaiming? Why, they'll say he is a hypocrite; they'll denounce him roundly for preaching one thing and practicing another. They will even bring charges against him. And, if his organization is really a Socialist organization, he will be expelled and justly so. But even if it does not come so far, he will have discovered that a Socialist party cannot play ostrich on the economic or trades union question. If it is a party of Socialism, it is a party of labor. In a party of Socialism the trades union is latent. It cannot be ignored. It will not ignore you."

"But suppose," I went on to say, "that, feeling a presentiment of what is in store for him if he votes to admit them into his party organization, he votes to keep them out. What will he have done then? He will have impressed upon his political organization, which wants large numbers, the characteristics of the backward pure and simple union with which he blandly floats along — another evidence that the trades union question is bound to assert itself."

Was not that the answer I gave your friend? With what face can you, then, come here tonight and ask the question that you did?

There is no such thing as a political party of labor "having nothing to do with the unions." It must have. It must either inspire the union with the broad, political purpose, and thus dominate it by warring on the labor faker and on the old guild notions that hamstring the labor movement, or it is itself dragged down to the selfish trade interests of the economic movement, and finally drawn down into the latter's subservience to the capitalist interests that ever fasten themselves to the selfish trade interests on which the labor faker, or labor lieutenant of the capitalist class, thrives.

The notion implied in the words of our friend who asked the question, the notion that numbers is the important thing and not soundness, often leads to bizarre results. A recent instance is striking.

At the late annual convention of Gompers' A. F. of L., Max Hayes, of the said so-called Socialist party, introduced a Socialist resolution. The resolution was snowed under by a veritable avalanche of something like 11,000 votes. About a month later, the Socialist Trade and Labor Alliance held its annual convention. The S.T. and L.A. is a trades union built strictly upon the Socialist lines of the resolution which Max Hayes introduced in Boston. But the S.T. and L.A. is a very much smaller body. At its annual convention it numbered barely twenty delegates. Now, then, what do we find Mr. Max Hayes saying about the S.T. and L.A. convention? He ridiculed it on account of its numbers. He, who had just been flattened out like a pancake by a huge anti-Socialist convention, seemed proud of having been in a big crowd, and peeping from under the numerous heels that trampled upon him, had jeers only for the smallness of the body that nevertheless upheld the principles which, in his hand, lay flattened out beside him, flattened out by a numerous body.

Such are the fruits, the mental somersaults, of a chase after numbers. It is nothing short of idiocy. The head of the lance that rushes forward shaftless, rushes forward uselessly. It should move no faster than its shaft.

The "Socialist" party that dances to the fiddle of labor-dividing pure and simpledom, may for a while get more votes than the Socialist Labor Party; but it never will "get there"; a miss is as good as a mile on the "get there" run.

Moreover, the slowlier going S.L.P., that is not a flypaper concern, and never sacrifices sense for votes, is a real educator. When the time for votes shall have ripened, that party will have them—will have the votes, plus the requisite knowledge—while the S. P. will have melted away, seeing it only had votes, and could not possibly, in view of its contradictory and flypaper conduct, have men back of its vote.

John J. Kinneally: We see what is going on in Colorado today. Pure and simple unionism is said to have over 2,000,000 members. I wish to ask the speaker if he thinks such outrages would be possible if those 2,000,000 were in the S.T. and L.A.?

Answer: Two millions of S.T. and L. A. men would mean 2,000,000 men swayed by S.L.P. sense, vigor, manliness and determination. It would mean 2,000,000 men moving, because they felt as one man, and, consequently, feeling and moving right. Large masses cannot feel and move as one if they are in error. Error is manifold; it scatters. Truth only is onefold, it alone unites. Such a number as 2,000,000 S.L.P. men in the land would produce such a sentiment and resulting actions that capitalism would melt like wax. The thing, then, is to build up S.L.P. men. Let that be all serious men's endeavor.

The Chicago Convention
(The IWW Founding Convention)

The *Daily People* June 27, 1905

Frederick Engels, next to Karl Marx the greatest Socialist philosopher, reiterates in his great work, *Socialism, Utopian and Scientific*, the old Greek philosophy first clearly enunciated by Heraclitus, who said, "Everything is and yet is not, for everything flows, is in constant motion, is in constant process of formation and dissolution." In other words, life is not a fixed but an ever changing and growing phenomenon. In no phase of life is this philosophy so applicable in its general features as in the economic and social spheres of man. There integration and disintegration are constant and incessant.

Today, a great portion of the working class of this country is turning its gaze in the direction of Chicago. In the Great Lakes city of the West there opens today a convention of workingmen, which, judging from the manifesto calling it, is destined to mark an important change in the history of labor in this country. This convention promises to launch an economic organization of the working class on the lines of the conflicting interests of capital and labor, in direct contradistinction to the prevailing organization, that is based on the principle of the mutual interests of capital and labor.

Such an organization necessarily demands integration and disintegration. It necessarily ignores those who regard the present form of trade unionism as fixed and stable, and proceeds to build up in conformity with sound principles, philosophical as well as economic.

That such promises as those of the Chicago manifesto have been held out before and have ended in comparative failure — that the Socialist Trade and Labor Alliance and the American Labor Union, for instance, have attempted the same thing with a measure of success less than that confidently expected — is no valid reason for discrediting such promises, or not aiding in the work that would fulfill them - integration and disintegration are processes that must often be accompanied by failure and experimentation in order to be finally successful. The fact that the efforts to launch a class-conscious organization of labor are attaining a certain cumulative force, despite their comparative failures, argues well for their final triumph.

Another fact, worthy of consideration, is the more favorable condition of affairs in which the new organization will be launched.

First, it is backed by a large number of weekly and monthly papers, free from the throttling influences of capitalist trade unionism that ever supported such a movement before. Headed by the *Daily* and *Weekly People*, and the Swedish, Jewish, German, Hungarian and Italian organs of the Socialist Labor Party, it has a press that wields a wide influence and can do much constructive as well as destructive, much defensive as well as offensive, work in its behalf. Again, the growth of Socialist sentiment and revolutionary Socialism are factors that cannot be ignored. They possess a power for good in combating the fallacious and treacherous workings of capitalist unionism, that was not so conspicuously present in the past attempts of the kind promised by the Chicago manifesto. With them present, capitalist reasoning and calumny no longer possess the field undisturbed, but are confronted by opponents whose increasing strength threatens them with overwhelming disaster.

Finally, the new movement has the existing disgust against the treachery and futility of Gompersism, combined with its disintegrating tendencies, to aid it. The working class look from Frisco to Fall River. They note mutual scabbery, bribery and defeat everywhere. They note the National Civic Federation and its malignant influence in their affairs, as exemplified in the subway strike. They are, accordingly, alive to Gompersism's impotency and treachery. Moreover, and above all, they note the organic changes in the system of capitalism itself, and the corresponding fallacy of the Gompers unionism. Hence, they are leaving the latter and are turning toward class-conscious unionism, with all that implies. When were the promises of such unionism ever more favorable and worthy of support? Never before in the history of the American labor movement.

It is to be hoped that the Chicago convention is alive to these facts, and will improve upon them. A step backward from the manifesto would be deplorable, while conditions justify many steps forward. The mere declaration of Industrial Unionism will not suffice without the determination to make class-consciousness the essence of the new movement.

Some sapient "Socialists" proclaim the International Typographical Union an Industrial Union, because it includes in its ranks many branches of the printing industry. The fact that these are the better paid branches, who use the inferior branches to raise their own salaries exclusively, as was done in the Brooklyn *Eagle* strike, doesn't affect the thinking apparatus of these wiseacres any. Nor does the International Typographical Union's endorsement of the "Krag-Jorgensen rifle" policy of settling the Labor question, have the slightest impression upon their "wisdom." They, now as always, are pleased with the form, for the essence is beyond them. Save us from such "industrial unionism." It is the old poisonous adulteration with a new label!

If the Chicago convention measures up to its duty and answers labor's prayer for relief, it will progress as it deserves. Otherwise retrogression will be its lot, while integration and disintegration will continue in the world of labor as of yore.

The Preamble of the IWW

An address delivered in Union Temple, Minneapolis, Minn., July 10, 1905

Workingmen and Workingwomen of Minneapolis:

Our chairman did not overstate the case when he said that the Industrialists' convention, which closed its sessions day before yesterday in Chicago after two weeks of arduous labors, marks an epoch in the annals of the labor movement of America. I may add, although his words imply as much, that the Chicago convention marks also a turning point in the history of the land.

What was done there? You will be able to obtain an approximate idea, a hint, from the public declaration—the Preamble to the Constitution—adopted by the convention.

The document is short; I shall make that shortness still shorter by picking out just three of its clauses, the clauses which I consider most important, and by the light of which the significance, not only of all the others, not only of the document itself, but of the movement which uttered it may be appreciated, gauged and understood.

The three clauses are these:

"There can be no peace so long as hunger and want are found among the millions of working people and the few, who make up the employing class, have all the good things of life."

The second clause:

"The working class and the employing class have nothing in common."

Lastly, but not least, the third clause is as follows:

"Between these two classes a struggle must go on until all the toilers come together on the political, as well as on the industrial field, and take and hold that which they produce by their labor through an economic organization of the working class, without affiliation with any political party."

The First Clause

I consider the first clause pivotal. Does it state a truth? Does it state a falsehood? Is it true that the condition of the working class is one of hunger and want? Or is the contrary statement, heard so often, the correct one? Upon this subject the men engaged in the social question are irreconcilably divided. Deep is the cleft that divides them.

On the one side stand those who were gathered, or were represented, at Chicago. They maintain that the condition of the working class is one of hunger, want and privation; that from bad it is getting worse and ever worse; that the plunder levied upon them mounts ever higher; that not only does their relative share of the wealth which they produce decline, but that the absolute amount of the wealth that they enjoy shrinks to ever smaller quantity in their hands. That is the Socialist position.

Over against that position is the position of our adversaries of various stripes — from the outspoken capitalist down to the A. F. of L.-ite. They assert that the condition of the working class is one of well-being; they claim that from good it is getting better and ever better; they maintain that both the absolute amount of the wealth that the workingman enjoys and his relative share of the wealth that he produces is on the increase; some of them, like the English organ of the New Yorker *Volkszeitung* Corporation, the *Worker* of February 5 of this year, go so far in their assault upon the Socialist position as to pronounce "a wild exaggeration" the claim that "the capitalist system filches from the working class four-fifths of all that class produces."

The two positions are irreconcilable. If the latter be true, or even approximately true, then the other two clauses that I am considering from the Preamble, aye, the Preamble itself, together with the whole work of the Chicago convention, fall like the baseless fabric of a nightmare; contrariwise, if the former; if the Socialist position is true, then all the rest are conclusions that cannot be escaped, and the Chicago convention built upon solid foundation. All, accordingly, centers upon this first clause. Is it true? Is it false? Let us see.

Let me introduce you to this document. You will find it excitingly interesting. It is entitled, as you see, "Uncle Sam's Balance Sheet." As you notice, it is full of figures. Be not alarmed by them. I shall need but two of these columns, the last two, for my purpose. I have not cut out the others, in order not to lay myself open to the charge of presenting a "garbled document." This poster is intended to give, both statistically and pictorially, a convincing presentation of the progress in affluence made by the people of this country.

Let me introduce you a little closer to the document. The columns of figures that you see were not gathered by me; they were not gathered by any Socialist; quite otherwise. This document was issued or circulated by the National Committee of the Republican Party during last year's presidential campaign. Seeing, moreover, that on this first column are given the successive Democratic and Republican administrations that presided over the nation's destiny during the last fifty years, it is fair to consider that the statistical, aye, also pictorial, presentation of conditions cast upon this canvas, is the joint product of both the ruling parties.

You may ask why I trot before you the figures of the foe; why not present you with my own. I shall tell you. If I say, "John Jones is a thief," the charge may or may not be believed: I would have to prove it. But if John Jones himself says he is a thief, then I am saved all further trouble. It is a fundamental principle of the law of evidence that a man's own testimony against himself is the best evidence possible. By tacking that poster before you, I have clapped the highest spokesmen of the capitalist class upon the witness stand. They cannot go back upon their own words. I propose to make them convict themselves.

I must earnestly request you to desist from applauding. The heat in this hall with this vast audience is intense. We must all be anxious to get out as soon as possible. These frequent interruptions by applause only deter the hour of our joint deliverance.

There is one more thing I wish to introduce you to on this document before I take up the figures. As I stated, the document is intended to be a pictorial, besides a statistical presentation of affairs. Let me invite your attention to this picture on the poster's extreme left. You will notice it is Uncle Sam—but how lean, how hungry, how poor, how shabby, how scraggy he looks! That is supposed to represent the country as it started. Now look at this other picture on the poster's extreme right. You will notice by the goatee and other tokens that it is still Uncle Sam—but how changed! No longer are his clothes in tatters; they must be of good material because they do not burst despite his immense girth. He has a gay, jaunty appearance; judging from that, from the tip of his hat, the twirl in the feather that surmounts it, and the twinkle in his eye, he is probably on a spree, half overseas—his face shining with the oil of contentment. That picture is intended to symbolize the country today. Now let us find out who this Uncle Sam is—the working man or the idle man, the capitalist. The figures will tell us exactly.

This first column is headed "Product of Manufacture." It gives, from decade to decade, the value of manufactured goods in the country, from 1860 down to 1900. I shall not read off the figures in detail; they would be too cumbersome to carry in your minds. Nor is that necessary. I shall mention them only in round numbers.

For the decade of 1860 the value of manufactured products amounted to nearly $2,000,000,000 in lump sum.

For the decade of 1870 it amounted to over $4,000,000,000.

For the next decade, 1880, it amounted to over $5,000,000,000.

For the decade following, 1890, it was over $9,000,000,000.

Finally, for the decade of 1900, the value of manufactured products was over $13,000,000,000.

This is a magnificent progression, as you will notice. From nearly $2,000,000,000 in 1860, the wealth produced by labor rose steadily, until in 1900 it reached the gigantic figure of nearly seven times as much—$13,000,000,000! This, no doubt, indicates a vast increase of wealth with a corresponding potential increase of well-being. So far, so good.

But be warned in time. The existence of a good thing is no evidence of its being enjoyed by the working class.

I must right here request you to get your thinking caps ready. Let me take an illustration. Suppose I say that in this hall, with a thousand people, there is $10,000 to be found. That fact alone is no indication as to how that $10,000 is distributed. It may be that, on an average, each one has about $10: It may also be that of that $10,000 I alone have $9,999.99 in my pocket, in which case only a lone copper would be left to straggle in the pockets of the remaining 999 people in this hall.

This first column of the poster informs us what the value is of the goods produced. It does not tell us how that wealth is distributed. It only gives us an idea of the increasing magnitude of labor's productivity. As to distribution, it is to the next column that we must look; and now make ready for the exciting interestingness that I promised you.

The next column is headed "Wages Paid." Here also the amounts are summed up from decade to decade. I shall run over them, again in lump.

In the decade of 1860, the total wages paid to the workingman was over $300,000,000.

In the next decade, 1870, the total wages rose $400,000,060"they were over $700,000,000.

In the decade of 1880, they rose by $200,000,000 more, and amounted to over $900,000,000.

In 1890 the increase in the total wages paid was double. The wages paid to the workingman was over $1,800,000,000.

Finally, in 1900, the wages were over $2,300,000,000, or $500,000,000 more than in 1890.

If we take a bird's-eye view of this wages column, its purpose is obvious. The way the figures are arranged they are meant to convey two ideas — first, that the share of the individual workingman is vast; secondly, that his rise toward affluence is steady and still vaster.

It is expected that when a workingman is told or sees, black upon white, that in 1860 his class received the gigantic pay of over $300,000,000, he feels quite sure that he has a big chunk of that amount. The largeness of the total is intended to act as an opiate on his feverishly pinched purse. And when, black upon white, that initial total is seen to swell and double, from decade to decade, until it reaches the giddy height reached in 1900, then he is expected to be so thoroughly dazed and muddled that he knows not whether he stands upon his feet or his head, and is utterly incapable of thinking. The gigantic wealth, that is supposed to be his, positively crazes him.

Now let us look closer at these figures. From now on until I get through with this poster, I must ask you put your thinking caps on, and keep them tied firmly to your heads.

Whenever figures of wages are presented to you, you must submit them to two tests. Not until you have done so will the figures convey to you any practical information. I propose to submit with you this column of wages to the two tests that I have in mind.

The first test is to ascertain the relative size, or percentage, that the wages bear to the total wealth produced. The test is easy. It merely involves a plain arithmetical calculation. Any fourteen-year-old child should be able to do the sum. Let us apply the test.

The poster informs us that in the decade of 1860 the wages paid were over $300,000,000. It also informs us that the wealth produced by labor during that same period was nearly $2,000,000,000. Applying that arithmetical calculation to the two full sets of figures, we ascertain that the wages were twenty percent of the wealth produced.

Now we are in possession of a fact. It is not a very cheering fact, but it is a useful fact to know. It is the first fact that conveys practical information. By its light the huge total wage of over $300,000,000 shrinks to its real, its social, dimensions. We now know, from the figures given by the poster itself, that in 1860, out of every $100 that he produced, the workingman got only $20: somebody else got $80; from it we learn that in 1860 the workingman was plundered out of $80 for every $100 worth of wealth that he brought into existence. Immediately a suspicion arises in our minds as to who this fat and festive Uncle Sam must be. But we snuff out the suspicion; twenty percent of one's product is not much; indeed, it is very little; but we remember that this is only a start, and that the soaring figures promise progress. Encouraged by this hope, we proceed to test the next decade.

Applying the same arithmetical calculation to the figures given on the poster for the decade of 1870, we again ascertain the percentage of labor's share—the relation that the increased total wage bears to the increased total production. What we there discover gives such a shock to our nerves that the pencil almost drops from our hands. Remember that in the previous decade the share of labor was twenty percent; remember also that we were promised progress. The expectation started by the promise justified the hope that we would be getting at least one percent more. Vain hope! The share of labor, as brought out by the test of the figures furnished by the poster itself, is—eighteen percent!

A curious progress, this. It is the progress of the cow's tail— downward. In 1860, the share of labor was $20 out of every $100 worth of wealth that it produced; in 1870, we find its share has gone down to eighteen percent. In 1860, the plunder levied upon the workingman was $80 out of every $100; in 1870, the plunder, as revealed by the figures furnished by the poster itself, is $82 out of every $100 worth of wealth produced by the workingman.

The suspicion, started in our minds by the revelations in 1860 as to who this stout and lusty Uncle Sam is, revives. But again we suppress it. Our hopes are buoyed up by the consideration that many a babe, instead of immediately growing, is assailed by the whooping cough, measles and bronchitis, and declines, but only temporarily; he rallies quickly, and then grows strong uninterruptedly. That may have been the case with us in 1870. Cheered by these thoughts we rush on to the next decade.

Again we apply that simple arithmetical calculation, now to the figures of the wages paid and the wealth produced in the decade of 1880. The percentage traced by our pencil looks absurd. We must have made a mistake. We go over the sum once more. No mistake. The workingman's share in 1880 is lower than the twenty percent that it was in 1860; it is lower than the eighteen percent that it was in 1870; it is now seventeen percent!

Arrived at this point, we are no longer able to suppress the suspicion as to who this rotund and jolly Uncle Sam is. Nevertheless, we do not yet lose heart. Still mindful of the promise held out by the poster regarding our progressive affluence we proceed to the following decade.

The same arithmetical calculation is gone through. We compute the ratio of the wages paid in 1890 to the wealth produced in that decade. Lo, a surprise! The decline has stopped, the percentage of labor's share in 1890 has risen above the percentage in 1880; it has risen above the percentage in 1870; it is now again twenty percent as it was in 1860.

Thankful for small favors, we look back. Having expected another decline our agreeable surprise almost makes us feel happy. Nevertheless, we wonder where the "progress" comes in.

The figures furnished by the poster itself reveal that we are in 1890 just where we were when we started in 1860. After thirty years of arduous toil; after thirty years, during which the soil of the land was literally drenched with the sweat and blood and marrow of the workingman; after thirty years during which the American working class produced more heiresses to the square inch than the working class of any other country, to purchase European noblemen for husbands; at the end of thirty years during which the working class, as this poster itself shows, produced a phenomenal amount of wealth—at the end of these thirty years the American working class is just where it was thirty years before, the wretched retainer of only $20 out of every $100 worth of wealth that it produced!

This is hardly a progress worth bragging about. It is conservatism of misery. Nevertheless, hope springs eternal in the human breast. Perhaps the long lean years are at last over. Perhaps a brighter day is suddenly to burst upon us, and we are suddenly to make up for lost time so as to look in 1900 like this affluent, well-fed, well-clad, jolly Uncle Sam who, according to the poster, typifies the worker.

And so we apply the test to the figures for 1900, the last ones furnished on the poster. The same arithmetical calculation is resorted to. Woe is us! Our hopes are dashed. The percentage of the share of labor comes down *kerslap*. It is as low as it ever was—seventeen percent! The temporary rise in 1890 was but the flicker in a dying man's eye—the precursor of collapse.

The lie attempted to be given to the Socialist regarding the outrageousness of the plunder that he maintains the working class is subjected to by the capitalist class, rolls down the throat of its utterer. Even making allowance for the value of imported raw material to which the labor of other countries has given value, even making generous allowance for all that due allowance should be made for, the figures to which this poster testifies establish the conclusion that the pittance of one-fifth of its product is a liberal estimate of the share that the working class is allowed to retain.

The first of the two tests, to which these figures of "Wages Paid" must be put, dispels their halo; it exposes a good portion of the naked and hideous reality; it points to the conclusion that, not this lusty Uncle Sam, but that other miserable being at the other end of the poster typifies the American workingman. The second test will establish the fact beyond peradventure.

Let me go once more over the figures on this column of "Wages Paid" so as to refresh your memory. The wages paid in the manufacturing industries are here given as:

"I do not think the country has any idea of the extent of the poisons that are administered in the food that is sold and eaten in this country. I think it is sapping the foundation of the constitution of our people. If we had to raise soldiers now as we did in 1861 I do not believe that throughout the country we could find as large a percentage of young men fit for hard service as there were at that time."

The proof of the pudding, in this as in everything else, ever lies in the eating. If wages really increase, and the cost of living does not rise, and the necessaries of life—food and clothing—do not deteriorate; if they remain good or even improve, what must be the result? Obviously the people who enjoy them must be hale and hearty; they must be healthy while they live, and their lives must be long. If, on the contrary, earnings barely increase and that increase is more than eaten up by higher prices and by the deterioration of such necessaries of life as food and clothing, the fact is bound to appear in the condition of the class that is affected thereby.

If you ever are in New York, take a walk in the evening on 42nd Street, or Fifth Avenue where the clubs are located of the Republican and Democratic parties, and of several other capitalist societies. There must be similar clubs here in Minneapolis; they are found in all our large cities, even in some smaller manufacturing towns. Peep through the large pier-glass windows into the gorgeous precincts. You will see grey heads abound. Is it that these gentlemen are prematurely grey? Is it that they are so poorly fed and clad that it has turned their hair? Hardly! I admit that their aged appearance is somewhat to be accounted for by their lives of dissipation, and their covert Mormon practices. Nevertheless, they have reached old age. Such is the good quality of the goods that they consume that all their dissipations and immoral practices do not prevent their reaching old age.

Having taken in that sight, move into the wards which the working class inhabit, and drop into the places where workingmen congregate. Make sure and take along a little pad of paper and a pencil. On that pad jot down a tally mark for every grey head that you come across. You will find few indeed to record. Why, look at this assemblage of workingmen. There is hardly a grey head among them. In an assemblage of half this size, but of capitalists, you would find the grey heads numerous. Among workingmen they are far and few between. Is it that the workingmen are so well-fed and so well-clothed that their hair preserves its color even into old age, and thus conceals their years? Oh, no! The grey heads are few among them because their hair is not given a chance to turn. Long before the season, they have sunk into early graves, the victims of intense toil, aggravated by small earnings, and this in turn aggravated by the adulteration of the goods that alone their earnings can purchase.

An interesting sidelight is thrown upon this subject by the official report recently made to his government by the British consul in Chicago. Speaking of the machinists in particular, he said that if a machinist in the United States is forty-two years of age and out of work, it is difficult for him to get a job; and he proceeds to explain why—said he, if the man has worked as hard as he is expected to, then he is worn out at forty-two; if he is not worn out, then it is a sign that he did not work so hard as he is expected to, and they have no use for him either way.

I wish to furnish one more piece of testimony under this head before I dismiss the subject. The man I am about to quote is not a "fire-brand agitator"; although he often spoke in public, his subject never was of the sort that might tempt a man to exaggeration. It is Huxley, the slow, plodding, accurate scientist. He said that four-fifths of the people die of slow starvation. There may be those among you who are of a statistical turn of mind. If such there be, they may have nosed among the statistics of mortality furnished by the census and other official sources. Such friends of statistical turn of mind may say: "Why, that's nonsense; a man or two may occasionally die of starvation; but hundreds and thousands of them, impossible! I have seen the statistics on mortality; I have seen the list of diseases; there are consumption, pneumonia, all sorts of other diseases; but I never saw starvation entered among the causes of death."

People holding such views are in error; in serious error. A man may be dying of slow starvation and not know it. His stomach may be full; he may never have felt the gnawings of hunger; and yet he may be dying of slow starvation. If in summer a man is not properly clad, he is emitting more heat than his system can stand—he is dying of slow starvation; if in winter he is not clad warm enough, he is consuming more heat than his system can afford—he is dying of slow starvation; his stomach may be replete, he may imagine himself well-fed, but if the matter in that stomach is adulterated food, then the organisms that carry the nutrition from the stomach, and spread it throughout the body, find no nutrition to carry, the tissues that are consumed are only partially replaced—that man is dying of slow starvation.

The fact is brought home to him when it is too late; aye, it is concealed from him and from his friends even then. He catches a cold; a robust constitution would cast off the distemper without difficulty; his constitution, however, is not robust; his constitution has long been drained by slow starvation; the slight distemper throws him on his beam ends; it develops into pneumonia; he dies; the physician reports pneumonia as the "cause of death"—but starvation it was.

And so down the line of consumption, rheumatism, diabetes and most of the other ills plentifully bestowed upon the working class by the "increased wages" that the capitalist class lavishes upon the working class. Because—never lose sight of this fact—it is the identical capitalist class which regulates wages, on the one hand, and, on the other hand, raises the cost of living, and adulterates the goods needed to live on, which, as you saw, is but another form of raising prices.

We are through with the witness. He stands convicted out of his own mouth. The condition of the working class has gone from bad to worse. Not this roly-poly of an Uncle Sam, but that other emaciated being typifies the wage earner of the land.

Some say, and I am of those, that craft or pure and simple unionism has promoted, aye, urged on these wretched conditions. Others, I know, claim that pure and simple or craft unionism is not to be held responsible; they claim that, on the contrary, were it not for pure and simple unionism, conditions would now be even worse. Those who are of this opinion hold that, instead of being decried, pure and simple unionism should be praised for what it does.

Even accepting this, the most favorable summary possible of the work of pure and simpledom, it would follow that pure and simpledom is, at best, a brake to check the downward run of the chariot of labor; it would follow that pure and simpledom not only is utterly incompetent to emancipate the working class, but that it is not even able to prevent decline; that all there is in it is the capacity to slacken or reduce the downward trend of things. Even accepting this most favorable of views, it would be an argument to cast the thing aside.

The mission of unionism is not to act as rear guard to an army defeated, seasoned in defeat, habituated to defeat, and fit only for defeat. The mission of unionism is to organize and drill the working class for final victory — to "take and hold" the machinery of production, which means the administration of the country.

I shall, however, prove to you that pure and simpledom deserves no credit whatever. I shall prove that it is directly responsible for existing evils, that it is an accomplice in capitalist crime, and has become a scourge to the working class.

The Second Clause

This takes me to the second clause of the three clauses of the Preamble that I proposed to take up with you, the last two of which are, as I stated in opening, pivoted upon the first which I have just demonstrated. The second clause — I shall read it again — is as follows:

"The working class and the employing class have nothing in common."

In a way, this clause also stands proved by the figures on this poster, together with the obvious conclusions that flow from them. Whatever the interests may be of a class whose material welfare steadily towers up, and the interests of the class whose material welfare, and all that thereupon depends, sinks perpendicularly and in even tempo with the former's rise, as illustrated by these figures — whatever these two sets of interests may be, they can have nothing in common. The relations between these two sets of interests are not even the relations of two, though opposing, yet supplementary forces, such as physics tells us of. They are the relations between the vampire and the victim, whose blood it drains — and such relations surely establish nothing in common. Of all one-sided relations, these relations "take the cake and the pie." Indeed, people who prate about the "mutuality," the "brotherhood," the "identity" of interests of the capitalist, or employing class, and the working class, demand of the workingman that for which they would spank their own children if they believed it possible. They want of you that you believe it possible to divide an apple between two men in such a way that each shall have the bigger chunk. An impossibility!

If the workingman produces four dollars and the capitalist takes two, there are only two left to the workingman; if the capitalist takes three, the workingman has to put up with one; if the capitalist appropriates three and a half, there is nothing but fifty cents left to the workingman. Inversely, if the workingman hangs on to a whole dollar, the capitalist's share is reduced to three; if the workingman pushes forward and keeps two, there are but two left for the capitalist; should the workingman preserve three, the capitalist would have to put up with one; and should the workingman "divide" in such a way that he "takes and holds" all that he produced, my capitalist will have to go to work. In other words, he would cease to be a capitalist.

Now, then, the figures on this poster quite clearly illustrate the law that underlies the capitalist system of production. That law does not aid the workingman to preserve an increasing share of his product; it aids, aye, it requires the capitalist to intensify his plunder increasingly. His chunk must be ever thicker, ever and correspondingly thinner must be the workingman's slice. No common interest there! As far as this aspect of the clause which I have just read is concerned, it is too obvious to require further proof. But weightier sense and meaning, meaning and sense of more immediate, practical pith and moment lie imbedded in that clause.

It is an inevitable consequence of the falsehood regarding the hand-in-hand prosperity of capitalists and workingmen that their relations are mutual, and, consequently, that they stand upon a footing of equality. Of course, if the two are getting along swimmingly, they must be peers, even if it be conceded that their peerage may be of different rank. Down from that parent falsehood, set afloat by the capitalist professors, politicians and pulpiteers, and zealously carried into the ranks of pure and simple unionism by the labor lieutenants of the capitalist class, a long line of descent of increasingly insidious and practically pestiferous falsehoods may be traced. The ancestral falsehood of the hand-in-hand progress of capitalist and workingman begets the son-falsehood of the equality of workingman and capitalist; the son-falsehood begets the grandson-fraud of "contracts"; and you will see how the grandson-fraud litters a prolific progeny of its ilk to labor's undoing.

What is a "contract"?

I am not going to give you any Socialist definition of the term. The term has nothing to do with Socialism. It is a term the meaning of which has grown up with the race's experience. The definition I shall give is the law book definition. It is the definition accepted and acted upon in all the courts of equity.

A contract is an agreement entered into by two equal parties; a contract is an agreement entered into between peers; a contract is an agreement entered into by two freemen. Where the parties to a thing called a contract fall within these categories, they are said to be of contracting mind and power, and the document is valid; where that which is called a contract lacks any of these essential qualities, especially if it lacks them all, the thing is null, void and of no effect; it is a badge of fraud of which he is guilty who imposes the contract upon the other.

Let me illustrate:

Suppose that some Minneapolis agent of a lecture bureau, anxious to secure my invaluable services as a speaker for this evening, had written to me in New York, asking for my terms; and suppose I had answered that I would come for $500. He would have written back wanting me to come down a peg or so. I would have replied. Suppose that after considerable chaffering I had agreed upon $400 and he had yielded, whereupon a document would have been drawn up reading somewhat like this:

"John Jones, party of the first part, and Daniel De Leon, party of the second part, have mutually covenanted and agreed that the party of the second part will deliver an address in Minneapolis on the 10th day of July, and the party of the first part will pay the party of the second part for his services the sum of $400 in U.S. currency."

This document being signed would be a contract. If on the appointed day I came, delivered the goods, and John Jones failed to pay me, I would have a just cause of action against him for breach of contract. If, on the other hand, I failed to put in an appearance, he could sue and recover damages from me on the ground of my breach of contract. Whatever people may think of the steepness of my price, the contract would stand. It would stand — why? Because both he and I were free to accept or reject; neither of us acted under compulsion; we were both free agents.

But now suppose that, instead of writing, he came down to New York, rushed into my office, whipped a Colt's horse pistol out of his hip pocket, cocked and held it with the muzzle an inch from my head, and said: "Sign this!" laying before me a sheet of paper containing this legend:

"The workingman does not stand upon a footing of equality with the capitalist; he is not of contracting mind and power with the employer. The latter holds over him the whip of hunger that the capitalist system places in the hands of the master, and with the aid of which he can cow his wage slave into acquiescence."

Why, among themselves, and even in their public utterances, when anger throws them off their guard, the apologists for capitalism blurt out the fact that "only the lash of hunger" can keep the workingman in the treadmill. At the bar of man and of justice the "contracts" that labor signs are null, void and of no effect.

And yet what do we see? The spectacle is of such daily occurrence that it has assumed the nature of a "system," of a deliberate maneuver, indulged in by employers jointly with their labor lieutenants to paralyze the labor movement; aye, worse yet, to give it the aspect of a rat pit.

This is the way it works. Say I am a railroad magnate. I make my "schedules" or contracts, not with all my employees together, but with each craft separately — and there cannot be too many autonomous crafts among them to suit me. Incidentally, let me call your attention to the circumstance that the A. F. of L. is steadily disintegrating its national and international unions into autonomous crafts. Its candle holders endeavor to make much out of some few exceptional instances, in order to make it appear that "the A. F. of L. itself is steadily becoming industrialist." The increasing volume of jurisdictional feuds tells the opposite tale. As I proceed you will be able to appreciate the meaning of the absolute craft autonomy tendency that manifests itself in the A. F. of L. But to return.

I make my separate contract with each of the separate crafts engaged on my railroad line — and there cannot be too many of them to suit me. My contract with my locomotive engineers is drawn up to expire, we shall say, on April 15; my contract with my switchmen is drawn up to expire on September 3; my contract with my firemen is drawn up to expire, say, on January 21; my contract with my trainmen is drawn up to expire, say, on November 30"and so forth, down the line of as many crafts as pure and simple unionism splits my workingmen into, and it can't split them into too many for my comfort. Each separate craft being tied up with a separate contract, expiring on a separate date, I have the industry at my mercy.

Say that, "contract" or no "contract," obedient to that underlying law of the capitalist endless screw, that economic law that neither capitalist nor his class can rein in, that relentless economic law which dictates their conduct in their wrestlings with one another and that causes the capitalists to interpret these contracts to suit themselves — say that my switchmen are driven to rebellion and strike. What do I do? I telephone to my chief labor lieutenants — the presidents, grand chiefs and superlative secretaries of the national unions — and, simultaneously, I touch the button and set the press agoing, both the capitalist newspapers and the labor papers, so called, edited by the pupils of the Civic Federation. My labor lieutenants hasten to respond to my call. Like blackbirds, they hie themselves to the scene from the four quarters of the compass. And then, to the orchestration of: "Infamous men, they have broken their contracts! Scandalous men, they have violated their sacred agreement!" and more to this effect from the press that I have set agoing, and that causes every old woman of both sexes and of all ages to look askance at my striking switchmen as so many serpents under the grass — to the tune of that artificial concert my national labor lieutenants fall to work. They do not turn their attention to the men on strike; the contract-breaking miscreants are below the contempt of my virtuous labor lieutenant. They call around them the men in the other departments — engineers, firemen, conductors, etc. — and with the aid of their understrappers, the local skates, address them in this language:

"Behold yonder sinks of iniquity! They have broken their contracts! It is a wonder the lightning of heaven does not come down and blast them. Surely the bones of the patriotic founders of this Republic are rattling in their graves at the discovery that there can be such lawless men encumbering this soil of freedom. Look at 'em! They broke their contracts! Surely you will not do the same? Surely you will not be so base! Surely you will be true!"

And the men thus addressed cross their arms over their manly chests, and bowing low to the Goddess of Contract, that has been conjured up before them for the occasion, make answer:

"Not we! We shall be loyal to our word. We shall respect our agreements. We shall not break our sacred contracts!"

Which, translated into English, means — "We shall scab upon our fellow wage slaves." And they do! And thus we have seen union locomotive engineers scabbing it upon union firemen, and union firemen scabbing it upon union brakemen, and union brakemen scabbing it upon union switchmen, down the line; and we have seen all of these jointly scabbing it upon union trolleymen and upon all manner of other union men on strike by transporting either the militia and military to dragoon the workers into submission, or the hungry unemployed to take the places of the men who went out. Thus we have seen union molders scabbing it upon machinists; union machinists scabbing it upon union elevator men; union cigarmakers upon waiters; union waiters upon brewers; union brewers upon glucose workers; union teamsters upon carpenters; union bricklayers upon cement workers; union soft coal miners upon hard coal miners — and so down to the very last and least of the craft organizations, and all against each.

It is a fact, deep with significance, though it seems to escape the observation of superficial observers, that it is not the unorganized scab who breaks the strikes, but the organized craft that really does the dirty work; and thus each craft when itself involved in a strike fights heroically, when not involved demeans itself as arrant scabs; betrays its class — all in fatuous reverence to "contracts"!

Only the other day we had a glaring illustration of this disgraceful performance in the city of New York, when the men on the Belmont Interborough struck for living conditions, and Gompers, together with the other lackeys of the Belmont Civic Federation, ably assisted by their local sub-lackeys, such as Mr. Morris Braun of the Gompers International Cigarmakers' Union No. 144, howled down the men on strike as contract breakers, revoked their charters as "unworthy of unionism," proclaimed directly to Belmont that "the men had done wrong," and meekly begged his pardon for the sinners.

Still another and even more pathetic instance was that of the strike of the New York newsboys, to whom Hearst had raised the price of his paper. These little tots, who by their very appearance herald in the open the merciless cruelty of capitalism even against the defenseless child; underclad, underfed, undershod; deprived of the innocent joys of childhood that are so essential to the building up of the future man; stunted in schooling; prematurely thrown into the temptation of vice; walking, running, yelling monuments of capitalist cannibalism, these waifs walked before Typographical Union No. 6 and asked for support, for the support of men, many of whom were fathers themselves and who, had they struck with the boys, certainly would have insured them victory. Did they? asks the scoundrel in Shakespeare.

"A contract! A contract! We have a contract in the pocket of our master Hearst! Shall we lay breach of contract upon our conscience?" asked the craft union compositors. Of course they wouldn't! They slobbered over the boys their "sympathies"; they bestowed upon them all the sweet words that butter no parsnips — and the boys went down in defeat.

It should be here added, although a digression, that when a year or so later the identical typographical union had its strike against the *Sun*, those bearded men went down upon their knees before the identical boys whom they had left ill the lurch, and implored their support. Let the fact be recorded as all evidence of the inherent nobility of the human heart, and in honor of childhood — the ever-renewing promise that human feeling and human instinct shall not perish from the earth — that when appealed to, the boys returned evil with good, and helped the printers fight their strike. It was a pure breath of industrialism.

And in Chicago, during recent months, what was the spectacle presented there? We saw the garment workers valiantly, with drums beating and colors flying, march to the fray. They fought bravely and were beaten off the field. Thereupon the teamsters put on war paint and fell to in support of the routed garment workers. They, too, fought with the desperation of heroes, and went down. Possibly after them some third division of labor may take the field to avenge the cause of the teamsters, after these went down in the attempt to avenge the garment workers after their fight was lost!

Do you know what would happen to the general who, in face of the embattled foe, instead of concentrating his forces for the fray, were to send first one small division into the field of battle; wait until that was annihilated; then send a second small division; again wait until that was routed; and then send a third, likewise to be wiped out, until his whole powerful army was demoralized and took to flight? Do you know what would happen to that general? He would be grabbed by the neck, court-martialed and shot in the back for treason.

Now I am no prophet, nor the son of a prophet; yet, concluding from the facts that are thronging to the bar, I venture the statement on this 10th day of July, 1905, that the day is nigh when the working class of America will court-martial the Gomperses, the Mitchells, the Stoneses whose generalship is sacrificing the army of labor—court-martial them for treason to the working class.

Thus we trace, in direct line of descent from the ancestral falsehood concerning the mutuality of relations between the employing class and the working class, a long genealogy of fraudulent principles, culminating in "contracting" the working class into paralysis, and the crop of evils that flow therefrom. Falsehood can only breed falsehood, and falsehood's spawn is evil; inversely, evil can be sired and damed by falsehood only. In the framework of the capitalist social system, the working class and the employing or capitalist class have nothing in common. The principle is a beacon on the track of labor's march to emancipation; the contrary principle is a false light that lures to social wreck.

The Third Clause

The third clause of the three leading and typical clauses in the preamble is the longest of the three; it is of special importance. I must bespeak your continued and close attention:

"Between these two classes a struggle must go on until all the toilers come together on the political, as well as on the industrial field, and take and hold that which they produce by their labor through an economic organization of the working class, without affiliation with any political party."

This clause contains two distinct ideas joined in two separate sentences. The two ideas are so distinct—the idea of the absolute necessity of political unity, and the seemingly contrary idea of the sufficiency of economic organization ultimately to strike the shackles from the wage slave—that they must be treated separately.

1. Political Unity

I cannot claim for the industrialist movement and its preamble, or declaration of principles, the palm of originality over craft unionism for the thought that is implied in the sentence that the toilers must "come together on the political as well as on the industrial field." The thought therein implied is that politics is a concern of unionism. This is no new thought. Strange as it may seem at first blush, it is a thought that pervades craft unionism as well; stranger still, it is a thought that the labor lieutenants of the capitalist class, in charge of craft or pure and simple unionism, have made themselves the special guardians of. On this head, the merit of industrialism does not lie in the utterance of a new thought. The great merit lies in uttering loudly a fact which, being kept secret by the said labor lieutenants, enabled them to profit by it at the expense of the membership. It is the case of a guardian concealing from his wards the hidden riches of their estate and, on the sly, trafficking upon those riches himself. Much lies in the thorough apprehension of these facts.

Who of you has not witnessed the sight of a labor leader jumping up at a craft union meeting, as if a torpedo had exploded under his seat, every time the economics or sociology of labor was expounded? The sight is common. Whatever the subject that presents itself to a union, it cannot choose but be handled from one of two viewpoints — either from the viewpoint of capitalism, or from the viewpoint of labor, that is, Socialist economics. Impassive, complacently smiling, perhaps even blissfully snoozing, the labor faker will sit in his seat so long as the discussion is carried on along capitalist lines. But let the first word be uttered that has the ring of Socialist, that is, labor economics, and you will notice a sudden transformation. Like a faithful watchdog of capitalism, the faker will snarl, jump up and bark.

I have more than once deliberately tested the thing at the meetings of craft unions with which I happened to be connected. I would join a discussion that was in progress, peacefully in progress, with the faker looking on unconcernedly — discussions on immigration, discussions on boycotts, discussions on wages, discussions on tenements, discussions on the liquor traffic, etc., etc. I would carefully avoid the word "politics"; deliberately would I avoid it. Neither the word "politics," let alone the name "Socialist Labor Party" would drop from my lips. They were as words tabooed, and alien to me while I spoke. But lo, no sooner did I deploy my argument so as to bring out the labor, which is the Socialist, viewpoint of the subject, than up would jump the watchdog of capitalism with the protest: "No politics in the union."

He was right; that is to say, labor or Socialist economics is politics. By the same token capitalist economics likewise is politics. Capitalist economics is at home, capitalist economics is tolerated, capitalist economics is safeguarded, aye, capitalist economics is fought for in craft unionism—who would dare gainsay that politics is a palpitating fact in the union? Or who would dare deny that the labor lieutenant of the capitalist class is the special custodian of that treasure? It is proven.

Upon this particular head—the head that politics is the concern of unionism—industrialism utters no new principle, leastwise a principle that it would lie in the mouth of craft unionism to dispute. Great, however, is the merit of industrialism in the consequences that flow from its utterance. Through craft unionism the watchdogs of the capitalist class keep the treasure a secret for their private gain. By openly proclaiming the treasure, industrialism renders it public property. The consequences that flow herefrom mark the turning down of an old and the turning up of a new leaf. That leaf is inscribed "political unity."

It is not a political organization—as the preamble indicates and I shall prove—that can "take and hold" the land and the capital and the fullness thereof. That—as the preamble proclaims and I shall prove— is the function reserved for the economic organization of the working class. Nevertheless, society moves from stage to stage, not via a succession of shipwrecks, but via evolution. Each succeeding social stage connects with the one preceding. Before the new is established and its methods are in operation, the methods of the old are perforce resorted to. They are the navel strings of the child aborning.

The evolution from the capitalist system to Socialism marks a revolution of first rank. The methods of the Socialist Republic will be methods that flow from its own material framework. The latter is so diametrically the opposite of the capitalist social framework that the two methods will bear no comparison. Capitalist society requires the political State; accordingly, its economics translate themselves into political tenets; Socialist society, on the contrary, knows nothing of the political State: in Socialist society the political State is a thing of the past, either withered out of existence by disuse or amputated—according as circumstances may dictate.

For all that, Socialism is the outgrowth of the higher development from capitalism. As such, the methods of the Socialist movement on its march toward Socialist society are perforce primarily dictated by the capitalist shell from which Socialism is hatching. Seeing that capitalist economics translate themselves into politics, Socialist economics cannot wholly escape the process. A part, the better, the constructive part of Socialist economics translates itself into the industrial organization of the working class: it translates itself into that formation that outlines the mold of the future social system; another part of Socialist economics, however, inevitably translates itself into politics: it inevitably takes that form that matches capitalist methods.

Upon that plane the Socialist movement crosses swords with the modern ruling class—these to uphold, it to dislodge them from and dismantle their robber burg. This is the fact that lies at the bottom of the Marxian tenet to the effect that the labor movement is essentially political. In a country like ours, where, in keeping with full-fledged capitalism, the suffrage is universal, the inevitable political character of the labor movement is rendered all the more marked.

The sentence of the preamble that we are now considering, and which urges the necessity of political as well as industrial unity, is planted upon these facts. Where, for instance, one set of workingmen imagine that they should pool their votes with their free trade employers, it is out of all question that they can be a unit on the industrial field with another set of workingmen whose economic views are that protection guarantees them work and better wages. Where, to take another issue, one set of workingmen share the capitalist economic notion that the gold standard means good wages, they cannot possibly be united on the political field with those of their fellow wage slaves whose political tenet on finance is that plentiful money means plentiful wages. These two sets cannot be industrially united, any more than politically, for the simple reason that they do not stand upon the bedrock of the class struggle. Trace their economic and their political views to their respective sources, and you will find them to be identical—the fundamental error that the employee's condition is dependent upon the condition of the employer.

The baneful result of the error is obvious: employers are economically divided into warring, competing clans; consequently, if the workingmen are appendages to their employers, they cannot choose but be likewise divided. Class ignorance, accordingly, scatters the ranks of the working class. The rupture produced upon the industrial field is reflected upon the political field, and there we see the labor vote likewise scattered — cast for all the scores of parties in the field, from the soundest Socialist down even to utopian prohibitionist; and, on the other hand, the rupture exhibited upon the political reacts back upon and intensifies the division on the industrial field where, thanks to the baneful policy of craft unionism, we see labor's hand at labor's own throat.

In this connection the speculative question has sprung up in some minds whether political unity is brought about by industrial unity, or industrial unity by political unity. As a question of speculative philosophy, it may be relegated to the realm of idle discussion. In natural philosophy a similar question appears in the conundrum: What was first, the hen or the egg? One man answers: "Of course, the hen: without the hen, there is no fowl to lay the egg"; another declares: "Nonsense, the egg must have been first: without the egg, there is nothing for the hen to be hatched out of." We know that in material life the evolutionary process is so gradual that result reacts back upon cause in such an endless chain that, in the limited span of man's observation, the exact line of demarcation is not always ascertainable. Cause and effect become relative matters, frequently dependent upon the viewpoint of the moment. It is likewise in social matters.

As an abstract question, it is idle speculation whether political clearness causes economic clearness, or, inversely, economic clearness brings about political clearness. We know that at certain stages of the movement political clearness may be ahead of industrial clearness, and will act upon and stimulate it; likewise do we know that at certain other stages, there is no political unity, consequently, no political clearness possible except as a result of economic unity, and that presupposes clearness. He who is engaged in raising poultry will get the eggs from which to hatch the hens; he who wants eggs for the market will get the hens to lay them; and he who wants both will cultivate both; he will not wear out his energies in speculations regarding the "original cause."

That is the posture of the preamble of the Industrial Workers of the World. It recognizes the necessity of both political and industrial unity; it proclaims the fact; nor does it conceal its opinion as to which of the two, at this stage of the movement, must precede in order to make the other possible. The construction of the sentence under consideration, proclaiming the necessity of unity "on the political field, as well as on the industrial field," amply indicates which of the two unities industrialism considers to be the necessary prerequisite at this stage of the labor movement in America. The sentence proclaims the fact that, at the stage reached by the labor movement in America, the political unity of the working class can only be the reflex of economic unity; it also proclaims the underlying, the pregnant fact that the political movement is absolutely the reflex of economic organization.

A brilliant passage in Marx's *Eighteenth Brumaire* casts a brilliant sidelight upon this particular subject. Referring to the conduct of the feudal lords of England during the British Revolution, Marx says they believed that the British Crown and the Church of England were the subjects of their enthusiasm, until the hour of danger wrung from them the admission that what they really enthused for was ground rent.

And so we see the editors of the privately owned press of the Socialist or Social Democratic Party in the land, called in this state Public Ownership Party, conducting themselves today. They believed that Socialism was the object of their enthusiasm, until the hour of danger — the issuing of the Chicago industrialists' manifesto, and the holding of the Chicago convention—has wrung from them the admission that what they really enthused for was the fleshpots of the A.F. of L. Political unity is a slogan of Industrial Unionism.

2. The Function Of Unionism

I shall now proceed to the second, the closing sentence of the third of the three clauses that we have been considering—the sentence which sets up the theory that the final, the consummating act of working—class emancipation must be achieved by the toilers "taking and holding" the product of their labor "through an economic organization of the working class, without affiliation with any political party."

In no country, outside of the United States, is this theory applicable; in no country, outside of the United States, is the theory rational. It is irrational and, therefore, inapplicable in all other countries, with the possible exception of Great Britain and the rest of the English-speaking world, because no country but the United States has reached that stage of full-orbed capitalism—economic, political and social—that the United States has attained. In other words, no other country is ripe for the execution of Marxian revolutionary tactics.

No wonder the theory has set all the owls, the pseudo-Marxists included, afluttering; no wonder it has set all the podsnaps of the A.F. of L., together with its kindred craft "brotherhoods," apondering and aconning the "contradiction" of demanding "political unity," and in the same breath proposing to take and hold the machinery of production through an economic organization "without affiliation with any political party."

In this sentence of the preamble is condensed what may be called the code of Marxian "tactics," as distinguished from the code of Marxian "economics"; the code of "action," as distinguished from the code of "theory." As a consequence, the sentence outlines the form of the governmental administration of the Republic of Labor. It involves the vital question of the function of unionism, a question that is so widely misunderstood that, on the one hand, we see the "intellectual" ever sneering at unionism and arguing, as is his wont, from partly correct and mainly false premises, that "the union is a passing institution," not worth bothering about; and, on the other hand, the "unionist," so-called, with a practical instinct that tells him the union is no "passing institution," but who blunders into the superstition of revering as "unionism" that which is purely a capitalist contrivance labeled "union" in order to deceive, and calculated to block indeed the path of unionism. The preamble of the Industrial Workers of the World is the first pronouncement on the field of practice that clinches this many-sided issue. As becomes her opportunities, therefore her duty, this fruit first ripened on the soil of America.

It does not lie in a political organization, that is, a party, to "take and hold" the machinery of production. Both the "reason" for a political party and its "structure" unfit it for such work. I have at considerable length dealt with some of the aspects of this question in the address I delivered last year in Newark, N. J., "The Burning

Question of Trades Unionism." I shall now take it up somewhat more in detail.

The "reason" for a political party unfits it to "take and hold" the machinery of production. As shown when I dealt with the first sentence of this clause—the sentence that urges the necessity of political unity—the "reason" for a political movement is the exigencies of the bourgeois shell in which the social revolution must partly shape its course. The governmental administration of capitalism is the State, the government proper (that institution is purely political). Political power, in the language of Marx, is merely the organized power of the capitalist class to oppress, to curb, to keep the working class in subjection. The bourgeois shell in which the social revolution must partly shape its course dictates the setting up of a body that shall contest the possession of the political robber burg by the capitalist class. The reason for such initial tactics also dictates their ultimate goal—the razing to the ground of the robber burg of capitalist tyranny. The shops, the yards, the mills, in short, the mechanical establishments of production, now in the hands of the capitalist class — they are all to be "taken," not for the purpose of being destroyed, but for the purpose of being "held"; for the purpose of improving and enlarging all the good that is latent in them, and that capitalism dwarfs; in short, they are to be "taken and held" in order to save them for civilization.

It is exactly the reverse with the "political power." That is to be taken for the purpose of abolishing it. It follows herefrom that the goal of the political movement of labor is purely destructive.

Suppose that, at some election, the class-conscious political arm of labor were to sweep the field; suppose the sweeping were done in such a landslide fashion that the capitalist election officials are themselves so completely swept off their base that they wouldn't, if they could, and that they couldn't, if they would, count us out; suppose that, from President down to Congress and the rest of the political redoubts of the capitalist political robber burg, our candidates were installed — suppose that, what would there be for them to do? What should there be for them to do? Simply to adjourn themselves, on the spot, *sine die*. Their work would be done by disbanding.

The political movement of labor that, in the event of triumph, would prolong its existence a second after triumph, would be a usurpation.

It would be either a usurpation or the signal for a social catastrophe. It would be the signal for a social catastrophe if the political triumph did not find the working class of the land industrially organized, that is, in full possession of the plants of production and distribution, capable, accordingly, to assume the integral conduct of the productive powers of the land. The catastrophe would be instantaneous. The plants of production and distribution having remained in capitalist hands, production would be instantly blocked.

On the other hand, if the political triumph does find the working class industrially organized, then for the political movement to prolong its existence would be to attempt to usurp the powers which its very triumph announces have devolved upon the central administration of the industrial organization.

The "reason" for a political movement obviously unfits it to "take and hold" the machinery of production. What the political movement "moves into" is not the shops but the robber burg of capitalism—for the purpose of dismantling it.

And now, as to the structure of a political party. Look closely into that and the fact cannot escape you that its structure also unfits the political movement to "take and hold" the machinery of production. The disability flows inevitably from the "reason" for politics. The "reason" for a political party, we have seen, is to contend with capitalism upon its own special field—the field that determines the fate of political power. It follows that the structure of a political party must be determined by the capitalist governmental system of territorial demarcations—a system that the socialist republic casts off like a slough that society shall have outgrown.

Take Congress, for instance, whether Senate or House of Representatives. The unity of the congressional representation is purely politically geographic; it is arbitrary. The structure of the congressional district reflects the purpose of the capitalist State political, that is, class tyranny over class. The thought of production is absent, wholly so from the congressional demarcations. It cannot be otherwise. Congress—not being a central administration of the productive forces of the land, but the organized power of the capitalist class for oppression—its constituent bodies can have no trace of a purpose to administer production. Shoemakers, bricklayers, miners, railroadmen, together with the workers in all manner of other fractions of industries, are, accordingly, jumbled together in each separate congressional district. Accordingly, the political organization of labor intended to capture a congressional district is wholly unfit to "take and hold" the plants of industry. The only organization fit for that is the organization of the several industries themselves—and they are not subject to political lines of demarcation; they mock all such arbitrary, imaginary lines.

The central administrative organ of the Socialist Republic—exactly the opposite of the central power of capitalism, not being the organized power of a ruling class for oppression, in short, not being political, but exclusively administrative of the producing forces of the land—its constituent bodies must be exclusively industrial.

The artillery may support the cavalry; the cavalry may support the infantry of an army in the act of final triumph; in the act, however, of "taking and holding" the nation's plants of production, the political organization of the working class can give no help. Its mission will have come to an end just before the consummation of that consummating act of labor's emancipation.

The form of central authority, to which the political organization had to adapt itself and consequently looked, will have ceased to be. As the slough shed by the serpent that immediately reappears in its new skin, the political State will have been shed, and society will simultaneously appear in its new administrative garb.

The mining, the railroad, the textile, the building industries, down or up the line, each of these, regardless of former political boundaries, will be the constituencies of that new central authority, the rough scaffolding of which was raised last week in Chicago.

Where the General Executive Board of the Industrial Workers of the World will sit there will be the nation's capital.

Like the flimsy card houses that children raise, the present political governments of counties, of states, aye, of the city on the Potomac herself, will tumble down, their places taken by the central and the subordinate administrative organs of the nation's industrial forces. Obviously, not the "structure" of the political movement, but the structure of the economic movement is fit for the task, to "take and hold" the industrial administration of the country's productive activity — the only thing worth "taking and holding."

The Ballot

The preamble of the Industrial Workers of the World poses well both the political and the economic movement of labor, and it places them in their proper relation toward each other.

Inestimable is the value, dignified the posture of the political movement. It affords the labor movement the opportunity to ventilate its purposes, its aspirations and its methods, free, over and above board, in the noonday light of the sun, whereas otherwise, its agitation would be consigned to the circumscribed sphere of the rat hole. The political movement renders the masses accessible to the propaganda of labor; it raises the labor movement above the category of a "conspiracy"; it places the movement in line with the spirit of the age, which, on the one hand, denies the power of "conspiracy" in matters that not only affect the masses, but in which the masses must themselves be intelligent actors, and, on the other hand, demands the freest of utterance. In short and in fine, the political movement bows to the methods of civilized discussion: it gives a chance to the peaceful solution of the great question at issue.

By proclaiming the urgency of political as well as of industrial unity, the preamble amply and sufficiently proclaims the affinity of the economic with the political movement. At the same time, by expressly proclaiming that the "taking and holding" is an act that falls wholly within the province of the economic organization, the preamble locked a dangerous switch, a switch into which to run there is grave danger, the danger of rendering the Socialist, which means the labor movement, illusory, and a roosting place for the "intellectual" riffraff of bourgeois society.

The ballot is a weapon of civilization; the ballot is a weapon that no revolutionary movement of our times may ignore except at its own peril; the Socialist ballot is the emblem of right. For that very reason the Socialist ballot is —

Weaker than a woman's tears,
Tamer than sleep,
Fonder than ignorance,
Less valiant than the virgin in the night,
And skill-less as unpracticed infancy,

— unless it is backed by the might to enforce it. That requisite might is summed up in the industrial organization of the working class.

Now, mind you, that might the labor movement needs, as much, I would almost say, against the political movements which its own breath heats into being as against the capitalist tyrant himself. It needs that might against the capitalist tyrant to put the quietus upon him; it also needs that might to prevent the evil consequences to which, in this corrupt atmosphere of bourgeois society, the political movement is inevitably exposed. The two points are vital. Much, infinitely more than appears at first sight, hangs thereby.

Despite the sharply marked economic feature of the labor movement, the principle that it is bound to take on a political form also, is founded on no fine-spun theory. Even discounting the force of the sociologic arguments that I have presented to you, and which point to the inevitableness of the political manifestation of the labor movement, there is a consideration that I have referred to only incidentally so far, and which, when properly weighed, places the matter beyond the peradventure of a doubt. That consideration is the existence of universal suffrage in the land.

The institution is so bred in the bones of the people that, notwithstanding it has become a gravel in the shoe of the capitalist, he, powerful though he is, dare not abolish it outright. Among such a people, chimerical is the idea of expecting to conduct a great movement, whose palpable aim is a Socialist revolution, to the slogan of "Abstinence from the ballot-box." The proposition cannot choose but brand its supporters as freaks.

Whether the economic movement wills it or not, its political phase will assert itself on the political field. Men from its own ranks, and men from outside of its ranks, will raise the standard of labor politics. Nor will the capitalist be slow in endeavoring, while humoring the thing, to draw the sting from it. Watchfully though he guards his political burg, he will, from time to time, carefully select some "promising" candidate from the labor ticket and allow him admission; or, maybe, he is sometimes taken napping, and some labor candidate slips through the fingers of his outposts at the ballot-box. Subjected to the lures and wiles at the disposal of the capitalist, these successful labor candidates in the parliaments of capitalism, ten to one, succumb. They succumb due either to their own inherently corrupt souls, or to their muddle-headedness. In either case they betray the working class; the effect is harmfully felt by the economic movement.

Against this danger there is but one protection—the industrial, that is, the class-conscious economic organization to keep that ballot straight. Nothing short of such an economic organization will prevent the evil, because nothing short of such an economic organization can keep sharp the edge of the special sword wielded by the political movement of labor. What that special sword is I have shown before. It is purely destructive. The economic movement may take a little at a time. It may do so because its function is ultimately to "take and hold" the full plants of production and save them for the human race. The political movement, on the contrary, has an entirely different function: its function is wholly to tear down the political burg of capitalist tyranny.

It follows herefrom that the political movement of labor may not even remotely partake even of the appearance of compromise. It exemplifies the revolutionary aim of the labor movement; it must be uncompromisingly revolutionary. This fact dictates the conduct of the successful political candidates of labor in the parliaments of capitalism.

The principle found expression in the celebrated maxim uttered by William Liebknecht, when he still was in the full vigor of his Socialist aspirations—"*Parlamentiren ist paktiren*"—to parliamentarize is to compromise, to log-roll, to sell out. When, in later years, experience brought home to him the unfortunate fact that the bourgeoisie of Germany had not finished their own revolution; when he discovered that that revolution had first to be completed and that there was none to undertake the task but the Social Democratic movement; when that hard reality faced him and his movement, Liebknecht wisely adapted his course to the requirements. To parliamentarize is legitimate tactics with the bourgeois revolution.

The parliamentarizing that the German Social Democracy thereupon, with Liebknecht at its head, has been constrained to practice, demonstrates that the movement in Germany has been constrained to adopt the tactics of the bourgeois revolutionist—precisely the reason why such tactics are wholly out of place, wholly inadmissible, aye, a badge of treason to the working class when applied in America.

Without the might of the class-conscious economic movement back of the political, the political movements that the labor movement inevitably promotes in America will not only be divided but, as a further result, will promote that confusion of thought that runs into corruption and that, reacting back upon the economic movement itself, helps to scuttle its efficiency. It surely is no accident that, without exception, all the labor candidates so far allowed by the capitalist class to filter through their garrisons at their election defiles, whenever the office to which they were allowed to be returned elected was of any importance, have uniformly "parliamentaryized," that is, "logrolled," in short, sold out the revolution. We saw it happen during the heyday of the K. of L.; we saw it happen more recently in Haverhill, in Brockton, in the Massachusetts legislature, in Paterson, in Sheboygan; we see it happening now in Milwaukee.

It is a matter of self-protection with the economic organization to watch and control the political. Skill-less as unpracticed infancy, a danger to labor itself, is the sword of labor's ballot without the might of the class-conscious economic organization to whet its edge, to keep it sharp and to insist upon its being plied over the skull of the foe, to insist upon that at the peril of the muddleheads, of the weakling, of the traitor.

There now only remains one point to consider, and I am through. It is the point with regard to the necessity of the industrial organization in order to supplement the right of the ballot with the might requisite to put the quietus upon the capitalist class itself. The point implies what is generally, but wrongly, meant by . . . .

The General Strike

. . . a term that, through misuse by its own advocates, who have hitherto placed the cart before the horse, is greatly misunderstood, and should be substituted by the more appropriate term of the general lockout of the capitalist class.

Political power is reached through the ballot box. But the ballot box is not an open field; it is a veritable defile. That defile is held by the agents of the capitalist class. The election inspectors and returning boards are capitalist appointees; they are veritable garrisons with which the capitalist class holds the defile. To imagine that these capitalist garrisons of the election defiles will complacently allow the candidates of the revolution, whose program is the dismantling of the political burg of capitalism, peacefully to file through, is to indulge in a mooncalf's vision. The revolutionary ballot of labor is counted out now; it has been counted out from the first day of its appearance; it will be counted out even more extensively in the future.

This fact is taken by some as a sufficient ground from which to conclude that the political movement is utterly useless. Those who arrive at that conclusion fall into the error of failing to realize that correct conclusions never flow from single premises. They can be arrived at only by considering all the premises in the case. While the Socialist ballot was, is and may continue to be counted out, the political movement accomplishes that which all the counting out will not be able to counteract.

A man may monkey with the thermometer, yet he is utterly unable to monkey with the temperature. Place a lump of ice to the bulb of the quicksilver in this room of suffocating heat, the column will sink below zero, yet the temperature remains at fever heat. Place a piece of burning coal to the quicksilver bulb in midwinter, the mercury will rise to fever heat, yet the temperature remains cold, unaltered. So with the election returns. They are the political thermometer. The political pickets of the capitalist class may monkey therewith to their heart's content—they will be unable to alter by the fraction of a degree the political temperature that prevails all around.

Now, then, that political temperature, for reasons that I have already explained, is preeminently the product of the political movement of labor. Wait, I have not yet proven the point. It still remains to be clinched. The question may still be asked, aye, it is asked: What does the hottest of political temperatures avail, if the capitalist class retains the power to nullify it by counting us out? It may avail much; here, in America, it may mean the consummation of that ideal so dearly pursued by the Socialist—the peaceful solution of the social question.

Look across at Europe. The feudal spirit still prevails there in an important respect, as a consequence of the continued prevalence there of large chunks of feudal institutions. In Europe, even the capitalist class is feudalized, let alone the surviving feudal heads. Though guilty of all the crimes of the decalogue, there is one vice that the feudal lord is substantially free from. That vice is cowardice. Valor is the burthen of the songs that rock their cradle; valor is the theme of the nursery tales to which they are raised; deeds of valor are the ideals set up before them. Take as a type the semi-crazy, semi-crippled Emperor of Germany. He will fight whatever the odds. In Europe a peaceful solution of the social question is out of all question.

But how is the lay of the land here, in America? Was it songs of valor that rocked the cradles of our capitalist rulers? Was it tales of noble daring that formed the themes of the nursery tales to which they were brought up? Were the ideals that they gathered from their home surroundings the ideals of manliness? In short, did they reach their present position by deeds of valor? No! Daily experience, confirmed by every investigation that one set of capitalists institutes against another, tells us that they reached their present status of rulers by putting sand into your sugar, by watering their stocks, by putting shoddy into your clothes, by pouring water into your molasses, by breaches of trust, by fraudulent failures and fraudulent fires, in short by swindle.

Now, then, the swindler is a coward. Like a coward, he will play the bully, as we see the capitalist class doing, toward the weak, the weak because disorganized, working class. Before the strong, the bully crawls. Let the political temperature rise to the point of danger, then, all monkeying with the thermometer notwithstanding, your capitalist will quake in his stolen boots; he will not dare to fight; he will flee. At least I, for one, expect to see him flee. But, indeed, he will not unless, back of that ballot that has raised the political temperature to fever heat is the might of the industrial organization, in full possession of the industrial establishments of the land, organized integrally and, consequently, capable of assuming the conduct of the nation's production. The complete industrial organization of the working class will then have insured the peaceful issue of the struggle.

But perhaps the capitalist may not flee. Perhaps, in a delirium of rage, he may resist. So much the worse—for him. The might, implied in the industrial organization of the working class of the land, will be in position to mop the earth with the rebellious usurper in short order and safeguard the right that the ballot proclaimed.

The futility of the ballot alone, however triumphant, was strikingly illustrated nine years ago during the first Bryan campaign. The political temperature against the plutocratic rulers of the land had risen to a point that they, for a moment, considered the battle at the ballot box lost in advance. That, however, did not disconcert them. Through their national mouthpiece, Mark Hanna, they threatened to stop production. In other words, they threatened to go on strike. The threat was no idle bombast. They could. It was known that they could. Craft unionism placed it in their power to do so. The threat had its effect. But let the capitalist attempt, under the pressure of the political temperature raised by the ballot of labor—let him attempt to strike. In possession of the might conferred and implied by the industrial organization of their class, the working class would forthwith lock out the capitalist class.

Without political organization, the labor movement cannot triumph; without economic organization, the day of its political triumph would be the day of its defeat.

Industrialism means might. Craft unionism means impotence. All the plants of production, aye, even the vast wealth for consumption, is today in the keeping of the working class. It is workingmen who are in charge of the factories, the railroads, the mines, in short all the land and machinery of production, and it is they also who sit as watchdogs before the pantries, the cellars and the safe-deposit vaults of the capitalist class; aye, it is they who carry the guns in the armies. But this place of vantage is of no avail to them under craft unionism. Under craft unionism, only one craft marches into the battlefield at a time. By their idly looking on, the other crafts scab it upon the combatant. What with that and the likewise idle onlooking of those divisions of the workers who man the commissary department, so to speak, of the capitalist class, the class struggle presents, under craft unionism, the aspect of petty riots at which the empty stomachs and empty hands of the working class are pitted against the full ones of the employing class. Was this ignorance? Was this treason? Whether treason or ignorance, the turning in the long lane has been reached.

Both the present conduct of craft unionism and the future conduct of Industrial Unionism was well portrayed by one of the delegates at the Chicago convention. Illustrating the point with the five fingers of his right hand far apart, he showed that to be the posture of the craft or autonomous unions—disconnected from one another for all practical work, and good only to act as a fan, a fan that had hitherto done nothing but scare the flies away from the face of the capitalist class; and, proceeding thereupon to illustrate the further point by drawing his five fingers tightly into a compact fist, he showed that to be the posture of Industrial Unionism—a battering ram, that would leave the face of the capitalist class looking materially different from the way it looked when it was merely fanned. The impotence wherewith the right of the working class has hitherto been smitten, is now to be organized into a might without which that right is but mockery. The signal for that organization was struck last week at the convention of the Industrial Workers of the World; and the word has gone out, as it could go out from no other country but America, in language that fits our fullgrown capitalist development -

"Unite! Unite on the economic field upon the only basis that economic unity is possible—the basis of the solidarity of the working class, the only solid fact from which political unity can be reflected! Unite! Unite upon the only economic principle capable of backing up the right of the labor ballot with the might to enforce it! Unite for the general strike at the ballot box, to overthrow the political robber burg of capitalism, backed by the general strike against, or, rather, the general lockout of the capitalist class from the industrial fields that it has usurped. Unite for the emancipation of the working class, and to save civilization from a catastrophe!"

Questions

Q. Do you not believe that the capitalist class will seek to prevent the growth of the Industrial Workers of the World by demanding from each employee a sworn affidavit that he is not a member of that organization?"

A. They may try that, but it will fail of its purpose. I showed you that the "contract" which I was made to sign by a pistol being held to my head was null. It was null because it was not I but the pistol that signed the contract. Likewise with such affidavits. They would not be sworn to by the workingman, but by the whip of hunger held over his head. The whip took the oath; let the whip keep it.

Q. If I were to join that new union, I would immediately be thrown out of work by the officers of my organization. What is a man to do?

A. Look across to Russia. Individual uprisings are speedily crushed. The individual's safety lies in mass uprisings. The tyranny of the grand dukes of the A.F. of L. and such kindred craft organizations can be overcome only by mass uprisings against them. Such a tidal wave of rebellion against the labor lieutenants of the capitalist class is now shaping, soon to burst over their heads.

As To Politics

Daniel De Leon, Editor, New York Labor News Co., 1907

Introduction

The contents of this pamphlet are a discussion that took place in the columns of *The People*, under the head "As To Politics," during the months of November and December, 1906, and January and February, 1907.

The discussion consisted of letters written to *The People* by correspondents who advocated the dropping of political action altogether, and reliance exclusively upon revolutionary, class-conscious Industrial Unionism; and *The People*'s answers. The letters are published in this pamphlet together with the answers given to each by *The People*, combating the error. An important part of the discussion consisted of a number of questions asked and answers to them by *The People*. These are also included, closing with an editorial from *The People* entitled "Supplemental" to the subject, and answering the last question put.

The subject matter of the discussion, besides being of deep interest, is timely. True to the Marxian observation that, contrary to the law of bourgeois revolutions, the law, obedient to which the revolutionary movement of the proletariat acts, is to "criticize itself constantly; constantly to interrupt itself in its own course; to come back to what seems to have been accomplished in order to start over anew; to scorn with cruel thoroughness the half measures, weaknesses and meannesses of its first attempts; to seem to throw down its adversary only in order to enable him to draw fresh strength from the earth, and again to rise up against it in more gigantic stature; to constantly recoil in fear before the undefined monster magnitude of its own objects - until, finally, that situation is created which renders all retreat impossible, until the conditions themselves cry out: "*Hic Rhodus, hic salta!*" — true to that Marxian observation, the Labor Movement of America is today thoroughly criticizing itself.

No more important subject of criticism can there be than half-measures - one time purely of physical force, another time purely of political action - which the movement has, in previous years, pursued. No more important a subject to be clear upon than the proper tactics of the movement. Means and ends supplement, they even dovetail into each other. No clearness as to ends is well conceivable without correctness of means; no correctness of means can well be hit upon without clearness as to ends. This principle is peculiarly applicable to the ends and the means thereto of the Socialist or Labor Movement.

The publication, in pamphlet form, of the discussion conducted during those four months in *The People* is intended to furnish in compact form the information whereby to arrive at the correct tactics wherewith to reach the goal of the Socialist Commonwealth.

Daniel De Leon

New York, July 8, 1907

First letter, by John Sandgren, San Francisco, Cal.

The most important issue confronting the working class today is the question of the proper method, the proper tactics to adopt in order to attain the aim upon which even the most hostile factions agree, namely, the overthrow of the capitalist system.

A discussion of this kind leads us immediately to the question: shall it be accomplished through political organization, or through economic organization, or through both.

It is imperative that this question should be openly, honestly, and widely discussed, in order to arrive at a solid basis upon which all workingmen may unite; it is imperative that the cloudiness and uncertainty, which now divides revolutionary workingmen and frustrates in part their best energies and efforts, should be dispelled. Having very decided opinions on the subject, I beg leave to submit my views, hoping they will be received in the same good faith as they are given, without prejudice or rancor, solely with the aim of benefiting the working class movement.

The first preamble of the Industrial Workers of the World says that "the workers must come together on the political, as well as the industrial field, and take and hold that which they produce by their labor, through an economic organization, without affiliation with any political party".

The second convention of the I.W.W., held this year, adopted an amendment to this clause to the effect that the I.W.W. does not wish to endorse or be endorsed by any political party, which amendment will no doubt be adopted by referendum vote. The amendment does not materially change the original clause. This clause declaring for political unity, but at the same time striking a *noli-me-tangere*, don't-touch-me, attitude to all political parties has been, is, and will be subject to an endless variety of interpretations.

A document like the preamble should be positive in its statements, not negative. It should outline a definite, absolutely definite, policy, which could leave no room for essential disagreement, between those who endorse its program at least. Its weakness on this point lies in enumerating two things out of the thousand and one things which it does not want, namely, it does not want to endorse any political party and it does not want to be endorsed by a political party. Instead of doing this, the preamble ought to state most positively what the I.W.W. *does* want and thus serve as a fixed star to steer by, instead of presenting us with a moving cloud to steer by, on this most essential point, the question of tactics.

However presumptuous it may appear, the writer will undertake to suggest an amendment for the next convention to consider, an amendment which will remove the apparent contradiction and express the ideas and the conception of revolutionary workingmen, and it would be as follows:

To strike out all reference to politics in the I.W.W. preamble.

In defense of a preamble thus amended, may I be allowed to submit the following reasons.

It is not in order to dodge or to escape a difficult situation, with which two I.W.W. conventions have unsuccessfully wrangled, that this amendment is submitted for discussion. It is submitted because *political activity may justly be considered of little or no value* for the overthrow of the capitalist system. If the following arguments in support of such a sweeping statement are defective to the point of making the conclusion wrong, they should be annihilated, in the best interest of the working class.

It is being asserted by the adherents of a revolution at the ballot box, that the working class outnumbers the other class as voters (some enthusiasts say "as 10 to 1"). If this statement is true, it would be theoretically possible to vote capitalism out of existence, provided nearly all workingmen could be made to vote solidly for revolution, and provided the class in power would count their vote, and provided the ruling class would abide by their vote, and provided that an economic organization is in existence to "back up" the vote, if the ruling class does not abide by it. But in the final analysis this contention is based upon the statement that the workers are a *majority of the voters*. The contention stands or falls with the question whether the workers are in a majority at the ballot box or not. Thus far nobody can disagree with me, except those who depend for political success upon the votes of people who do not belong to the working class.

The writer maintains that the working class is not in a majority at the ballot box, which he will proceed to prove in the following simple manner, by the aid of statistics.

According to United States statistics, as summed up in the Socialist Almanac, page 101, the working class was in 1870, 62.81 percent of the population, in 1880, 58.91 percent, and in 1890, 55 percent of the total population. Later statistics I can unfortunately not quote, my little library having been destroyed in the great San Francisco fire. But I am certain that later statistical figures are not such as to wreck my conclusions, as we will find further on.

Taking the figures of 1890 the wage working class 55 percent of the population and the plutocrat, middle, and professional class 45 percent. Assuming that we have universal and equal manhood suffrage it would then be correct to assume that the working class controls 55 percent of the votes and the master class 45 percent.

But these 55 percent are by no means all voters. In this percentage of workingmen are included men of foreign parentage who have not become voters and the disfranchised Negroes, and many other non-voters.

Considering first the foreign-born, included in the 55 percent we find that in 1900, according to my best recollection, they were about 18 percent of the whole population. Of these approximately 12 percent may be counted as belonging to the working class, and the other 6 percent to the other class. These 6 percent being nearly all citizens and voters. Of the 12 percent belonging to the working class only a small part are voters. A large percentage are not in the country a sufficient time to be citizens, and outside the Celtic and Teutonic races comparatively few foreigners acquire citizenship, partly because they do not learn the language well enough to become citizens, partly because their imperfect knowledge of the language makes them indifferent to citizenship "privileges," partly on account of the difficulty in securing witnesses in accordance with law, partly because they have lost faith in the ballot in the country where they came from. Taking all these factors into consideration it is safe to assume that of the 12 percent counted with the working class about 8 percent have no vote.

Subtract 8 from 55 you have 47 percent., as against the 45 percent. of the other class. Your majority is dwindling dangerously already.

Now we come to the Negroes included in the 55 percent. They number about 10 percent of the population. Most Negroes being wage workers about 7 percent of them are included in the 55 percent. Of these approximately 5 percent are disfranchised directly.

Subtract 5 percent from 47 percent and you have 42 percent. as against the 45 percent of the other class. Now where is your majority? You are already in the minority, and I have already proven my statement that you do not outnumber the other class at the ballot box.

But in addition to these large groups who have no voice in the nation's affairs we have an immense number of citizens, who are counted in the 55 percent, who lose their vote through poll tax, property and residence qualifications and through the nature of their occupation. About 200,000 seafaring men can not vote. Hundreds of thousands of workers, aye over a million, who work in railroad construction, in the woods, or drift from Manitoba to Louisiana with the harvest season, or between the different crops in California and the Northwest, or from mining camp to mining camp or from one industrial town to another, are disfranchised. It is safe to deduct 5 percent more from the 55 percent. Deducting 5 percent from 42 percent we get 37 percent as opposed to the 45 percent of the other class. You are now 8 percent behind, which leaves a generous margin to cover any errors made in this argument. That the figures will not stand essentially different in 1910 or 1920, counting by percent, is also safe to assume. It may be said with some truth that since 1890 the working class has been largely swelled by accessions from a dying middle class, and that nearly a million wage workers (largely disfranchised) come to this country every year, and that the working class as a consequence is now more than 55 percent of the population. But as stated above the figures were for 1870, 62.81 percent, for 1880, 58.91 percent, for 1890, 55 percent. If the pendulum has swung the other way since 1890, it is still hardly probable that it has swung far enough to give the working class a majority at the ballot box. It is up to my critics to prove that it has, by quoting later, authentic statistics.

It is proven, then, that the working class does not outnumber the ruling class at the ballot box. And a miss in politics is as good as a mile. To fall short 100 voters of a majority is, for all practical purposes, as bad as getting only 100 votes in all.

Rut this argument against the value of the ballot as a working class weapon is so strong that I can afford to be generous. I will grant, for the sake of argument, that we do outnumber the ruling class at the ballot box.

Can we, then, judging by past and present success, entertain the hope of gathering, in any reasonable time, that problematical working class majority upon one program, under one revolutionary banner? Probably not. The ruling class holds the strings of the bread and butter of millions of slaves so tightly that they can not vote for revolution. Furthermore the ruling class controls the schools and poisons the young minds of the children. It owns the press and controls the minds of the fullgrown. It controls the pulpit, and there pollutes the mind of child and man. What becomes of your working class majority before these facts?

Again, granting for the sake of argument, that we now outnumber the master class at the ballot box, is there any reasonable justification for hoping that the master class will cease to impose new restrictions upon the right to vote, when that has been their course for the last ten years, as witness Texas, Louisiana, Mississippi, Georgia, North Carolina, Virginia and other states? Or is there any guarantee whatsoever that our ruling class will not resort to gerrymandering or election geometry, that is, redistributing of districts and representation as has been done in Germany, Sweden and other countries, in order to curtail the effect of a working class vote?

Granting, again, that we not only outnumber the ruling class, but have actually succeeded in getting a majority vote, what hope is there that they will not count us out, as is being done in every election, not only against workingmen's parties but between the masters themselves? What would it matter if we had the vote "backed up with an economic organization"? As long as we insist on accomplishing our aim "legally," so long can the master endure the game of showing us black on white that we are in the minority, and if we were to attempt the "backing up" of this minority, we would be "illegal" in the eyes of the ruling class anyhow, is long as they are in power.

Having granted so many impossible things, for the sake of argument, let us grant one more. Let us assume that a revolutionary political party carries a national election, and is allowed to take possession of all offices from President down. What will be the result?

As has so frequently been demonstrated, that day of our political victory would be our political funeral. The function of government is to make and enforce laws for the running of the capitalist system and to safeguard it against all comers. Or in other words, the sole purpose and function of government is to regulate the relations springing from the private ownership of the means of production and distribution, and everything connected therewith. But the new form of society, which we are preparing for, does not recognize this private ownership, it proposes to recognize production and distribution on collective lines, a function which can not possibly be filled by politicians, by a President, a Secretary of War, a Secretary of the Navy, a House of Representatives, a Senate, a Custom House Department, an Internal Revenue Department, etc. Like Shakespeare's Moor, the politicians would find their occupation gone. There would be positively nothing for them to do, unless they were to continue to run society on capitalist lines, the very thing they were supposedly elected to discontinue.

Neither can it reasonably be suggested that these men, thus elected, should instantly sit down and reorganize society on co-operative lines. Society may be *reformed* by decrees and resolutions, but a *complete organic change*, a revolution, as we contemplate, must begin at the bottom, is a matter of evolution within the constituent parts of the organism itself, is a building of cell upon cell until the organism is completed. The so-called political organization does not occupy itself with this task. This task is left to the economic organization such as the I.W.W. which is even now grouping and arranging the individual human units as cells in the future organism of society. Such an organization as the I.W.W. will, when the proper time comes, pass society over from private to collective ownership with no more jar, than when a railroad train, after crossing a steel bridge, glides over the narrow slit which separates the bridge from terra firma, no matter what its struggle may be before it reaches that point. And such an organization, instead of having to abdicate on the day of victory, reaches first then its perfection, and becomes the permanent form of the new society.

Of course I realize that little, if any, objection will be made to this manner of stating the function of the economic organization. The objection I anticipate is that we need the political movement as an auxiliary, at least in the every day battle with the master class. Against this objection I maintain, and will try to prove, that the political propaganda, far from being needed as an auxiliary for the overthrow of capitalism, is positively harmful to true working class interests. Such propaganda fosters and maintains the illusion that all the evils of society can be mended at the ballot box, which I have shown not to be the case. *Reforms* can be enacted through the ballot, but not revolutions contrary to the interests of those who control the ballot. Political activity puts us on a par with the capitalist parties and places us in a position where we have to tacitly endorse and cooperate in maintaining the capitalist system. I will illustrate.

Suppose Jackson of the S.L.P. had been elected governor of New York, Haywood of the S.P. governor of Colorado, or Lewis of the S.P. governor of California, and all three suppositions are unreasonable, for the capitalist class is not going to allow us to play at governing, simply for the pleasure of having us demonstrate our impotency.

What would happen if these three men had been elected together with their whole tickets, controlling state legislature and everything else?

Could they have declared the cooperative commonwealth in existence? Everybody answers no. The legislature would have to sit down and tackle the bitter tasks of making, amending and improving the laws pertaining to the private ownership of the means of production and distribution. To do anything else would bring upon them the U.S. Supreme Court and eventually the U.S. regular troops. They would perforce have to be accomplices of the capitalist class in administering capitalist law to the workers. Could they even shorten the hours of toil or increase the pay of the workers? Experience tells us no. Ten-hour laws have been declared unconstitutional in the State of New York. An eight-hour law was passed by a referendum by the people of Colorado, but it never was taken up by the legislature, so it never had a chance to be declared unconstitutional, but nobody doubts that it would have been so declared had the legislature passed it. Even a local victory would thus be futile. Oh, but you will say, we could keep the militia off in case of strike. Yes, but could you keep the federal troops off? No, we could not.

In the meantime the Western Federation of Miners, and many unions of the American Federation of Labor even have an eight-hour day and a minimum wage. Have they been declared unconstitutional? No, and they did not gain it through political action, but through economic organization.

The advocates of political working class activity predicate their success upon being "backed up" by an economic organization which is to take the chestnuts out of the fire for them. The economic organization stands on its own legs and declines political "assistance". The economic organization makes just such demands as it is able to enforce, and it is able to make demands and to enforce them from the very first, it does not have to wait for that hazy day when we shall have a majority. For them to waste their energy on the building up and maintaining a political organization, which they afterwards would have to "back up," only to awaken to a realization of its impotency, would be like crossing the river to fill your water bucket, when you can just as well get your water on this side.

One more objection I will anticipate and meet. It will be said perhaps: "The workers have the right to vote, and, if we do not give them a chance to vote for revolution, they have no choice but to vote for capitalism." But this objection has only a sentimental value. Some workingmen may feel some satisfaction in teasing the bear with a vote for revolution. I, for one, do not any longer. I do not enjoy practical jokes, and still less do I enjoy being insulted by having my ballot counted out. I wish to see my fellow workers quit wasting their time and energy on an illusion, drop politics, and unite on a plan of action which will bring about the results we desire, and that plan of action I find expressed in an economic organization on the lines of the I.W.W.

You will then, finally, ask: "What are we going to do with the political working class organizations already in existence, the Socialist Labor Party, and the Socialist Party?"

The question is simple and easily answered. Both these organizations maintain that there is war between the two classes. In the war both of them have rendered splendid service, especially the S.L.P., in educating the workers up to the point where they were able to see the necessity of, and to form an economic organization like the I.W.W. They have done well as propaganda societies, but that is all they have ever been, their names and platforms notwithstanding. That they should have originally chosen the political field was natural, due to the deep rooted idea that all social evils can be cured at the ballot, in a "free" country. But their role is now played.

In war, success depends often upon a complete change of front, upon a swift flank movement, upon abandoning one position and taking up a new one. Such movements are often necessary to avoid exposing your own men to your own fire. Such is the position of the S.P. and the S.L.P. now. They are right in the line of fire. Their war cries are confusing and demoralizing the gathering proletarian army and may cause a temporary reverse. What kind of organization is theirs for war purposes! It is a machine, a general staff, composed of sections, of locals, calling on their army (and an unreliable army it is) every two or four years for parade and review at the ballot box and then dismissing it. What sensible man could any longer participate in that sort of stage war? It is up to you to break up camp and take up the struggle from a point of vantage in the I.W.W. and get out of the line of fire. Turn over your funds and your institutions at the earliest possible date to the I.W.W. and let us join in the drilling and perfecting of the revolutionary industrial army which is never dismissed, but fights and forges forward irresistibly to the goal, the overthrow of capitalism and the establishing of the new society.

Before closing allow me again to request that my arguments be considered exclusively on their merits, and that every critic give as much time and sincere thought to the subject as I have.

Answer

Sandgren's article falls within the general province of the burning question of Unionism, with a special eye to political activity, as its title indicates. The writer plants himself upon the industrial form of organization, or the I.W.W., as essential to the emancipation of the working class, and proceeds to present a chain of reasoning from which he concludes that the political movement is worthless, harmful and should be discarded, and he calls upon the Socialist Labor Party and the Socialist Party to "break up camp," and to "turn over their funds and institutions" to the I.W.W. Finally, the writer makes an earnest appeal for the serious consideration of his arguments, and invites discussion thereupon.

The writer's premises are in the main wrong, and his conclusion is not only wronger, but not even logical, his own premises being defective. Nevertheless, the article is timely. Due to its timeliness, seeing that a perceptible anti-political sentiment has latterly broken out in several quarters, the article is published. Moreover, in honor to the good spirit which prompts the article, and for the purpose of systematizing the discussion which it invites, and preventing the same from degenerating, as such discussions unfortunately but too frequently do, into an indefinite rambling that wanders more or less from the conclusion or the premises under consideration, the article will here be divided into its two main component parts, and these dissected.

I—Working Class Strength At The Ballot Box

After the first four introductory pages which can be safely left undiscussed, whether pro or con, the writer devotes much space to prove statistically that the working class does not outnumber the capitalist class at the polls, and hence the workingman's ballot can never win. The figures are wrong. For one thing, part of them are nearly twenty years old; for another, the deductions are made only from the figures for the working class, whereas many a deduction should also be made from the figures for the voting strength of the capitalist class. Here are, for instance, a few serious discrepancies between the writer's figures and the figures of the Census for 1900:

The writer estimates the foreign born population in 1900 at 18 percent; the census states 23.7. The writer estimates the number of citizens among the foreign born at considerably below 10 percent (6 percent as capitalists and all voters, and of the remaining 12 percent, workingmen, he says, "only a small part are voters"); the census for 1900 gives 80 percent of foreign born males as citizens, and only 20 percent as remaining aliens. The writer climaxes his errors under this head by subtracting his deductions, not from the working class population in 1900 (about 70 percent), but from the working class population in 1890 (about 55 percent).

Again, the writer deducts in lump from the voting strength of the working class "about 200,000 seafaring men as unable to vote"; the census for 1900 gives less than one-half that number, only 78,406 as the total for "boatmen and sailors," exclusive of U.S. sailors and marines who are comparatively few, seeing that, together with the soldiers, they number only 43,235 men.

Again, the writer overshoots his own mark. He points to the influence, physical and mental, that the ruling class exercises through "the strings of the bread and butter of millions of slaves" which that class "holds tightly," as well as through its schools, press and pulpit, and concludes therefrom that these slaves "can not vote for revolution". If these influences, which no doubt must be reckoned with, are so absolutely controlling that these wage slaves will be too timid to perform even such a task as voting, a task that the veriest coward could perform with safety, and they must be deducted in lump from the voting strength of the working class, upon what ground can the writer feel justified to enroll those same slaves as reliable material for the revolutionary act of the I.W.W.? If they must be excluded from the former, they can not for a moment be thought of in the latter.

No doubt deductions must be made from the voting strength of the working class; but the necessary deductions are not the slashing ones made by the writer. So overwhelming is the numerical preponderance of the working class that, all justifiable deductions notwithstanding, it preserves an ample majority at the polls. Moreover, the revolutionary working class ballot may safely count with reinforcements from the middle and kindred hard-pushed social layers. While corrupt and vicious is all attempt to secure split votes for the revolution from classes that vote the rest of capitalist tickets, legitimate is the attempt to induce hard-pushed middle class elements to tear themselves from their class prejudices and plump their vote for the revolution - and justified is the expectation that big chunks of that class will hearken the summons. If the decision for or against politics were to depend exclusively upon the numerical strength of the working class at the polls the decision would have to be for, not against.

II — The Mission Of Politics

The second of the two main component parts of the writer's article is devoted to proving that even if the working class ballot were more numerous than the ballot of the foe, the former would be counted out by the latter; and that, even if it were not counted out, working class political victory would be a Barmecide's Feast, in that the Socialist Republic has no use for the political or modern form of government.

Both these points have been enlarged upon and proven in detail in De Leon's address on "The Preamble of the Industrial Workers of the World"; they were proved so thoroughly that the pure and simple political Socialists, who felt the cold steel of the argument enter their bourgeois souls, have handled the argument like a hot potato, and confined themselves to vapid slurs about "vagaries," or the more vapid indulgence in "calling names" against the maker of the argument. That argument, however, was made in *support* of the I.W.W. position regarding the necessity of uniting the working class on the "political as well as upon the industrial field"; the writer of the article under discussion, on the contrary, makes the argument *in opposition* to the I.W.W. position.

The opposite application of the identical argument brings out the basic error that underlies Sandgren's reasoning — he confuses *political agitation* with the *ballot*. The two are distinct.

How completely the vital distinction is missed by those who oppose political action is graphically illustrated by a favorite argument among them, an argument that Sandgren reproduces in beautifully pictorial style when he says that for the working class "to waste their energy on the building up and maintaining of a political organization, which they afterwards have to 'back up,' only to awaken to a realization of its impotence, would be like crossing the river to fill your water-bucket, when you can just as well get your water on this side". This is begging the question. The very point at issue is whether that economic organization, able "to fill the water-bucket," can at all be brought together without the aid of political agitation; the very point at issue is whether the politics—ignoring economic organization has hitherto accomplished anything of lasting value to the working class at large; or to put it in yet a third and summary form, whether the decline of power with the economic organization is not due to its contradictory posture of "voting" for one thing and "striking" for its opposite. Of course, if such a thing is conceivable as the bringing together of an industrial organization, able "to fill the bucket" without the aid of political agitation, it were folly to waste time, energy and funds in building up and maintaining a political organization. But the thought is visionary. To him in whom such a thought can find lodgment the blood spilt in Russia during the last sixteen months is blood wasted—and the error is born of the confusion of "political agitation" with the "ballot".

The value of the "ballot" as a constructive force is zero; the value of "political agitation" is immeasurable.

Not everything that capitalism has brought about is to be rejected. Such a vandal view would have to smash the giant machine of modern production as well. Among the valuable things that capitalism has introduced is the idea of peaceful methods for settling disputes. In feudal days, when lords fell out, production stopped; war had the floor. The courts of law have become the main fields of capitalist, at least internal capitalist battle, and production continues uninterfered with. It matters not how corrupt the courts have become, or one-sided against the working class. The jewel of civilized or peaceful methods for settling disputes is there, however incrusted with slime. Capitalism, being a step forward, as all Socialists recognize, can not help but be a handmaid, however clumsy, to civilized methods. Of a piece with the court method for the peaceful settlement of disputes is the political method. The organization that rejects this method and organizes for force only, reads itself out of the pale of civilization, with the practical result that, instead of seizing a weapon furnished by capitalism, it gives capitalism a weapon against itself.

The "filling of the bucket" must be done by the million-masses. The agitation for force only clips the wings of the agitation for the "filling of the bucket". The inevitable result is that the agitation has to degenerate into "conspiracy"; conspiracy can be conducted in circumscribed localities only, such localities exclude the masses - and the wheels of time are turned back. *The bringing together of the physical force organization becomes impossible.* Political agitation equips the revolution with a weapon that is indispensable. Political agitation enables the revolution to be preached in the open, and thereby enables the revolution to be brought before the million-masses— *without which there can be no "bucket" fashioned to do the "filling".*

In short, political agitation, coupled with the industrial organization able to "take and hold," or "back up" the political movement, or "fill the bucket," places the revolution abreast of civilized and intelligent methods—civilized, because they offer a chance to a peaceful solution; intelligent, because they are not planted upon the visionary plane of imagining that right can ever prevail without the might to enforce it.

Of course, "political agitation" implies the setting up of a political ticket, and that, in turn, implies the "ballot". Indeed, the "ballot" may be lost; let it; the fruits, however, of the "political agitation" are imperishable. *Under the shield of that agitation the "bucket" is shaped.* To Father Time the final issue may be safely left. No doubt there are many thorns to the rose of the political movement. No rose is without them. Irrelevant is the enumeration of these thorns. What the adversaries of political action in the I.W.W. should do in the endeavor to convert their fellow workers of the opposite view is not to indulge in the superfluous repetition regarding the folly of the political movement when the "bucket" is in shape, but how the "bucket" can be put in shape without the aid of the agitation and education which the political movement places in the hands of the revolution.

The Socialist Party will as little "break up camp," by the argument, however crushingly convincing, of the futility of the "ballot" only, as the capitalist class will break up camp by the argument, however crushingly convincing, that it is doomed. For that the S.P. is too legitimate an off-shoot of bourgeois thought, which is clogged with "reform" notions, and for which the pure and simple ballot is a useful weapon. The S.P. will break up camp only when the revolutionary element in its ranks discovers that it is upon their shoulders that such a caricature of Socialism actually rests, and that it is from them only that the caricature draws its strength. The S.P. will "break up camp" only when this revolutionary element, by withdrawing, removes the plug from under the concern.

As to the Socialist Labor Party, it never will need to be appealed to "to break up camp" after the "bucket" of the I.W.W., having gathered sufficient solidity, will itself have reflected its own political party. That day the S.L.P. will "break up camp" with a shout of joy—if a body merging into its own ideal can be said to "break up camp."

-Ed., *The People*.

Second letter, by J. A. La Bille, St. Louis, Mo.

I have been much interested in the discussion under the heading of "As to Politics"; so much so that I was sorry to see it stop almost before it started. The article by John Sandgren was very good except in regard to the vote, which does not affect the question. All we need to know is that the working class is in the majority. We *do* know they will be counted on the economic field. So I will take a stand in this discussion that working class political action, parliamentary or agitation, is not only harmful to the marshalling of the working class, but that the industrial organization is all sufficient, hence, I contend the I.W.W. should change its preamble by declaring against political action.

Comrade De Leon says we confuse "political agitation" with the "ballot," so we will analyze "political agitation" and endeavor to determine if its value is "immeasurable"; also if "the bringing together of an industrial organization able 'to fill the bucket' without the aid of political agitation" is impossible. Political action may be summed up as follows: Political organization, business meetings, mass meetings, conventions, propaganda meetings, placing tickets on the ballot, watching at polls, burning midnight oil studying election laws and tricks of the professional politician, spending tremendous sums of money, all of which means a great deal when the organization attains any size of importance. Then Mr. Workingman is in politics so confused and befuddled that he don't know whether he is a workingman or a professional politician.

Comrade De Leon is correct when he states: "In feudal days, when the lords fell out, production stopped; war had the floor; the courts of the law have become the main field of capitalist, at least internal capitalist, battles, and production continues uninterfered with." Thus showing the capitalists have good reason to settle their disputes by the courts through politics because they are property owners and needs must have their revenues uninterrupted. The working class, on the other hand, are propertiless, giving them advantage on the economic battlefield, having nothing to lose but their chains. It is there where the struggle must be, and it is there and there only where the working class will reach the heart of capitalism.

Every victory won, every hour of leisure gained, every "supply wagon" captured, will be of unlimited more value to the revolution than the conquering of a piece of paper called the ballot. Then what is political agitation but the urging of the working class to go into politics, and when you do that you can't give it any material reason for so doing because the fight of the working class is economic in character, not political. The economic organization can "back up" the political, but the political can not back up the economic, in this country any more than in Germany or Russia. Those expecting to secure power on the political field will some day find themselves chasing the rainbow which appears very beautiful, but always out of reach. The workingman is not exploited by the political "burg" of capitalism, but through the private ownership of the means of production, hence his malady is not a political disease but economic. His environment in the mills, factories, mines, fields, etc., gives him an economic character out of which it is folly to lure him into a field of battle entirely foreign to his characteristics and environments for no other purpose than agitation. The reason he first took to the "ballot" was from an illusion that all that was, was the result of the ballot. The slave saw his master feed the slaves, hence, he thought the slaves were supported by the master. The workman today kisses the hand that pays his wages and believes he is exploited as a consumer because he sees the prices go up. He sees the police, soldiers and the politicians in office come after him with "fixed bayonets," so he thinks his struggle is a political one. He does not know that, like Russia, the army and police are here to stay until the end of the struggle and the only way to get the best of them is by cutting off their base of supplies.

I further contend the I.W.W. is all sufficient, both as to education and force. Comrade De Leon says: "Of a piece with the court method for the peaceful settlement of disputes is the political method. The organization that rejects this method and organizes for force only, reads itself out of the pale of civilization with the practical result that, instead of seizing a weapon furnished by capitalism, it gives capitalism a weapon against itself." The impression seems to be that the economic organization, the embryo of the coining republic, is physical force only. I take the position that it not only has the force, but all the means of educating the working class necessary, in fact, it is only through the industrial organization that the proletariat can be educated to its true class interests. And if they go into politics, the longer they are there the more befuddled they become. If they must have politics let them have it in the I.W.W. as the Socialist Republic, where a vote qualification will be had. "No producer, no voter." The worker does not need political agitation in order to reach the masses, and I believe at this stage of the game the capitalist "committees" will have their hands full suppressing agitation by the industrially organized workers. If it be the case, that agitation will be hampered, and the economic organization can not protect itself, then how is it to protect both itself and the "fiat of the ballot"? The idea of a "general strike" entailing many hardships on the part of the working class, to defend the ballot, in my opinion is absurd. *We are not fighting for the privilege of registering our votes on capitalist books. We are fighting for bread and butter now, and our emancipation as soon as we are well enough organized* to take charge of the various industries and operate them entirely in the interests of the workers therein. If the worker centralizes his struggle for liberty on the economic field only, then his education need be very simple. Yea; he could travel the path of his class interests almost by instinct; but if he divides his fighting forces, one on the political, one on the economic, then his education will require years of study and experience to know which one of the many paths is safe for him to walk over (these remarks apply to the working class as a rule). We must remember also that only a small percentage of any organization must shoulder the greater part of the work, and when the strength of these valiant workers is divided between two organizations it handicaps the general movement to a great extent.

As I said before, if the working class devotes its efforts to the building up of the industrial organization, the foundation of the future republic, his education need be very simple and along such lines as: (1) Labor is the source of value, therefore should have full product; (2) Capital does not produce value, therefore the capitalist is not entitled to any part of the product, and show him how he is exploited, and the method to his emancipation, as we do today, except cut out all agitation for politics, and show him the fallacy of expecting to derive benefits from political action.

It appears to me that the honest workingman who would go into political action for agitation is a pure and simple borer from within as much so as the honest man who votes and agitates in the A.F. of Scabs and S.P. who also works and agitates to educate the rank and file of those organizations. The result, in all three cases, is the same. Will we smash the capitalist institution of politics by boring from within or smashing from without? Let the workers do their voting in the I.W.W., a place the capitalist can not vote. Let them do their fighting in that army, and, when the industries have been thoroughly organized, let them move the I.W.W. in the capitol building if they so will, and if there be senators and representatives of capitalist hell there, sweep them with the rest of the rubbish into the sewer if necessary, and remember it won't require a single workingman in political office from president up to dog catcher to do it, either, for the moment the source of the capitalists' existence is cut off by the industrially organized workers the dome of capitalism will crumble and fall of its own weight. In the meantime, let the capitalists have the ballot all to their precious selves. Let them fill their offices with all the rotten eggs in the country, let them make the laws to their hearts' content, yes, all the laws, and fill their political citadels with law books, lawyers and jurists, too. We will rest at ease, knowing their laws and interpretation of laws will be as a bullet without force to propel it, *their politics will be impotent.* It matters not how many laws or what they are, the whole question is in their ability to enforce them and their ability to enforce them depends not on their political supremacy but on their economic supremacy over the working class. It is the same with the working class whose demands will be limited only by the full product of their toil and their ability to enforce.

So with these few suggestions (I could make many more but do not wish to abuse a privilege), I will say in conclusion that it is practically the same for the pioneer to attempt to be an Indian in order to capture their war councils as for the worker to be a politician in order to capture the war councils of the capitalist class; in other words, we want the pig, we will not waste energy following echoes trying to capture the squeal; when we get the pig we've got the squeal, too.

The S.L.P. undoubtedly has done and is doing a great service for the revolution and deserves to be called the "Fighting S.L.P". But its *real great service lies in its economic teachings*.

A little discussion on this subject will be beneficial for the members of the S.L.P. and I.W.W., myself included. We should all study it thoroughly and know the whys and wherefores and avoid taking things for granted.

Answer

The above is published out of excess of courtesy to the side that our correspondent holds with. The columns of *The People* were held open for a month to the matter and not one contributor to the discussion having sustained the anti-political action position the discussion was closed. Out of courtesy to views different from those of *The People*, the discussion is re-opened to the extent of allowing space to the above.

There may be those who suppose that some slight perfidy is alloyed with our courtesy. Perhaps these are not wholly wrong. The courtesy may be perfidious that allows the great space which our correspondent takes and yet leaves unanswered the only question that is pivotal to the issue — how are the masses to be recruited and organized into capacity to take and hold if the agitation is to be conducted upon lines that wholly reject the peaceful theory of "counting noses"?

It is time wasted to point out the thorns on the political stalk. They are all admitted beforehand. The question is, Is that stalk all thorns and no rose? Nor do we get any nearer to the truth by incorrect definitions. Our correspondent's definition of what political action embraces is woefully deficient. That is the system of "giving a dog a name and then killing him".

The rose on the stalk of "political action" is the posture it enables a man to hold by which he can preach revolution without having to do so underground; in other words, by which he can teach the economics and sociology of the Social Revolution in the open, where the masses can hear, and not in the dark, where but few can meet.

The nomination of tickets, together with all the routine that thereby hangs, is but an incidental—like the making of a motion to which to speak, and without which motion being before the house, speaking degenerates into disorder.

Simply to assert that the masses can be reached, educated and drilled for the revolution by any other process does not remove the fact that it can not be done; at any rate it does not enlighten those who hold otherwise, and who, having no hobby to serve, but only a goal, the emancipation of the working class, to reach, are ever ready to learn. Assertions teach nobody.

Finally, the just compliment our correspondent pays to the "Fighting S.L.P." should cause him to ponder and overhaul his anti-political-action views. He will have a hard time to explain how it comes about that it is the S.L.P. that has been teaching the real fighting economics, if political action is the worthless thing that he takes it for.

The theory of preaching revolution against the capitalist class only by brandishing the sword, in a country where the suffrage is in vogue, leaves unexplained the phenomenon of the unquestionable hatred that the capitalist press manifests for the S.L.P.—for that political organization that admits its impotence to carry out its program, unless the working class is organized into possession of the national machinery of production, in other words, that is aware of and admits the fact that it is only a shell, but the necessary shell, within which the physical force is to be hatched whereby to enforce the demands peacefully made by the ballot. The capitalist class of the land dotes upon pure and simple political Socialism (the hollow shell, without the substance); it likewise dotes upon pure and simple, or non-political Unionism (the amorphic substance, amorphic because shell-less within which the mass can grow and gather shape). For that combination that combines both shell and substance - for that combination the capitalist class, together with its pickets of all grades, has only the hatred which it manifests upon the slightest provocation for the S.L.P. and for the I.W.W. with its political clause.

- Ed., *The People*.

Third letter, by Jos. Wagner and Leon Vasilio, Springfield, Ill.

It is with doubt as to being allowed space in the columns of *The People* that the undersigned take the decision to express their opinion in regard to Comrade Sandgren's article.

We realize the degree of annoyance that we are causing the editor by our action; and were it not for the fact that we have seen in *The People* so many reflections cast at the privately owned press of the S.P. in regard to refusals to publish whatever is not to their heart, we would, most assuredly, try to kill our temptation to give out what is our honest and sincere conviction.

We know that our opinion is that of thousands of members of the Industrial Workers of the World, and consequently ask for the same privilege that we both have been granted in the past, when our views were not at variance with the attitude of *The People*.

After both reading and rereading carefully Sandgren's article, and the answer of the editor of *The People*; after giving the matter earnest consideration from all viewpoints for the last three weeks, we arrived at the conclusion that, of all the answers that Comrade De Leon has made in his life in capacity of editor of *The People*, the one just mentioned must be the poorest and the weakest one. Not that he is no more the same brilliant writer, but that the time has come when he is in the wrong, defending a wrong cause. Why and how is this thus? We shall see.

In order to be better understood, we would like to refer the reader to the two articles in question, which are published in the *Weekly People* of December 1, 1906, under the title "As to Politics". But as every one who will happen to lay hands on this number may not be in position to get that one, we shall give here the quintessence of Sandgren's article.

His contention is that the political activity is useless and harmful, and that the emancipation of the working class can be accomplished through economic revolutionary organization only.

In the first part of the article, which in our opinion is a complete failure, Sandgren endeavors to prove that the working class are not in the majority at the ballot box. Unless Sandgren wanted to be altogether "original" we can not understand how a man of his calibre could have ventured such an absurdity. This we consider a waste of time to take up for discussion.

In the second part of the article, he admirably shows the impotence of a political organization, and also how fitted an economic organization is to bear the struggle.

"Ten-hour laws have been declared unconstitutional in the State of New York.... In the meantime the Western Federation of Miners and many unions of the A.F. of L., even, have an eight-hour day and a minimum wage. Have they been declared unconstitutional? No, and they did not gain it through political action, but through economic organization. The advocates of political working class activity predicate their success upon being 'backed up' by an economic organization which is to rake the chestnuts out of the fire for them.

"The economic organization stands on its own legs and declines political 'assistance'.

"The economic organization makes just such demands as it is able to enforce, and it is able to make demands and enforce them from the very first; it does not have to wait for the hazy day when we shall have a majority."

And now comes De Leon's answer. He says that "the basic error that underlies Sandgren's reasoning" is the confusion of the *political agitation with the ballot*. The two are distinct, says the editor.

"How completely the vital distinction is missed by those who oppose political action is graphically illustrated by a favorite argument among them, an argument that Sandgren reproduces in beautifully pictorial style, when he says that for the working class to waste their time on the building up and maintaining of a political organization which they afterwards have to 'back up' only to awaken to a realization of its impotence, would be like crossing the river to fill your water-bucket when you can just as well get your water on this side."

First of all Comrade Sandgren—as well as all of us, industrial workers, who dropped ballot box activity—gives the Socialist political agitation its due credit when he says: "Both these organizations (the S.P. and the S.L.P.) maintain that there is a war between the two classes. In the war both of them have rendered splendid service.... They have done well as propaganda societies, but that is all they have ever been, their names and platforms notwithstanding.... Their role is now played."

This means that Sandgren does not confuse political agitation with the ballot; he only rejects the ballot, which, as a constructive force, even in the opinion of the editor is zero. In order to make this point clear, let us analyze the nature of a Socialist political party activity.

In the first place it is an incessant criticism of the actual system of society based on the private ownership of the means of life, for which it intends to substitute another system, based on the social or collective ownership of those means – the cooperative commonwealth. This is the political nature of it.

On the other hand, this Socialist political party activity consists of a laborious propaganda for the attainment of that social system, a propaganda for the class struggle on the political field, which "implies the setting up of a 'ticket,' and that, in turn, implies the 'ballot'".

But if the ballot, as a constructive force is zero, so must necessarily be all the amount of work spent in getting that ballot, such as holding nomination conventions, caucuses, getting signatures on petitions, watching at the polls, etc., etc. And we know that most of the energy of a Socialist political victory is wasted on that zero proposition. A revolutionary organization of the working class that aims at the overthrow of the capitalist system and the establishment of the cooperative commonwealth is essentially political in character and such is the I.W.W., as Comrade De Leon himself ably proved in his Chicago speech on September 12, 1906.

The one who does confuse the political agitation with the ballot is De Leon. On page 32 of the Preamble of the I.W.W., he says: "A part, the better, the constructive part of Socialist economics, translates itself into the industrial organization of the working class; it translates itself into that formation that outlines the mould of the future social system; another part of Socialist economics, however, inevitably translates itself into politics." Should he not confuse the political agitation with the ballot, he would never dismantle a revolutionary industrial organization "that outlines the mould of the future society" of its sufficiency to carry on the political agitation of the working class, and give this function to another organization which, as we have seen is spending its energy on a zero proposition - at the working class expense.

The Industrial Workers of the World sufficiently fulfills that role of a political party of Socialism by that, that it aims at the cooperative commonwealth and it teaches the class struggle on the industrial field where every victory is a step towards the social revolution - and doesn't waste the energy of the working class on a zero proposition, on something that not only may be lost, but that is always lost.

So much in regard to confusing the political agitation with the ballot.

Now to "the point at issue". "The very point at issue," the editor says further, "is whether that economic organization, 'able to fill the bucket,' can at all be brought together without the political agitation; the very point at issue is whether the politics - ignoring economic organization has hitherto accomplished anything of lasting value for the working class at large; or to put it in a third and summary form, whether the decline of power with the economic organization is not due to its contradictory posture of 'voting' for one thing and 'striking' for its opposite. Of course, if such a thing is conceivable as the bringing together of an industrial organization able 'to fill the bucket' without the aid of political agitation, it were folly to waste time, energy and funds in building up and maintaining a political organization."

Let us ask Comrade De Leon, why is he beating around the bush? What does he mean by politics—ignoring economic organization? Does he mean the Industrial Workers of the World, or the American Federation of Labor? His allusion to "the decline of power with the economic organization" on account of "its contradictory posture of voting for one thing and striking for its opposite" conveys to our minds the A. F. of L., and not that economic organization "able to fill the water-buckets," the "I.W.W.," which is now under discussion.

And since when is Comrade De Leon willing to admit that the A. F. of L., as an organization, is doing on the economic field the opposite of what its members are doing on the political field? This sounds very familiar to those who have heard the pure and simple political Socialist appeal to the pure and simple craft unionist to vote as he strikes. But let us not indulge any longer in these non-essentials.

The question is "whether that economic organization able to fill the bucket can at all be brought together without the aid of political agitation". Before answering this question, let us consider the nature and the activity of an economic organization, such as the I.W.W.

Like the political party of Socialism, it aims at the overthrowing of the present System: it aims to take possession of the tools of production from the capitalist class and operate them for the benefit of the working class, which will be the whole of society.

But for the attainment of this end, the economic organization fighting the class struggle on the industrial field, it organizes the workers in their various locals, industries and departments in order to make them able to cope with modern capitalism in their everyday fight, and wrest concessions from that class locally, industrially or generally, as the case may be — concessions, which, unlike the politician's reforms, are steps towards the revolution, as they put the working class more and more in control of the industries in which they are working.

It is founded on the recognition of the fact of the division of society into two classes, between which a struggle must go on, until all the toilers will come together and take over the means of production. Its aim is revolutionary, its activity *political*. It is revolutionary and political because its aim is to change the foundation of this society from an exchange of commodities to the co-operative commonwealth. In other words, it is not like the pure and simple union, which acts as buffer between the opposing forces — the capitalist class and the working class — but it is one of these forces organized.

Such an organization as the I.W.W. is brought about by the modern economic conditions, that is, by the industrial development and the revolutionary propaganda, absolutely independent of any ballot party activity, which has an altogether different function, as we have seen.

In all that preceded we can not see at all where the role of a ballot organization comes in. In his attempt to answer Comrade Sandgren, the editor tells us of the "jewel" of "civilized or peaceful methods of settling disputes". If this is the only argument left to defend an organization which wastes our time, energy and funds, then we can rest assured that the industrial organization is the only thing able to fill the bucket or to accomplish the revolution. He might as well tell us about those lovely seances of looking each other in the eyes. They are more to the question.

But it is an irony of fate to hear men telling us of settling disputes. Is that the reason for which we are organizing? We are organizing to struggle, and not to settle disputes, which have never been settled in the interests of the working class.

Nothing could settle disputes better than a powerful organization—able to strike terror in the heart of the capitalist class would. Confronted with such an organization the capitalist class would either have to submit or bear the consequences.

The methods employed by the revolutionary industrial organization are peaceful and civilized enough for the working class. We are assembling peacefully and in a civilized manner discuss matters of our class interest which we afterwards submit to the capitalist class in form of demands. We can not understand how Comrade De Leon jumps at the conclusion that the I.W.W. agitation—which he terms "agitation for force only"—has to degenerate into conspiracy, which excludes the masses. The industrial agitation is not and can not degenerate into a "conspiracy" for the simple reason that it is preached in the open, and thereby enables the revolution to be brought before the million masses. Not only does the industrial organization bring the revolution before the million masses, but it also draws the million masses to its ranks and keeps aloof the hard pushed middle class element, with its lawyers, priests and intellectuals in general—in a word, all that is foreign to the working class. It draws all the toilers of all nationalities; citizens and non-citizens; all the disfranchised, all the cramps and "coffee-and-doughnut-bums," which are able to beat their way from Frisco all the way through the "wild west" to Chicago in order to do their own business.

As far as the "chance to a peaceful solution" goes, we are very little concerned about it. It does not depend on the working class how the last blow will have to be struck. If the capitalists will not be satisfied with a decree to step out, we can rest assured that they will, most likely, get worse.

The events that have taken place in the last sixteen or seventeen months have taught us more than the preceding two decades. They have taught us not only that the political party agitation is useless, but harmful to the industrial organization from the Pacific to the Atlantic. We have seen men eagerly listening to the industrial speaker, accidentally being an S.L.P. man, start to show the "difference" or something of that sort, then the men would turn away with a sneer at "the politician".

That the ballot agitation is harmful to the bringing together of an economic organization able to fill the bucket, is obvious; so obvious is this fact that, at the last convention of the I.W.W. we have witnessed Comrade De Leon make a motion to the effect that no organizer of any political party should be employed as organizer for the Industrial Workers of the World. Yes, one year of I.W.W. agitation and experience has brought about great changes in the revolutionary thought in this country.

Men that but a few months ago were feeling as touching an extremely delicate spot when speaking of the non-party affiliation clause of the I.W.W. preamble, are now dropping politics without any *reservatio mentalis*.

And let us not for a minute fool ourselves and think that this is merely a passing crisis, a temporary manifestation of a few over-heated brains. No! This let-alone politics tendency that we now are noticing in this country is the American expression of a general tendency of the revolutionary working class the world over. In Italy, Spain, Switzerland, and France and even Germany with its great three-million-strong-paper-party we can see the same thing.

In a lengthy article by our Parisian comrade, A. Bruckere, recently published in *The People*, we can see how the working class of France, tired of political parties, is gathering in a revolutionary organization, "The General Confederation of Labor," after dropping politics altogether and adopting the "direct action". The history of this let-alone-politics tendency in Europe would make a mighty interesting and instructive work, which would considerably help in the understanding of the great change that is going on in the revolutionary thought of the working class of the world.

Before closing we would like to say that, in writing this article, we have not been actuated by any prejudice against any particular man or party; that in speaking against ballot activity we have meant all Socialist parties of the world.

We have been good, faithful members of Socialist parties in Europe and in America for many years, but our experience as wage slaves has shown us that we have been in the wrong. We expressed our opinion, which, we are sure, will not meet with the approval of those who have forgotten nothing and learned nothing by years of bitter experience.

Answer

The question repeatedly asked of the advocates of physical force only, who have favored us with their contributions, remains unanswered:

How do you expect to recruit and organize your Industrial army if you begin by rejecting the peaceful method of solving the Social Question, to wit, the political method? It is significant that none of our opponents has cared to meet this point. They all give that question a wide berth. Instead of covering the only point that is decisive they go into a vast number of subjects that may or may not be so, but have nothing to do with the real point - *how?*

The nearest our above esteemed contributors come to an answer on this particular point is the passage: "The I.W.W. sufficiently fulfills the role of a political party of Socialism by that it aims at the cooperative commonwealth and teaches the class struggle on the industrial field." This statement is doubly defective.

If to "aim" at a thing is enough, then to "wish" for it should be equally sufficient. Every practical mind knows that wishes and aims, like steam, must be in the boiler of a properly organized machine before results can be obtained. Wishes are good, aims still better. Without the organization to realize them they are, well, so much hot air. The question is how to recruit the elements that will constitute the requisite organization.

The second defect in the passage is still more marked. It is fatal to the contention of the anti-political agitation. Indeed, the I.W.W. "teaches the class struggle," and can teach it freely, and freely can proclaim its purpose to "take and hold"; but it can do so only because it plants itself upon the non-Russian, that is, upon the civilized principle of solving social difficulties. The I.W.W. expressly recognizes the necessity of working class unity "on the *political* as well as upon the industrial field". So doing, the I.W.W. can preach and teach in the open. Its posture is clear — to organize the economic body that shall be able to reflect its own political party, whereby to give a chance to the peaceful settlement of the present social "unpleasantness," and that shall, withal, have the requisite power to enforce the fiat of its ballot. To say that the I.W.W. can freely teach the class struggle, now that its preamble is so wise and sound, is a substantial denial of the claim put forth by our correspondents that political agitation is worthless. Let the I.W.W. follow our correspondents' views and strike out the political clause, that moment they will find out that the present revolutionary agitation conducted by the I.W.W. will have come to an end. Having placed itself upon the plane which the Russian revolutionists are constrained to agitate on, the I.W.W. will be treated to a dose which it will itself have invited, a dose of Russian governmental terrorism. So far from having contributed to raise the tone of the country, the I.W.W. will have helped the capitalists to drag that tone down to the level from which the Russian revolutionists are now seeking to raise their country.

This disposes of the only remotely relevant argument made by our correspondents. There are, nevertheless, two others that should not be ignored, however irrelevant.

Our correspondents say: "We can not understand how Comrade De Leon jumps at the conclusion that the I.W.W. agitation—which he terms 'agitation for force only'—has to degenerate into conspiracy."

The answer to this is: Either our correspondents claim that De Leon has said that "the present I.W.W. agitation has to degenerate into conspiracy"; if that is their meaning then they will have a hard time to prove that De Leon made any such statement. The I.W.W. is what the I.W.W. is today, not what our friends, who sign the letter published above, seek to turn it into. They are not yet so far. If, however, our correspondents merely made a slip in their statement, and what they meant to say is that De Leon holds that by removing the political clause from the preamble of the I.W.W., *and retaining the "take and hold" clause*, then the I.W.W. would have to degenerate into conspiracy—if that was their meaning, then they have quoted De Leon correctly. A simple denial of this conclusion does not refute a conclusion drawn from the irrefutable historic experience from which the conclusion flows.

At this point a serious illusion seems to reveal itself as taking possession of the minds of our esteemed contributors. They seem to believe that the preaching of the "industrial" form of organization would be sufficient to drill a revolutionary economic organization. We would like to hasten to dispel the illusion by suggesting to them the following principles:

1. The exclusion of the political clause from the I.W.W., leaving the "take and hold" clause extant, would drive the agitation into the narrow quarters of a conspiracy, with all the evil results thereof.

2. The exclusion of both the political clause and the "take and hold" clause, leaving extant only the "industrial" form of organization, would fatally steer the I.W.W. into the quagmire of the Gompers-Mitchell A.F. of L.

The other of the two irrelevant arguments that should be taken up is the one contained in the passage: "So obvious is this fact [the harmfulness of the ballot agitation] that, at the last convention of the I.W.W., we have witnessed Comrade De Leon make a motion to the effect that no organizer of any political party should be employed as organizer of the I.W.W." — De Leon is correctly quoted there; the purport of his motion is, however, misinterpreted. So far from his motion being an evidence of the harmfulness of the political agitation, it is an evidence of his position that such agitation is essential to success. Considering such agitation essential to success, he is earnestly bent upon the bringing together of a revolutionary economic organization powerful enough to reflect its own political party, that is, its own forerunner that may afford a chance to a peaceful solution. Consequently, recognizing tile fact that there are today in this country two rival and hostile political parties, both flying the colors of Socialism, it should be obvious that organizers of either of the two parties, acting simultaneously as I.W.W. organizers, could not choose but hamper, rather than promote the growth of the I.W.W.

- Ed., *The People*

Fourth letter, by Arturo Giovannitti, New York

I have read very attentively the articles by Comrades Wagner and Vasilio in *The People* of Tuesday, and the few remarks by Comrade De Leon, and, as a result, I should like to give my humble opinion and try to answer the still unanswered questions of *The People*'s Editor.

It seems to me that both Sandgren and De Leon have given a wrong definition of what they term "the political activity of the working class," an error which has been but partly redressed when they drew a line between ballot and agitation. Yet although Sandgren and his followers want no politics, they want a revolution, and whilst De Leon excommunicates the ballot, he still persists in having an S.L.P. ticket on the very same ballot. The first forgets that a revolution must be essentially political before it can be anything else, the latter is a little afraid to reconduct the revolutionary method on the straight road of the "outside political action," to wit, the general strike and the revolt.

The question is not whether we should bother about politics or not, but how we should conduct our political fight; should we remain even temporarily within the orbit of legality, or should we get out of it altogether and enforce our rights and will with new means and weapons adequate to the opportunity of the historical moment which we cross? In Europe, to define this legal fight, for to be peaceful it must be legal, we have coined a new word: parliamentarism - and all the question, according to me, lies in that word, that is to say, the political struggle of the working class within the capitalist state machine.

Does then Comrade De Leon mean parliamentarism when he speaks of a peaceful method of solving the Social Question? If not, where is then the necessity of having a ticket in the field so far as we don't expect and don't want to send our "Honorable Comrades" to Washington?

I shall consider only the first hypothesis and endeavor to prove as briefly as I can that parliamentary action, to use an imported word, spells simply reform and not revolution, in the real historic sense of the word.

Parliament is a bourgeois institution, the cornerstone of capitalism, as it is the very same organ with which the republic struck the monarchy and through which capitalism emerged from feudalism. Previous to and through the insurrectional phases of the French Revolution, the rising bourgeoisie knew that it could not fight feudalism with the legal weapons that were then possible, and realized that in order to transform society it needed first the absolute destruction of the existing State, and therefore forced and developed a new form of State that had nothing in common with the old one, i. e., the Parliament. It must be so of the proletariat as it was of the bourgeoisie.

"The proletariat does not escape the common rule of all the revolutionary classes that preceded it. It also forms itself an organ for the representation of its collective interests. This organ is the labor organization, the trade syndicate. Not a class truly revolutionary can think that the use of legal machines of the existing regime can be enough to guarantee the collective interests. It must form itself its own organ and strive to make it prevail on those of the existing society." (Labriola)

In other words, a class that really intends to fulfill its historical function must be revolutionary, not in aim, but in methods and means. The task of revolution is not to construct the new society but to demolish the old one, and, therefore, its first aim should be the complete destruction of the existing State so as to render it absolutely powerless to re-act and re-establish itself. When revolution fails to do so, the old regime may absorb some of the new ideas but will always remain, as it was the case in Italy and Germany, and as it will happen in Russia if the working class does not strike violently at the root of the monarchy and forcibly impose its own political organs against both the Czar and the Duma.

In other words, when the revolutionary process gets off the track of violence and insurrection without having achieved its destructive function and comes to argue and discuss within the circle of legality, when it does not strike at the existing political machine from the outside, but comes to bore from within, it utterly fails to its new ideal, but a new action to realize historical mandate and does nothing but a mere act of reform.

"To use the organs of the existing society to transform the same society means to collaborate to defend and guarantee it, to wit, do a work openly anti-revolutionary." (Sorel)

Consequently, if the S.L.P. goes to Congress, it means that it recognizes its usefulness, and in so doing it will cooperate to its perpetuation and give the State, and therefore capitalism, a longer lease of life. Therefore, it is not only an organization with a revolutionary aim that we need, but one ready to follow the revolutionary process in not only a new ideal, but a new action to realize the same. By this, it is evident that such an organization can not and must not employ legal and lawful methods, neither can it hope in a peaceful solution, as the simple fact that a class is revolutionary implies that it is outlaw.

This, Comrade De Leon does not discuss, neither does he answer arguments with arguments and facts with facts. He does not say that such an organization would not lead the working class to victory, but he is simply worried as to how we are going to recruit it if we abandon the idea of a possible peaceful solution of the Social Question.

This peaceful solution could be attained only through parliamentary action, but, again, if capitalism has opened its Holy of Holies to an enemy class that wants not less than its head, it means that it is no more afraid of the proletariat when the latter is willing to visit capitalism at home and talk matters over. My enemy is my enemy and I fear him while he waits for me outside with a gun or a stiletto, but, when he comes in and sits down to expose his reasons I cease to fear him, and the whole quarrel is liable to end with a merry supper and abundant glasses of wine with relative toasts and madrigals. How can we believe that even with the most rigid logic, and with the fear of a strong revolutionary organization, we could convince the master class to give itself up into the hands of the rival class that knows no Christian charity and will not commute the death sentence of capitalism? Are we then to understand that capitalism will commit suicide rather than to face the I.W.W. executioner? Is there an example in history than can justify such a sweet dream of peace and love? Not even the Holy Father, who believes in turning the left cheek when somebody slaps his right one, ever refrained from the sweet help of the hangman and other Christian accessories any time he saw his throne and holy purse attacked. Suicide is not the act of a normal being, neither have we any reasons yet to believe that the capitalist class will get crazy all at once in the last moment.

It is then by main force and through violence only that we can transform society, but collective, organized violence, not as it is now in Russia but as it was in this country fifty years ago. It is not a conspiracy, but an open and loyal fight, not an assault but a regular duel, and it will not be a riotous outbreak but a good and proper civil war, if you wish to call it so. If an act of Congress can prevent all that and yield to the working class the land and the means of production and distribution, so much the better, but this is their business, not ours.

How can we get the men together for this glorious proletarian epopee? Well, how did the International get them? How did we build Local 199, Tailors' Industrial Union, the strongest and most numerous in the city, where not even once was election mentioned, although every member is fully acquainted with the take and hold clause? *How*? Why, by going to them and telling them all about it without considering them either tigers or rabbits, but men who, once having understood, can prove that they are right in the good old American fashion, and put up a good fist fight when words and arguments fail.

Are then the S.P. and the S.L.P. so necessary to the I.W.W. that, without the former, the latter could not exist? Are the polls the only means to convince them to unite, to go on strike, to resist, and to press their action so on the political field (political agitation) that those from above will let something drop every once in a while before the whole edifice tumbles down?

Why should we speak to the working class of a peaceful settlement when probably not *one* of the S.L.P. members believes in it?

Fifty vacant seats in Congress will frighten capitalism more than fifty "Honorable" Socialists sitting there and doing nothing, and if we must use the ballot for something let us use it for the sole purpose of emptying their ranks.

The future of Socialism lies only in the general strike, not merely a quiet political strike, but one that once started should go fatally to its end, i.e., armed insurrection and the forcible overthrow of all existing social conditions. It may be objected that it is yet too early to throw the alarm of parliamentarism in America, but the fact is that the Socialist movement has degenerated so in all European countries on account of parliamentarism that it would be simply foolish not to take advantage of their lesson and follow another road. Let us not strike out the political clause from the I.W.W. constitution, but let us understand that the I.W.W. must develop itself as the new legislative and executive body of the land, undermine the existing one, and gradually absorb the functions of the State, until it can entirely substantiate it through the only means it has: The Revolution.

Answer

First of all let the fact be once more recorded that this week's opponent of the S.L.P. posture, like each and every one who preceded him, leaves unanswered the practical question put by *The People* at the beginning of this discussion - how can the ranks of the I.W.W., of the revolutionary army intended to take and hold the means of production, recruit the necessary forces for that eventful and final act of the revolution, if it starts by rejecting the civilized method of settling disputes, offered by the political platform, and plants itself instead upon the principle of physical force exclusively?

Surely this is a question worth answering. It is essential to a common understanding. Why is the question persistently evaded? Every evasion thereof can only be construed as an evidence of inability to answer it; consequently, as demonstration of the soundness of the practical principle that it implies. The demonstration is only made all the stronger by the indulgence in vast digressions, and the taking up of space on side matters.

In the instance of this week's correspondent the evasion is all the more marked. Giovannitti starts with the admission that the question put by *The People* has not been answered. Indeed, it is for that very reason that he asks for space to "try to answer the still unanswered questions of *The People*'s Editor." Does he answer that question? With not a word.

Or is this sentence, perhaps, an answer: "How can we get the men together for this glorious proletarian epopee? Well, how did the International get them ?" — The sentence implies that the International did get the men together for this glorious proletarian epopee. That's news to us. If the International had "got the men together for this glorious proletarian epopee" there would be no capitalist class today to overthrow; the epopee would have been enacted. That it has not been enacted, that Giovannitti recognizes the epopee has yet to be enacted, is ample refutation of the implied claim that the International "got the men together".

Or is, perchance, this other sentence the answer promised by Giovannitti: "How can we get the men together for this glorious proletarian epopee? Well... how is the I.W.W. getting them ?" This sentence is of a piece with that analyzed last week from the correspondence of two St. Louis opponents. That sentence does not "answer" *The People*'s question; the sentence confirms *The People*'s question; the sentence is fatal to the posture of *The People*'s opponents. This discussion was initiated by Sandgren's proposition "to strike out all reference to politics in the I.W.W. preamble". Upon that *The People*'s question, re-stated above, was put, and the contention both of Sandgren and of all who sided with him, this week's correspondent included, was and is, logically enough from their premises, that political agitation should be excluded as harmful and unnecessary. No opponent of *The People*'s position can quote the successful agitation of the I.W.W., whose platform has the political clause, as an evidence that the ranks of the I.W.W. can be recruited with the necessary numbers upon the principle of physical force only.

Giovannitti, accordingly, leaves unanswered the question he promised to answer; and strangest of all he closes by opposing Sandgren's proposition to expunge the political clause from the I.W.W. platform! Inextricable are the contradictions that this week's opponent tangles himself in.

We might stop here. The gist of the above letter is disposed of. Nevertheless our correspondent incurs a number of collateral errors that we trust he will thank us for calling his attention to. And this we do for reason of the knowledge that frequently it happens that collateral errors are responsible for central ones. So long as the former becloud the mind, the latter remain unperceived.

Giovannitti says: "A class that really intends to fulfill its historical function must be revolutionary, not in aim, but in methods and means."

This sentence sins doubly against social science.

Its first sinfulness lies in the use of the expression, "revolutionary methods and means". 'There is no such thing as "revolutionary means" or "methods". Means and methods may be good or bad, wise or unwise, timely or premature—"revolutionary" never. Physical force, the revolutionary methods and means meant by our correspondent, is by no means essentially revolutionary, it may be archly reactionary. If physical force were the test of "revolution" the palm for revolutionariness would have to be awarded to the Czar's establishment. Unconsciously Giovannitti himself acts obedient to this view of the matter. If he did not he would not now be in the revolutionary camp of the I.W.W.; he would have fallen with the Sherman crew of reactionists who resorted to physical force.

The second sinfulness of the sentence lies in its first part, the notion that the function of the proletariat "must be revolutionary, *not in aim*, but in methods and means". In other words, that the aim is a negligible quantity in determining the revolutionary or non-revolutionary character of a body. Such a conception of Social Evolution or of the march of human events is untenable. Marx well said that "force is the midwife of every old society pregnant with a new one". According to our correspondent's idea of things, however, all that is needed for the birth of a child would be the midwife; the functions of the father and the mother count for nothing. There is a violent clash of physical force now in progress in Russia. If physical force were the test of "revolution" then both the contending sides would be revolutionists. We all know this is false. How do we all determine which is the side of revolution and which that of reaction? Why, by their respective aims.

This serious error on the part of Giovannitti leads to the following other error, which runs like black warp through the woof of his argument. He says in one place: "Should we remain even temporarily within the orbit of *legality*"; in another place: "the *legal* fight, for, to be peaceful it must be *legal*"; again: "the use of *legal* machines of the existing regime"; still in another place: "such an organization [the organization that we need] must not employ *legal* and *lawful* methods"; and so forth. The continuous iteration and reiteration of the terms "legal," "legality," "lawful," betray a misconception of *The People*'s posture. Giovannitti will not find the words used once by *The People* in this discussion.

The People is not troubled with the thought of "legality". *The People* planted itself upon the principle of "civilization".

Giovannitti and the Editor of *The People* are civilized men. Being civilized men they are discussing the subject politely. Were the two a couple of barbarians they would have begun by breaking each other's heads.

Giovannitti's confusion of thought in the matter is such that he has read "legal" for "civilized," "legality" for "civilization," and that has interfered with his understanding of *The People*'s arguments in this discussion, beginning with the answer to Sandgren where the principle of civilization was treated at large. Political action is the civilized, because it is the peaceful method of social debate and of ascertaining numbers. He who rejects that method places himself upon the barbarian plane, a plane where the capitalist class would be but too glad to see him, seeing that he thereby would give the capitalist class a welcome pretext to drop all regard for decency and resort to the terrorism that would suit it.

But civilization is *civilization*. It implies not only the effort for peace, but also the knowledge of the fact that Right without Might is a thing of air. *Accordingly the civilized revolutionary organization proclaims the right, demands it, argues for it, and willingly submits to the civilized method of polling the votes - and it organizes itself with the requisite physical force in case its defeated adversary should resort to the barbarian's way of enforcing his will.*

The civilized man answers force with force; the barbarian begins with force. "Civilization", not "legality", demands the political clause.

A third collateral error committed by Giovannitti happens in the passage in which he quotes Labriola in support of what Labriola does not hold. Labriola belongs to the "Syndicalist" (Unionist) wing of what? Of the Socialist *Party* of Italy. The quotation from Labriola becomes a misquotation in the place where it occurs. It is perfectly sensible in connection with Labriola's position, which is as exactly that of the S.L.P. as two positions in two different countries can be.

Finally a luminous insight is obtained into the loose methods of thought of our opponents by the following passage from Giovannitti's letter: "Fifty vacant seats in Congress will frighten capitalism more than fifty 'Honorable' Socialists sitting there and doing nothing, and if we must use the ballot for something let us use it for the sole purpose of emptying their ranks," - a notion that can only proceed from a mistaken comprehension of facts in the case. Even if the whole Working Class abstained from voting, there would be *not one single seat vacant*, the capitalist candidates would then be elected unanimously by the capitalists themselves.

The theme of this discussion is serious. It should be approached, not with anger or preformed thoughts, but with a mind open to apprehend the facts and to reason from them.

- Ed. *The People.*

Fifth letter, by H. B. Hoffman, New York

Whether the debate on the political situation is closed or not it is up to the editor of the *Daily People* to reply to the following trite questions and answers. And, as no comment can be made without presenting the matter from which the argument is drawn, I would be pleased to see this contribution printed in full:

The questions are addressed to an S.L.P. man:

1. "Are you a revolutionary body?" "We are and decided so."

2. "Very well. If, then, you are a political party you are organized to enforce or evolve legislative enactments?" (Hesitatingly). "Yes, we are organized for legislative purposes."

3. "And yet you call yourself revolutionary. Legislation within the capitalist State, in order to be declared valid, must be of a mild constitutional nature. It must partake of the capitalists' notion of validity. It must harmonize with the existing order of things, must it not?" "Yes."

"So that if you harmonize with the capitalist State you can effect reforms, radical or ultra radical, but such reforms are drawn within the boundary lines of private property. In fact, you succeed in palliating rotten conditions, you ease the lot of the workingman and make him able to bear up. You unconsciously harmonize the workingman to existing conditions because you build up a hope in him that you are there to help him, and that through legislation. You are in fact doing the work of the reformer, which he, as a useful lieutenant of the capitalist, can better do himself. Hearst can bring about more reforms through legislation in a shorter time than can five revolutionary parties.

"You furthermore build up a false hope which the working class will not forgive you, when they realize the emptiness of it. As a conscious Socialist you know that the capitalist is well entrenched; legislatures, courts and police make up his armaments of war, all effective legislation can be nullified by the courts which are generally not of an elective nature. You know the helplessness of your situation and yet you would goad the workers on and make them believe in the strength of legislation."

"No! No! We are in politics for agitational purposes," answers the disturbed S.L.P. man.

"Ha! ha! in politics for agitational purposes! Were I not fully conscious of your extreme honesty I would call you a knave. As it is, I am content to think you are in the wrong.

"A political party means something. It has its classical mission which is popularly understood. A political party is a body either in office or trying to get in office. It nominates men for especial offices. In coming before the electors it makes certain specific promises which it also promises to enforce if elected. Absurd is it not to imagine that it can masquerade as a political party with no political intentions. Absurd is it not to simply spread agitational propaganda and yet go to the trouble of organizing a political body. It is misrepresentation, culminating in a farcical tragedy. And how absurd would it be to practice both politics and agitational propaganda through a political party and yet sustain its revolutionary character of the body. It is a reformer's carnival with the fitting mask of the masquerader."

Answer

Again let, first of all, the significant fact be recorded that, along with his predecessors, this week's opponent of the S.L.P. position also leaves unanswered the question put by *The People* at the beginning of this discussion—how can the ranks of the I.W.W., of the revolutionary army, intended to take and hold the means of production, etc., recruit the necessary forces for that eventful and final act of the revolution, if it starts by rejecting the civilized method of settling social disputes, offered by the political platform, and plants itself instead upon the principle of physical force only?

Surely none can claim the question to be a trick, or unfair. Men who aim at the overthrow of the capitalist system; men who recognize the necessity of a revolutionary economic organization of the working class to accomplish the revolution; finally men who reject the civilized method of social warfare, political action; such men certainly owe to the public, the working class public, an answer to the question put above—how do you expect to recruit your forces?

The persistent avoidance to answer this question justifies the conclusion that it is unanswerable; that it knocks the bottom from under the notion of rejecting political action; that indeed, the question needs but to be put in order to expose the error of the notion. Nor is the evasion at all concealed by an answer which puts other questions and, as Hoffman does this week, himself furnishes a series of answers unwarranted, in the main, by the exhaustive answers given by *The People* to previous correspondents on the subject, and the well known posture of the S.L.P. in the premises.

The facts in the case are simply these:

The Socialist Party asserts that political action is all-sufficient to emancipate the Working Class. "Elect us to office," it says, "and we will emancipate you."

Whatever there is intellectually clear and clean in the Labor Movement readily sees through the error; it even sees deeply and perceives that such a body, if it does not start corrupt, must inevitably degenerate into a fraud upon the proletariat.

The emancipation of the proletariat, that is, the Socialist Republic, can not be the result of legislative enactment. No bunch of office holders will emancipate the proletariat. The emancipation of the proletariat can only be the mass-action of the proletariat itself, "moving in," taking possession of the productive powers of the land.

This correct, this indisputable position leads directly to the principle that the revolutionary proletariat can not fulfill its historic mission unless it is so organized economically, that it can take possession integrally, shed the slough of the capitalist political State, and assume the reins of industrial administration of the country.

The industrially organized revolutionary Union, in short, the I.W.W., was the product of this insight into things.

This position, by reason of its very purity, brought its lees along with it. An element there arose, which — whether nauseated by the unavoidable corruption in the pure and simple Socialist party; or whether, dazzled by the very brilliancy of the position itself, disabled them from seeing aught but that — contends that political action should be wholly discarded; accordingly, that the I.W.W. should drop the political clause from its preamble where it expresses the necessity of uniting the working class "on the political as well as on the industrial field".

The I.W.W. denies the soundness of such a position. It goes further; it points to the fatal error involved in the same. The rejection of political action would throw the I.W.W. back upon the methods of barbarism — physical force exclusively. Where, as in Russia, no other method exists, none other can be taken up. Where, however, as in the rest of the Western Civilization, especially in America, the civilized method exists of public agitation, and of peaceful submission to the counting of ballots that express the contending views; where such methods exist, the man or organization that rejects them does so at his or its peril. This is especially the case in the capitalist America of today. The capitalist class, however powerful, is not omnipotent. It feels constrained to render at least external homage to the Genius of the Age. The Genius of the Age demands free speech and a free vote. So soon, however, as a Labor Organization were to reject the peaceful trial of strength, the capitalist class would be but too delighted to apply the system of Russian Terrorism. The long and short of it all is that the revolution could not gather the necessary recruits. On the other hand, clad in the vestments of civilized, fully civilized conflict, the I.W.W. recognizes the indispensable usefulness of political agitation whereby it may demand the unconditional surrender of the capitalist class; whereby it may preach and teach the reasons thereof; whereby it may express its willingness to abide by the fiat of the ballot, that is, by the peaceful trial of strength; and by reason of such conduct, recruit, drill and organize the physical force which it may need in order to safeguard the civilized because peaceful victory that it has striven to win.

Putting the matter in a nut-shell—without the revolutionary economic organization of the Working Class the day of the Socialist political victory would be the day of its defeat; without the revolutionary political action of Socialism, the revolutionary economic organization of the Working Class can not be fully shaped for action.

The Socialist Labor Party represents this view. Though recognizing its preponderatingly economic importance, it perceives its incidental political necessity.

"Ha!" cries out Hoffman, our this week's opponent, "A masquerade!"

The ways of civilization are no mask on the face of civilized man. The ways of civilization are part and parcel of the civilized man's being; they sharply mark the profile of his face.

For the same reason, and by the identical principle, that Sherman's defeat in the I.W.W. could be encompassed only by the policy of those delegates who went to last September's convention sincerely believing, not masked with the belief, that the man was honest, but who soon as they found him out a scoundrel, grabbed him by the slack of his reputation and threw him out of the Convention and the I.W.W., for the same reason, and by the identical principle, the overthrow of the Capitalist Class will be the work of those men only with whom the ways of civilization are not a mask but part of their nature; men who insist upon exhausting the ways of civilization, and who, when Capitalism shall have dropped its mask, will be found ready to resort to the ways of barbarism—all the more determinedly so because the method is repellent to the civilized cause that they are the apostles of.

For the same reason, and by the identical principle, that Sherman would have remained in possession of both the convention and the I.W.W. if the policy of those delegates had prevailed who went to the convention convinced in advance of the man's scoundrelism, and who wanted to throw him out from the start, for the same reason, and by the identical principle, the Capitalist Class would remain enthroned if the policy were to prevail of that impatient and angry element who reject in advance the expectation of a peaceful trial of strength, and would start with resort to physical force.

The S.L.P. ballot demands the unconditional surrender of the Capitalist Class. The S.L.P., accordingly, preaches the Revolution, teaches the Revolution, and thereby enables the recruiting and organizing of the physical force element requisite to enforce the Revolution. The S.L.P. does all this, including the latter, because it strikes the posture of holding the Ruling Class to the civilized method of a peaceful trial of strength.

Maybe the S.L.P. will triumph at the hustings, that is, win out and be rightly counted. In this case the S.L.P. would forthwith dissolve; the political State would be ipso facto abolished; the industrially and integrally organized proletariat will without hindrance assume the administration of the productive powers of the land. Is this impossible? We admit it is highly improbable.

More likely is the event of S.L.P. triumph at the polls, but defeat by the election inspectors, or resistance, as the Southern slaveholders did at the election of Lincoln. In that case also the S.L.P. would forthwith dissolve into its economic organization. That body, having had the opportunity to recruit and organize its forces, and the civilized method of peaceful trial of strength having been abandoned, the Might of the proletariat will then be there, free to resort to the last resort, and physically mop the earth with the barbarian Capitalist Class.

Most likely, however, the political expression of the I.W.W. will not be afforded the time for triumph at the polls. Most likely the necessities of capitalism will, before then, drive it to some lawless act that will call forth resistance. A strike will break out; capitalist brutality will cause the strike to spread; physical, besides moral support, will pour in from other and not immediately concerned branches of the Working Class. A condition of things—economic, political, social-atmospheric—will set in, akin to the condition of things in 1902, at the time of the great coal miners' strike, or in 1894, at the time of the Pullman-A.R.U. strike. What then? The issue will then depend wholly upon the degree, in point of quality and in point of quantity, that the organization of the I.W.W. will have reached. If it has reached the requisite minimum, then, that class-instinct of the proletariat that Marx teaches the Socialist to rely upon, and the chord of which the Capitalist Class instinctively seeks, through its labor fakers, to keep the Socialist from touching, will readily crystallize around that requisite I.W.W. minimum of organization. The Working Class would then be organically consolidated. Further efforts for a peaceful measuring of strength would then have been rendered superfluous by capitalist barbarism. Capitalism would be swept aside forthwith.

For this consummation, however, in the eventuality under consideration, be it remembered, the I.W.W. must have reached the requisite quantitative and qualitative minimum of perfection, *and that in turn will depend upon the freeness of its previous agitational work, a freedom that it never could enjoy except it plants itself upon the principle that recognizes the civilized method of peaceful trial of strength - the political ballot.*

Accordingly, it all comes back and boils down to the question, How is the I.W.W. to recruit and organize its forces if it starts with the absolute rejection of the political ballot?

All talk concerning the thorns that beset the political stalk are beside the question. Such talk our opponents should reserve for the pure and simple political Socialist party men. Addressed to the S.L.P. men, such talk is superfluous and inconsequential—as inconsequential as would be extensive dissertations on the stench that periodically is felt in dissecting rooms, and of the diseases such stenches occasionally breed: *the dissecting room is necessary*; as inconsequential as would be extensive dissertations on the accidents and discomforts that result from ocean travel: *ocean travel is requisite*. The pure and simple political Socialist man is on the political question what a man would be who favors the dissecting room for the sake of its stench, or the man who favors ocean travel for the sake of its perils and discomforts.

That, our physical force opponents know, is not the S.L.P. position.

The S.L.P. knows that the political State is worthless, and can not legislate the Socialist Republic into life. The S.L.P. man clings to political action because it is an absolute necessity for the formation of that organization - the I.W.W. - which is both the embryo of the Workers' Republic and the physical force that the proletariat, may, and in all likelihood will, need to come to its own.

-Ed., *The People*.

Sixth letter, by John Sandgren, San Francisco

Having been granted the privilege of answering the criticism of my views "As to Politics," I shall gladly avail myself thereof.

First, as to the strength of the working class at the ballot box, I have no alternative but to accept the figures given by the Editor of *The People*, namely that the working class in 1900 constituted seventy percent of the population and that we would, theoretically, be able to muster a majority at the ballot box. But it must be admitted that the change from 1890, when the working class were fifty-five percent, with a downward numerical tendency, is so astonishing, that one may justly question the correctness of at least one set of the figures.

However, seeing that little importance is attached by my critics, who must be considered to represent the S.L.P. position, to the ballot as such, and to the question of our strength at the ballot box, discussion on this point may be dropped.

But, from another point of view the figures I gave under this head, somewhat amended, are of great significance in attempting to determine the proper posture toward political activity on the part of the working class, namely in the following sense:

Out of the whole mass of actual wage workers, men, women and children, there are approximately eighteen millions who can in no manner be directly interested in politics, to wit: 1,700,000 children wage workers, 4,800,000 women wage workers, 3,500,000 foreign wage workers, 5,000,000 Negro wage workers, 3,000,000 floating and otherwise disfranchised wage workers; total, 18,000,000 approximately. And nobody will deny that in the building up of the economic organization and constructing the framework of the new, collective form of society, we will sooner or later have to take account of every one of these eighteen million wage workers. In fact, they are "grist for our mill," but what is to be done with them politically?

This open admission on the part of spokesmen for the S.L.P., although not new or brought out for the first time in this discussion — this admission that the ballot counts for little or nothing, will come as a shock to many faithful adherents of the ballot, who with one of my critics bravely exclaim: "Outvote them we shall!" This admission is another sign of the fact that working class "parliamentarism" has come upon evil days, the tendency throughout the whole world being to bring economic organization to the forefront and relegate politics to the rear.

It may be hard for those who have seen and helped the revolutionary movement grow on political lines to vigorous manhood to now discard politics; the new tendency to reorganize the forces on exclusive economic lines, entering the political arena only in the negative way of "direct action" may strike them as unholy violations of sacred principles. But as Marx says in effect: "The proletarian movement ever comes back to its starting point, ever retraces its steps and begins anew, until it has finally struck solid foundation." So it is now. Parliamentary experience having brought out the weak points of the political method, a revolt from the "million masses" brings into existence an organization in which the workers shall meet the master class face to face (direct action), thus realizing, as Comrade Bruckere says, the Marxian motto: "The emancipation of the workers by the workers themselves."

In regard to the position that we needs must continue political organization for the sake of political agitation, to be used as a shield under which to mold and form the working class movement proper, i.e., the economic organization, I am far from convinced of its correctness.

Political organization and agitation without faith in the ballot or without, as in Russia, demanding the ballot, or as in Sweden, an extension of the franchise, is like running a windmill without any grain to grind or without any millstones to grind it with. The position being an artificial one it will soon become untenable. It *will fail* to accomplish what it was intended for: to deceive the master class as to our purpose; it *will* accomplish what we least desire: to deceive our fellow workers and confuse. Such is the penalty one always has to pay for one of the gravest tactical errors in the revolutionary movement: double sense, dissimulation upon which see page 85 in De Leon's work: "Two Pages from Roman History."

Political organization and agitation becomes an absurdity without the ballot, without parliamentarism. On this score allow me to quote from a recent article in the *International Socialist Review* on the Italian movement:

"Parliaments are not and can not become organs of social revolution. The inherent social and economic qualities and tendencies of parliamentarism limit the possibilities of reforms.... It is a most ridiculous utopian supposition that a Socialist party ever can obtain a majority in the parliaments of any country. The social revolution which shall establish 'the autonomous government of production man' aged by the associated working class' (Labriola) is above all a technical and economic fact which can not be called into existence by an incompetent assembly such as the parliaments of all countries are, but must result from the autonomous development of the capacity, and from the spontaneous initiation of those who attend to the process of production."

Again, I hold that my critics have not established the fact that the I.W.W. needs any shield, or that the political organizations have any shield to offer. While the I.W.W. certainly needs the well trained membership of the S.L.P., I can not but see that we must respectfully decline their offer to hold a shield over us to protect our coddling infancy.

The I.W.W. can do, and is doing, everything in the way of agitation that the political organization is doing, it can address by word of mouth, it can distribute and sell literature, it can organize, and what more can the S.L.P. do?

In fact, it would be a direct advantage to have the shield out of the way, as we could then address our fellow-workers somewhat in this way:

"Politics is the game of capitalism; it is a flimsy shell game in which your very lives are the stakes played for. As long as you workingmen are allowing yourselves to be bamboozled into pinning your faith to the ballot, the capitalist class does not want any better snap. For no matter how you vote, capitalism is perfectly safe. 'Praise be to God,' the capitalist class whispers, 'the blamed fools are still voting!' Therefore, throw away that old weapon of times bygone, the boomerang vote, and spring into the ranks of the militant industrial army, where shoulder to shoulder with our fellows we shall gain victory through organized strength."

But here are some of the best fighters of the I.W.W., one night fearlessly proclaiming emancipation through organization and the next night "holding the shield" and exhorting street audiences to vote the S.L.P. or S.P. ticket, when they well knew that such course is about as fruitless as an Eskimo dog's barking at the moon.

No, the shield is not needed, not appreciated, and does not shield.

Past has shown that the political agitator enjoys no more immunity or security than others. He may be "legal" and "constitutional," but legal opinions and supreme court decisions are made to order and cost only the paper on which they are written, so we are as much exposed to "law and order" if we parade in the mask and disguise of politicians as if we come openly forward as an economic organization, not to speak of the advantages of an open, straightforward course.

To those who defend political organization and agitation, because it would suggest to the ruling class our willingness to adorn ourselves in the conventional garb of legality, civilization, peace, etc., I would put the question: when did economic organization cease to be a legal, civilized and peaceful weapon? In fact, I would maintain that it is one of the newest and most perfected products of modern civilization.

To those who plead for a much to be desired peaceful solution of the social problem, I wish to say that economic organization even with the purpose of taking and holding is primarily a peaceful organization, and it is a straining at gnats to maintain that politics is more civilized, more peaceful weapon, when the political organization proposes to carry behind its back "the big stick" of the economic organization, with which to emphasize its civilized and peaceable intentions. The whole difference is the difference between direct and indirect action.

The question of peace or war is optional with the master class, it is not for us to decide which it shall be. But it is our duty to be prepared for both. Only the economic organization can do this. The political organization is capable of preparing for neither. It is incompetent to bring about a peaceful solution, because society will have to be reconstructed on economic lines; it would be incapable of preparing for war because its organization is only a general staff without a regular army.

But why speak of peace or war! The capitalist class has already chosen war. Our blood has run in torrents, as in the Paris Commune, or bespattered the road to Hazelton and Cripple Creek; the rope has strangled some of our early champions and is in preparation for others. To speak of a possibility of peaceable settlement between us and the master class is the same as the mutual agreement between the man flat on his back and him who holds the dagger to his throat. The war has been going on these many years and is raging fiercely now. How can anybody suggest a peaceable settlement, especially as we demand complete surrender?

Another thing which seems to worry some of my critics is that if we were to discard politics and have only an economic organization, we would, Peter Schlemil-like, be without a shadow or reflex, which is against the rule, as no economic manifestation should appear in public without its political reflex or shadow, any more than a self-respecting citizen would go out without his shadow. These critics seem to forget that a revolutionary, economic organization with an aim to reconstruct society, has its reflex or shadow projected forward, and that no true reflex could be contained in the frame of politics. In so far as the organization also serves the incidental purpose of fighting the every-day battles of the working class, it is entitled to a shadow on the political field. But that shadow will be thrown as indicated in Bruckere's report of the French movement; our organized strength will cause the ruling class to fall all over themselves in an attempt to "reflect" us on the political field, in order to save themselves from a worse calamity.

For these and other reasons I still maintain that the Preamble of the I.W.W. should be so amended as to exclude political action. Only thus will we have found a solid basis upon which all workingmen can unite. The operation may be painful, but it must be endured.

Answer

Again, for the sake of keeping the record clear, the first thing to be done is to record the fact that the question asked by *The People* at the incipience of this discussion remains unanswered, to wit, how are the ranks of the I.W.W., of the revolutionary army, intended 'to "take' and hold" the means of production, etc., to recruit the necessary forces in America for that eventful and final act off the revolution, if the I.W.W. were to start by rejecting the civilized method of settling social disputes, the method of a peaceful trial of strength, offered by political action, and plant itself, instead, upon the principle of physical force only? This is the issue. Sandgren, like the others who hold with him, leaves it untouched.

We say Sandgren leaves it untouched. That is putting the case mildly for him. In so far as he can be said to have at all touched it, he overthrows himself. What, was Sandgren's motion, so to speak? *It was that the I.W.W. drop the political clause from its preamble.* He who comes with such a proposition, and is met with the question, How are we to recruit our forces if we start by discarding the political, or peaceful trial of strength? He who comes with a motion such as Sandgren's, and is met with the question just put, can not do, as Sandgren does, show that the I.W.W. today, with the political clause which he would strike out, is doing the very work that we claim it could not do in the long run without that clause. If such a statement was meant as an answer to our question, the answer overthrows the original motion. It yields the point at issue.

We may again stop here. All that is essential to the issue is covered by the above observation. Nevertheless, again mindful of the experience that central errors often derive their nourishment, if they do not actually rise, from collateral errors, we shall here take up the principal mistakes in Sandgren's reply—mistakes, which, though irrelevant to the real issue, are important, relatively and absolutely.

First—Those critics of Sandgren, who agree with him against political action, but find fault with his looking for support in statistics, do him and their cause injustice. There is no theory but should be based upon facts. Sandgren yielded to a correct instinct in seeking the support of figures for his conclusion. Who knows to what extent his erroneous conclusion was due to the erroneous figures that he quoted. Yielding to the same correct instinct he correctly returns to statistics.

Again his statistical reasoning is at fault. The array of items that foots up eighteen million, child, woman, foreigner, Negro, floating, and otherwise disfranchised wage workers by no means warrants the conclusion that they "can in no manner be directly interested politics". Far from it. The conclusion reveals one of the false notions that dominate the anti-political action mind. That mind can not disengage itself from the notion that political action begins and ends with conventions, nominations of tickets and voting. This is false. Political action, conducted by revolutionists, consists in something else besides those acts; it consists in something else infinitely more important than any or all of those acts; it consists in revolutionary agitation and education upon the civilized plane that presupposes a peaceful trial of strength: that is, settlement of the dispute. "What is to be done with them [these child, woman, foreign, Negro, floating and otherwise disfranchised wage workers] politically?" asks our friend. What? Fully sixty percent of them, that is, all except the infants and the sick, can be made the carriers of the agitational and educational propaganda of the revolution conducted upon the civilized plane. Though they be not entitled to cast a single vote, they can distribute literature, and those who have the gift - though foreign, female, Negro or otherwise disfranchised - can by speech promote the revolution by teaching it on the political platform. We all know that this actually happens.

Second—The indisputably correct and, indeed, cheering fact mentioned by Sandgren concerning the widespread revulsion from "parliamentarism," or be it pure and simple Socialism, by no means warrants his conclusion that, therefore, the other extreme, total rejection of political action, is correct. Such a conclusion is a "non sequitur," is illogical from his own premises; indeed, his own premises warn against the conclusion. The knowledge that the pendulum just was at one extreme is a warning against, rather than an argument in favor of the point which the pendulum is bound to strike immediately after—the other extreme.

Aye, Sandgren correctly alludes to Marx. The proletarian revolutions as Marx says, "criticize themselves constantly; constantly interrupt themselves in their own course; come back to what seems to have been accomplished, in order to start over anew; scorn with cruel thoroughness the *half-measures*, weaknesses and meannesses of their first attempts"; etc. The proletarian revolution started with exclusive physical force attempts; it "criticized," "interrupted" itself, and swung over to the other extreme of exclusive politics; it is again "criticizing" and "interrupting" itself and receding from that second extreme posture. The experience it has been making teaches it to "scorn with cruel thoroughness the *half-measures*, weaknesses and meannesses of its first attempts". Experience teaches it that all extremes are *half-measures*; that all half-measures are *weakness*; that all weakness leads to *meanness*—corruption and treason. What corruption and treason the half-measure of pure and simple political Socialism leads to is palpably shown by the record of the Socialist party Careys of Massachusetts, Hillquits of New York, Buechs and Bergers of Wisconsin. At the same time, written in the blood of the workers is the corruption and treason that flows from the half-measure of exclusively physical force, or so-called "direct" action. The names of the McParlands, of Molly Maguire fame, and of the McKenneys, of modern Colorado fame, should suffice as hints—to say nothing of what the more recent Dumases and Petriellas are capable of.

The S.L.P. seeks not patronizingly to officiate as a shield to the I.W.W. The endeavor of the S.L.P. is directed toward promoting the vigorous development of the I.W.W., to the end that the I.W.W. may, schooled by the experience of previous half-measures, itself set up its own shield and itself hold up that shield which will protect it, in front, against the pure and simple politician; in the rear, against the "agent provocateur".

Third—Sandgren slips badly when he quotes, against the S.L.P. attitude, page 85 of De Leon's "Two Pages from Roman History," wherein the warning is correctly uttered and illustrated against the practice of double sense and dissimulation in revolutions. The passage is recommended to our readers. It describes Gaius Gracchus as bent upon overthrowing the power of the Senate, but keeping the secret "locked in his breast," and indulging in a bit of pantomime that could not throw his foes off their guard, and only succeeded in confusing, thereby "keeping away forces needful to his purpose, whom straightforward language would have attracted".

We take Sandgren for too honest a seeker after truth to wish to imply that anything the S.L.P. has done, said or printed, whether with regard to the economic or the political action, can even remotely be compared to that *half-measure* of Gaius Gracchus. The ballot of the S.L.P., and the ballot of that political reflex which the I.W.W., as a full-measure body, is bound to reflect, demands and will demand plump and plain the unconditional surrender of the capitalist class; that ballot does, and will, place the revolution on the civilized plane of a peaceful trial of strength; last not least, and above all, that ballot, equipped with all the experience of our Age, will school the proletariat in the absolute necessity of organizing the physical force - the integrally industrial Union of the working class - which it may and in all probability will need in order to enforce its program in case the capitalist class resorts to the brute measures of the barbarian. There is no "double see" or "dissimulation" in that posture.

Fourth—Not unless Sandgren would make out of Marx a sort of Bible—a compilation of scraps from different periods of civilization, and therefore often contradictory - can he quote the Marxian saying "the emancipation of the workers by the workers themselves," as an argument against political action, seeing that the same Marx stated "Only the Trades Union can give birth to the true party of Labor." Was Marx's idea that the Union would give birth to a useless thing? If "the emancipation of the workers by the workers themselves" excludes the thought of political action, then Marx floundered when he made the latter utterance.

Marx was not infallible. If he is found to have erred the error should be specifically pointed out. Otherwise, in quoting Marx, he should be quoted fully.

Fifth—The next slip made by Sandgren is closely related to the previous one. He quotes Labriola. The quotation is a misquotation. It is that because it is put in a way suggestive of the idea that Labriola wholly spurns political action. The idea is wrong. Labriola's syndicalists (substantially the attitude of the S.L.P.) are affiliated with — what? — with the Socialist *Party* of Italy! — *a political organization!* The sentiments in the quotations from Labriola are not different from those of the S.L.P. Such sentiments recognize the necessity of the ballot, without "pinning our faith" to it. They recognize in the ballot a potential means of a peaceful trial of strength, and they, so far from "pinning their faith to the ballot," provide for the organization of the physical force, which the political agitation enables us to organize, and which in all likelihood will be needed, but which the Movement will not allow itself to be heated into the blind passion of pushing out of the proper perspective.

Sixth — We must frankly admit our utter inability to handle Sandgren's contention that an economic organization, determined to ignore the political ballot, is "a peaceful organization". Either he is color blind, or we are, on the subject.

Seventh — Finally, Sandgren's closing paragraphs, declaring that there is *war* now, consequently, what is the use of considering peaceful solutions, reflects the unfortunate psychology of our anti-politics friends. Why spend so much time with claims about the peacefulness of the revolutionary economic organization, quotations from Labriola and Marx, statistical figures, parallels in history, etc., etc.? What they mean is that there is *war* now, and consequently we might as well fight. *There is no war now.* Unreliable are the conclusions of men who take a word, used in a technical sense, transfer that word to another technical sphere, and then give it, in the second, the meaning it has in the first sphere.

There is *class war* today; but the word *war* in that sense means something essentially different from the word *war* in the sense used by Sandgren when he says we might as well wage *war* now against the capitalist class. War, in the sense used by Sandgren, has not yet broken out. If it had, his articles could not be published in *The People,* this discussion could not be going on, the capitalist institutions would not be available for the transportation of our thoughts, and neither could write with the peace and comfort that we do. There is no such *war* now. If there were, the discussion would be superfluous; the very fact that Sandgren has raised his anti-politics point is proof that there is no such *war* now. The only justification for Sandgren's contention would be the actual existence of war. Seeing there is none, the ground fails on which to sustain his point.

In the absence of the only reason why political action should be dropped - the existence of actual war - the only question of moment is how to equip ourselves for that war that we are all agreed we shall in all likelihood be involved in. The question put by *The People* at the incipience of this discussion remains unanswered. The glove, thrown down to our anti-political friends, remains on the field challenging to be picked up.

-Ed. *The People*.

Seventh Letter, By V. H. Kopald, New York

At the time Comrade Sandgren started the discussion. "As to Politics," I was in complete accord with the Editor. Since, I have gone over to the other side, and I wish to give a few reasons why.

In actual fact we live now in a state of war, a war of classes. It was always a maxim of war: Do what the enemy does not want you to. The capitalist class let you do all the political agitation you want, but use all obstacles possible, even force and gallows against economic agitation.

No matter what anybody thinks, the end of all political agitation must be the ballot; and the ballot and election is one of the principal assets of capitalism. After every election the whole capitalist class is elated, the proletarian is depressed. Naturally so. The sight of even a would-be people's tribune, like Hearst, getting "defeated" by a majority of 75,000 makes Comrade Sandgren argue that the capitalists are more numerous than the proletarians, and makes thousands of proletarians think, Socialism is hundreds of years away. It puts at the disposal of the capitalist the unanswerable argument, We'll give in to Socialism, whenever the majority of people want Socialism. As to civilized argument and agitation:

What is "civilized agitation"? Are we in a state of war, or not? If we are in a state of war, then war is hell and civilization is impossible. We have only one object in view: emancipation of the working class. Civilized agitation between bandits and victims! Nonsense!

With all my means in my power I shall still support *The People*, as *The People* is more industrial than political. But I shall support no political party. The little energy I could give to the former before I shall now turn to the Industrial Workers of the World.

Answer

The distinguishing feature of this week's contribution against the position of the Industrial Workers of the World, whose preamble proposes the unification of the working class "on the political as well as on the industrial field"; or that correlative position of the S.L.P., whose literature announces that, without the economic organization the day of the political victory of Socialism would be the day of its defeat, and that, without political action, which places the Social Revolution in America upon the civilized plane of endeavoring to reach a peaceful trial of strength, the emancipation of the workers would be indefinitely postponed, and could then be reached only by wading through a massacre, both the delay and the then assuredly vast amount of bloodshed being brought on and rendered necessary by the workers themselves; in short, the distinguishing feature of this week's contribution against all political action and in favor of physical force only—that distinguishing feature lies in that this week's contribution indulges in no feints. Kopald wastes no time upon the corruption that politics engender; he consumes no space with recitals of the dangers that beset politics; he resorts to no needless quotations concerning the revolutionary character of the Labor movement; he leaves alone all attempts at statistical display; he gives a wide berth to phrases and to controversial finessings; he says plump and plain what he means. What he means is that there is *actual war today*. If all the previous contributors against politics and in favor of physical force only had been as clear in their minds upon the thought that was working upon them, then they would have taken less space; they would have saved us much work; and the question—how are the ranks of the Industrial Workers of the World, of the economic revolutionary army intended to "take and hold" the means of production, etc., to recruit the necessary forces in America for that eventful and final act of the revolution if the Industrial Workers of the World were to start by rejecting the civilized method for settling social disputes, the method of a peaceful trial of strength, offered by political action, and plant itself, instead, upon the principle of physical force only? This question, put by *The People* at the inception of the discussion, and left unanswered up to date, would not have been put. It would have been unnecessary. The question could be met only in one of two ways—either by answering it straightforwardly, or by pronouncing it preposterous. Kopald is the only contributor who can not be charged with having evaded the question. His contribution amounts to pronouncing the question preposterous. From his premises he is right. But his premises are wrong.

Of course, if indeed our present state were one of actual war, then a question that proceeds from the premises of there being actual peace, would be preposterous. Of course, if actual war had already broken out, then none but a lunatic would strike the posture of a possible "peaceful trial of strength". Such a posture would not rest upon the elevation of civilization; it would be a mockery of civilization. Such a posture would rest upon the depths of stupidity. With bullets flying around, and the "dead line" established by pickets, there is nothing left but force. Woe would be to the proletariat of America, woe to the emancipation of the proletariat of the world, whose emancipation depends upon that of their American fellow wage slave, if the outbreak of actual war found the working class of America as disorganized as now they are.

Were that to happen, then that which *The People* has been warning against, as the inevitable result of a system of organization that started with the rejection of the civilized method of striving for a peaceful trial of strength, which political action alone offers—then, that result would not be questioned by our opponents. The movement of the American working class would find itself dwarfed into a conspiracy; and they could see their actions reflected in the actions of the Russian revolutionists: compelled to move about in disguise, creeping stealthily at night to place bombs in the chimneys of the residences of the American Wittes, the heroines among their women sacrificing their chastity upon the altars of Freedom as the only means to gain access to the soldiery of the Despot class, in order to stir them to mutiny, as was done by several heroic Russian revolutionary women in the fortress of Kronstadt.

We are confident in the belief that Kopald thanks his stars that actual war is not yet. The statement that the "Capitalist class use all obstacles, even force and gallows against economic agitation" is mere rhetoric. The issue in this discussion can not be settled by rhetoric. Obstacles? Yes, many; force? yes, quite often; the gallows? that also, occasionally; these and other devices does the capitalist class apply against the economic agitation—and it has applied them, though not yet the gallows, against revolutionary political agitation as well. It has done all that in the course of the *class war*. But the "class war," that socioeconomic term, is not *actual war*.

All reasoning, proceeding from the premises that there is *actual war* now, proceeds from incomplete premises; being incomplete, the reasoning is premature; such reasoning can not choose but be false in consequence, and, by every operation, multiplying into wider error.

There is no actual war now. The question put by *The People* at the incipience of the discussion stands.

We rely upon it that the sense of right on the part of our opponents will do us the justice to admit their side has been treated with fairness. The contributors have not been limited in space; their contributions have not been mutilated; the subject has during these months been thoroughly and courteously ventilated; an impartial and thoughtful audience, bent upon ascertaining the best in behalf of our common cause, will have read and reflected. Further discussion on the subject should be unnecessary. There must be an end to the best of things. Moreover, there are imperative calls upon the limited space of the *Weekly People* for other matters.

Accordingly, the *discussion* is closed with this issue. We say the *discussion*. The columns of *The People* will remain open under the head "As to Politics" to any reader who will furnish a direct answer to the question that *The People* has propounded, and which has been repeated above; what that question purports, the discussion has made clear. None but *direct answers* will be accepted; such answers, if forthcoming, need occupy but little space. If the question is answerable, the movement is entitled to it.

The S.L.P. is not nailed to any special "means"; it is bent upon a "goal". The S.L.P. will hail any "means" that will stand the test of reason and experience, and would give justifiable promise of reaching the goal more swiftly than the means of combined political and economic action, to which the Party now holds.

There still remain unpublished five communications. Four of them—George F. Spettel's of St. Paul, Minn.; O. Eherich's of Oakland, Cal.; Charles Rice's of New York; and Julius Kiefe's of Cincinnati, Ohio—will be successively published in the course of the next two weeks. With the exception of Kiefe's, these communications contain bona fide questions exclusively. Under ordinary circumstances they would have been answered in the Letter Box. It is, however, preferable in this instance to publish the questions themselves. They will appear under the head "As to Politics," with the answers attached.

Kiefe's communication, while embodying questions, might be justly excluded, seeing that it trends on the controversial, and also wanders from the question. Nevertheless, its shortness assists in giving it the benefit of being considered as bona fide questions only. It will go in.

The fifth communication, from Goldie Karnoil, St. Louis, Mo., is barred by the decision to close the discussion. It is a lengthy, eleven-page closely written and merely controversial production, that merely repeats past assertions made by the lady's side of the issue, and that, although it is the last one received, having come in only last week, again evades the question put by *The People*. Phrases like these— "every lost strike is a lesson ; since our planet revolves through space nothing of lasting value for the working class has ever been accomplished through preaching"; etc., etc.—are no answer to the question. Of course, every event is a lesson: even the Thaw trial is a lesson. Of course, preaching alone is worthless: aims without "organization" to carry them out are, as *The People* has shown before, just so much hot air. Still less are phrases of which the following is a type—"once class-conscious and organized, there is no power on earth to keep the working class from taking over production"—an answer to the question. That is a begging of the question. Finally, and least of all, is the repetition of the statement that the Industrial Workers of the World (with its present preamble proclaiming the necessity of working class unity "on the *political*, as well as on the *industrial* field") is organizing grandly—least of all is that an answer to the question, especially when the "answer" comes from those who wish to remove the political clause from the Industrial Workers of the World preamble. It does not follow that because a man, in possession of both his legs, walks steadily, *therefore*, one of his legs being sawed off, he will be able to keep from hobbling and falling. Reason dictates an opposite conclusion. The *discussion* is closed.

-Ed. *The People*

Eighth Letter, By C. F. Spettel, St. Paul, Minn.

In your answer to Arturo Giovannitti you say, "Accordingly, the civilized revolutionary organization proclaims the Right, demands it, argues for it, and willingly submits to the civilized method of polling the votes. And it organizes itself with the requisite physical force in case its defeated adversary should resort to the barbarous way of enforcing his will."

Now my question is: How is the organization to know when its adversary is defeated? Is there any probability that the political machine that counts the votes will become good or terror-stricken, and honestly count the votes, and thereby proclaim the defeat of the idle class by the working class?

Answer

A political movement knows from a thousand and one sources whether its numerical forces are strong or weak. In this city, for instance, Hearst was elected Mayor two years ago. Everybody knows that. The reason he is not in the City Hall today is that he was not equipped with the physical force to enforce his victory. The counting out of Hearst deceived nobody.

The above answer is on the supposition that the political movement of Labor would triumph, and the Capitalist Class then attempt the trick played on Hearst. The chances are against such a contingency. The chances are as stated several weeks ago in the answer to Hoffman. Some capitalist outrage on the economic field will precipitate war. In that case the issue will depend upon the degree of integrally industrial organization that the proletariat may find itself in.

If they should find themselves in so weak a degree of integrally industrial organization as they now are in, or in a stronger one, yet not possessed of the minimum of strength needed for resistance, cohesion and attraction, then the armed force of the capitalist class will mop the earth with them. Then there will be born an "Underground America," as there has long been an "Underground Russia". The handful of revolutionists will be forced into surreptitious propaganda, and the Revolution will have to raise itself above ground by its own boot-straps.

If, however, the proletariat should, at such a time, find themselves organized to such a degree of integral industrialism (and the more strongly the better) that sufficient resistance could be offered to the capitalist, and sufficient attraction could be exercised upon the rest and not yet organized workers, then the proletariat would mop the earth with the capitalist class. It would be able to do so because its industrial form of organization would not only furnish it the required physical force, but would also enable it forthwith to conduct production.

But that possibility, or eventuality, is out of all question if the industrial organization were to start upon the theory that there is *actual war now*. If it did, it would be throttled in short order. Only by recognizing the civilized method of peaceful trial of strength, implied in political action, will the proletariat be able to recruit the physical force (industrially organized workers) with the aid of which, under the first supposition, it will be in position to enforce its political triumph; or with the aid of which it may be able, under the second supposition, to meet successfully capitalist brutality.

Thus, in either case, political action is as necessary as industrial organization is indispensable.

- Ed. *The People*.

Ninth Letter, By O. Eherich, Oakland, Cal.

Since the controversy as to politics has tapered down to this point, I feel constrained to ask the question of the Editor: "Have the workers in reality the choice left as to effective tactics?"

Granted the validity of the assertion by the Editor, that without open political agitation the working class movement will narrow down to conspiracy, is it not being driven that way by the tactics of the ruling class? And must not the ruled class adopt the same methods if it wishes to meet and vanquish the opponents? Was it any more or less than a "conspiracy" that the mine-owners resorted to in the war in Colorado? Did it not burst through the thin veneer of constitutionality and brag of it in words? Did not the men in Colorado express their political will in regards to an 8-hour law by a majority vote of 47,000, for a constitutional amendment? If all the laborers in that state had been organized in as sound and solid an organization as the W.F. of M., could they not have borne the brunt of the battle without the political movement? Could an utterly irresponsible autocratic power in Russia have gone any further after the same amount of provocation? Could these things not happen in any other State than Colorado, after the late Supreme Court decision? Let us not deceive ourselves, but do we really live in a constitutional country, or is it only an illusion? The powers in Colorado were only provoked to the extent of being compelled to employ three shifts of men instead of two, yet when they could not starve the men into submission, did they not play their last trump? Could they have done any worse in the face of an existing conspiracy on the part of the miners? Is it not a merit for the W.F. of M. to have unmasked the law and order brigands by tearing the mummery of hypocrisy from the faces of the plutes and shown the working class with what kind of an enemy they must reckon? Is there a possibility of emancipation by peaceful methods after these experiences? Will not the ruling class provoke violence if the demands for better conditions of the workers threaten the profits of the former? Has the working class really a choice left as to tactics, or is not the manner of resistance determined by the methods of oppression?

Fully realizing the importance of keeping the proletarians from indulging in a headlong reckless, unheedful rush, can the class-conscious workers be trusted enough to learn from past experiences and shape their course accordingly? Have we any choice?

Answer

Boiled down to their substance, the above questions proceed from the error of holding that actual war exists now. In last week's answer to Kopald the error was exposed. Eherich himself would recognize his error if he allowed his eyes a wider sweep of the horizon.

It is true that the capitalist class has violated the constitution in the instance of the Colorado men. But that is not evidence enough of the existence of actual war. The rest of us are doing what Haywood was kidnapped for, and yet we are at large. The kidnapping and other outrages had taken place, and yet the convention of the Industrial

Workers of the World met and worked in peace, although the capitalists aimed at its destruction, and evidently had their agents there to do their bidding.

Of identical nature is the error implied in the question whether the workers should not "adopt the same methods" as the capitalists. In this, as in the instance just touched on above, Eherich just sees one thing, but overlooks other things that are necessary for a correct conclusion. Eherich correctly points out the barbaric methods resorted to by the capitalists. He overlooks another thing that these self-same capitalists resort to, and without which their barbaric methods would not work in the manner they do. That other thing that capitalists resort to is external homage to the ways of civilization, external homage to the Genius of the Age. He who says the workers should adapt themselves to the methods of capitalism and cites their barbarism may not exclude their external homage to civilization. Adaptation in this instance would consist in a hypocritical posture towards political action, plus preparation of the means of barbarism. Adaptation, accordingly, would reject Eherich's suggested repudiation of political action. The bona fide Movement of Labor may not "adopt" the methods of the capitalist class in the class war. The Labor Movement must, on the contrary, place itself upon the highest plane civilization has reached. It must insist upon the enforcement of civilized methods, and it must do so in the way that civilized man does. Civilized man acts equipped with experience. Experience teaches that Right is a toy unless backed by Might; experience teaches also that the capitalist class is a brigand class bearing the mask of civilization, and that it is helped in the cheat by the undoubted circumstance that it has been a promoter of civilization. Equipped with this experience and knowledge, the civilized man will take up political action as the only means that, theoretically, promises a peaceful trial of strength; and he will simultaneously organize the integrally industrial union as the only available and the all-sufficient Might to enforce the Right that his ballot proclaims.

As to the question, whether or not the capitalist does not now "conspire" and "act in secret," and whether the worker should not adopt that method also—that question, partly answered above, deserves special treatment. *No; secrecy is the bane of the union generally; it would be the destruction of the revolutionary union!* The Mahoneys and Shermans wanted secrecy. The widest publicity is essential to safety. Secrecy leaves the majorities in the Unions in ignorance of what happens at Union meetings; secrecy promotes the trade of the police spy, the "agents provocateurs," those raw-boned "anti-political revolutionists," like McParland, in the pay of the capitalist politicians. Left in ignorance of what happens in the Union, the majority of the membership is ever dependent upon private information; the informant may be honorable, he may also be dishonorable; the revolution must not be exposed to trip upon misinformation. On the other hand, the "agent provocateur" will find his occupation gone if publicity is enforced; the blood and thunder ranter, knowing his words would be published as coming from him will love his neck too well to indulge in crime-promoting declamation. Secrecy is *death*; publicity, *life*.

Has the Movement any choice? Certainly it has.

- Ed. *The People*.

Tenth Letter, By Julius Kiefe, Cincinnati, O.

The S.L.P. members of the Industrial Workers of the World always claimed, that political (parliamentary) action is an absolute fluke: except, if it is backed up by economic organization on the lines of the Industrial Workers of the World. They also tell us in word and print, that people, believing the economic organization to be the sole factor, by using the general strike tactics are just as wrong in their theory as the Socialists from the Socialist party who are of the opinion that the ballot only will bring them economic and political liberty. Another argument we hear at present quite often and that is: How could we (non-parliamentary Socialists) organize the workers on general strike tactics without being jailed or hanged at present? Indeed very easy to answer. We tell the working class that the Industrial Workers of the World (and that is the reason we belong to it) is a revolutionary economic organization, whose ultimate object will be to free the workers, who are robbed under the capitalist system of exploitation in the production of wealth by not owning the necessary tools to produce commodities for themselves. For this reason the Industrial Workers of the World was organized and not like pure and simple unions a la American Federation of Labor to get for the workers an increase in wages and possibly a shortening of hours. If the capitalist class fears this proposition so much, that it would not tolerate such an organization, because it trains its members for the Social Revolution, how is it that it allows a political party such as the S.L.P. or even S.P. to make propaganda for Socialism? In my opinion this looks very funny indeed, or is it perhaps that the capitalist attorneys and the leaders of the different parliamentary Socialist parties have some kind of an agreement to blind the workers if you please, when the day of the social revolution arrives and is declared by the working class themselves by refusing to work any longer for the capitalist parasites? In fact Mr. Iglesias of Spain and also Mr. Vandervelde of Belgium, two of the prominent members of the international political Socialist parties, blinded the workers of their respective countries, when they were in conflict several years ago, while the social general strike was tested there. (This information I received by reading a leaflet on the general strike by Walter Arnold about a year ago.) As far as the preamble of the Industrial Workers of the World in regards to organizing the workers on the political as well as on the economic field is concerned, it is, to say the least, confusing and should be changed at our next convention to read: The workers should be organized on the economic field to overthrow the economic and the political State of capitalism.

Answer

Upon a more careful reading of the above the impression that it asked some questions was found to be false. Had a first glance at the communication conveyed the correct impression, it would have been excluded by last week's decision to close the discussion. Kiefe's contribution not only evades the question repeatedly put by *The People* to the total opposers of political action, but it is cast in an unhappy controversial mold, unhappy because in not a single instance are its premises correct, the whole thing reveals a woeful confusion of facts and rashness in arriving at a conclusion. The promise of an answer having been made last week, the promise will be kept.

When ten years hence — 'tis to be hoped sooner — Kiefe, a member of last year's Industrial Workers of the World convention, may happen to read his above argument, he will feel quite charitable towards those workers, who, notwithstanding they have frequently heard his arguments against the American Federation of Labor and the capitalist class in general, still keep coming back with retorts that prove they still are muddled, still remain tangled in previous misconceptions, still continue stuffed with prejudices, and still have failed to learn the lesson that reckless accusation can only work against the unification of the working class.

If Kiefe can still use the term "parliamentary" action as identical with "political" action in this discussion; if he can still venture to insist that, without political action so as to recognize the civilized method of peaceful trial of strength, the *working class* (not a handful of men behind closed and barred doors) can organize itself for the revolution, and to insist by simply insisting; if he still does not see the difference between the power that a political body (a body recognizing the peaceful method of trial of strength) enjoys, by the mere fact of its civilized posture, to force the capitalist class to draw in its horns against it, and the contrary power which a body, that preaches physical force only, does, by the mere fact of its own uncivilized posture, suicidally exert to furnish that same capitalist class a welcome excuse to draw out and sharpen its horns against it; if he still does not see that, and can only consider "funny" the arguments of those who do see, explain, and declare the difference; if he still is so confused on the subject at issue that he perceives not the radical difference between a "strike" and a "general strike"; if he still is so reckless as to repeat, wholly without verification of the charge, such slander against the integrity of Iglesias and Vandervelde, as he hurls at them and insinuates indiscriminately against all other Socialist political parties, is satisfied with merely stating the source from which he borrows his slanderous conclusion, is ready to appear as a swallower of the untested charge of somebody else, and ventures to make such a sequence the basis of his stand; if notwithstanding his contribution is dated as late as February 7, months after the discussion started, and enjoying better opportunities than the average worker, whom he addresses in behalf of the Industrial Workers of the World, Kiefe himself is found guilty of their foibles, himself comes back with retorts that prove he still is muddled, still remains tangled in previous misconceptions, still continues stuffed with prejudices, and still has failed to learn the lesson that reckless accusation unaccompanied with even a vestige of evidence, can only work against the unification of the working class—if this is thus, Kiefe should not despair of the "dullards".

Taking up Kiefe's statements seriatim we shall rapidly run through them.

"Parliamentary" action is not "political" action. Without "political action," true enough, there could be no "parliamentary" action. But the latter need not follow the former. For instance. There was a campaigning and election for delegates to last year's convention of the Industrial Workers of the World. Some of the delegates tried to parliamentarize at the convention. Those were the ones who favored compromise with treason and corruption. The revolutionists refused to "parliamentarize". They stood to their guns. They neither compromised nor bolted, and they triumphed.

Superfluous to heap up further proof that a body that organizes for war only can expect to remain unbattered by the capitalist, from above, or unscuttled by the McParland "agents provocateurs," or their kindred the Dumases and Petriellas, from below. The style of argument adopted by the woman who *insisted* against her husband that a knife was a pair of scissors, and who, when finally ducked under water, stuck out her arm, and with her fingers made the motion of scissors, will not stead in the discussions of the labor movement - least of all by folks who evade a direct answer to a pointed, legitimate and fair question.

If the ballot, an acquisition of civilization for peaceful trial of strength, is a concession from the capitalist class, then all other conquests of civilization are concessions, *the right to organize economically included*. If it is "funny" to utilize the concession of political action, it must be side-splitting for any inflexible non-accepter of concessions to start Unions. Consequently, if "funny" is the claim that the capitalist class should "allow a political party such as the S.L.P." but will not tolerate an organization that repudiates the civilized method of trial of strength, if that claim is "funny," then roars-provoking must be the hint that the S.L.P. and all Socialist political bodies indiscriminately are in the pay of the capitalist class.

The organizing for the ordinary strike is no social act; the organizing for the general uprising of the working class is an act of high social significance. The latter is a political act in that its purpose is the remodeling of society. Consequently, though "physical force," after a fashion, rather than the "ballot," is the means for the trial of strength in ordinary strikes, civilization does not condemn the Union that organizes for such "physical" demonstration. In the instance of the so-called "general strike" (a most infelicitous and contradictory term in the mouths of those who mean the dispossession of the capitalist class) the union that organizes for that to the tune of "down with political action!" would today, in America, tactlessly and uselessly bring down upon itself the condemnation of civilization.

Walter Arnold libeled Iglesias and Vandervelde. As to the latter, *The People* has more than once expressed its opposition to his methods. To suspect his integrity, however one may suspect his judgment, is gratuitous insult. As to Iglesias, the gratuitousness of the insult is still crasser. Spanish conditions are among the most backward. Difficult is there the part of the revolutionist. So difficult that suffering has bred unreasoning rage in many heads and breasts. Not even of these would it be fair to say they "blinded the workers" by "some kind of agreement," although they have more than once led the workers to useless slaughter - and then themselves escaped over the mountains into France, or over the water to Italy. The charge that Iglesias "blinded the workers" by "some kind of agreement" is an unqualified libel.

- Ed. *The People*.

Eleventh letter, By Charles Rice, New York

The controversial columns "As to Politics" have proved intensely interesting and suggestive even to workers outside of the ranks of the Socialist Labor Party or the Industrial Workers of the World. Quite a notable element, ever growing numerically, of the Socialist party men, members as well as non-members (the writer among them) are on the point of turning a new leaf in Socialist theory and tactics. Many of us are disgusted with the untenable, double-faced hobnobbing of the Socialist party organizations and its prominents (a la Hanford, Hoehn, etc.) with the A.F. of L., not to speak of campaigning methods frequently resorted to by the Socialist party in different States that nauseate by their stench of the Rep-Dem vote-catching. We are now taking stock of our traditional parliamentarian Socialism and are looking around us for a new light.

I am confident that I voice the sense of a great number of Socialist party members and sympathizers in propounding the following questions for our especial benefit:

I. What is the exact position of the *Daily People* on the question of so-called political action in connection with a class-conscious labor consolidation of the Industrial Workers of the World type? So far, unfortunately, we have not been able to cull from the columns of The People a *definite* and *exhaustive* exposition of *The People*'s attitude on this head, an exposition *definite* as to the terms involved (e.g. "political action") and as to practical steps to carry out that attitude. Let the Editor take the trouble to give an exhaustive statement of all that his position implies, taking care to *define* preliminarily *every doubtful,* or involved, or ambiguous term or expression, and assuming nothing for granted until he has covered *this* part of his work (i.e., definition) and he will have cleared the way for a much more effective and beneficial discussion of this question of the utmost importance to all wage slaves.

II. Is the position taken by the *Daily People* on this question identical with that of the S.L.P. itself?

III. This query is put here simply as a hint to the Editor to take account of it in formulating his answer to the first query, as the answer to the third is necessarily involved in the answer to the first. The platform of the S.L.P. states that "The time is fast coming when, in the *natural course of social evolution* [italics are mine], this [capitalist] system, through the destructive action of its failure and crises, on the one hand, and the constructive tendencies of its trusts and other capitalist combinations, on the other hand, will have worked out its own downfall," and "We, therefore, call upon the wage workers of America to organize under the banner of the Socialist Labor Party into a class-conscious body, aware of its rights and determined to conquer them."

In view of this, the following queries under this head are legitimate:

(a.) *What* is there to conquer and from *whom* to conquer, if this system will *naturally* work out its own downfall?

(b.) If some conquering has to be done, who will do it — the Socialist Labor Party or the Industrial Workers of the World (through a political organization of its own)?

(c.) What shall we, in quest of new and certain light in our sea of doubts, meanwhile do? Shall we join the S.L.P., build it up, get ourselves drilled for the final "conquering" and then disband and walk over to the political organization that the Industrial Workers of the World will have by that time evolved?

(d.) Will the Industrial Workers of the World at all be likely to evolve such an organization if we persist in building up the S.L.P.? If we are to join the Industrial Workers of the World and to try to steer its course away from politics, that is, from endorsing any existing Socialist political organization, and at the same time band ourselves outside as a body of staunch S.L.P.-ites, then where will our Industrial Workers of the World political expression through an organization of its own come in?

(e.) Shall we not join the S.L.P., but stay in the S.P. and try to do what we can to counteract the semi-bourgeois tendencies and dubious methods of the Bergers, Wilshires, and their ilk, and wait till the Industrial Workers of the World *will* work out its own political machinery for "taking" and afterwards "holding" the means of wealth-production and distribution, as we will have to at any rate; to disband, to strip ourselves of our S.L.P. or S.P. garments in order to don the full revolutionary dress suit of the Industrial Workers of the World?

Answer

Answer to I: A rapid sketch of the social evolution that underlies the word "political" may aid in understanding the different shades of meaning that the word conveys.

Genesis 2:24, proclaims this maxim: "Therefore shall a man leave his father and his mother, and shall cleave unto his wife"; the same Genesis 3:16, proclaims this other maxim: "And thy desire shall be unto thy husband, and he shall rule over thee."

The two maxims are obviously contradictory. They can not stand abreast of each other. They were not reflected by the same, they were reflected by different social stages. The first was reflected by an earlier, the second by a later social stage. At the earlier social stage a male of one gens marrying a female of another gens (marriage was not allowed within the same gens) went over to and was absorbed by his wife's gens; at the later social stage it was the wife who left her own and passed over into her husband's gens. At the earlier social stage inheritance was in the female line; at the later social stage it was in the male line. At the earlier social stage property was communal, at the later social stage it became private.

Hand in hand with these changes went a series of institutional changes. "Government," "administration," or whatever name may be given that central guidance found indispensable in organization, was revolutionized. The original system, under which "government" rested upon the *people*, not upon *territory*, was reversed. "Government" resting upon *territory*, not upon the *people*, reached the latter only through the former, only as they came within the territorial property demarkation. This change of institutional "government" was in keeping with the change that property had undergone. Natural enough the institutional change culminated in the building of cities and the establishment of class-rule. The word "political" has its root in the Greek word for city. For fuller information read Lewis H. Morgan's "Ancient Society". It furnishes the ethnic groundwork for Socialism, and at the same time sheds light upon terminology.

Obedient to its origin, the word "political" has more than one application.

The word occurs, for instance, in the Socialist maxim: "The 'political' concept dominates the economic aspirations of a Union; hence no Union is worth the name whose economic aspirations are not dominated by Socialist thought." Sloven users of words have misconceived the meaning of the word "political" in the maxim; self-misled, they have come to cite the maxim as follows: "The political organization must dominate the economic organization." This is nonsense. Political organization neither does nor can dominate economic organization. Such a notion is at war with the Morgan-Marxian materialist conception of history and the error leads to grave false steps in tactics. The word "political" in the maxim, as correctly quoted, means the conception that a Union may have regarding the social structure. A Union whose conception of society is capitalistic will find its economic aspirations dominated accordingly. Ignorant of the wage slave nature of its membership, it will seek to deal with the employers as peers. At first blush this view also may be considered at war with the Morgan-Marxian principle of the material basis of thought. There is no contradiction. It is a fact, insisted upon by these scientists, that thought lingers behind newly formed and forming material bases. Indisputable is the fact that most of the economic efforts on the part of workingmen today—despite their material conditions, which no longer furnish a basis for "conservatism"—are conservative. The circumstance is only additional argument why such efforts are fatedly ineffective. On the other hand, a Union whose conception of society enlightens it on the wage slave status of its membership, together with the rest that thereby hangs, such a Union will not circumscribe itself to conservative aspirations. There is no economic organization without a "political" concept, consciously or unconsciously. The word "political" in that connection has no reference to voting. It simply means conception appertaining to social structure. In identical sense, the word "political" recurs in the term "political economy".

The word "political" occurs also in the expression "political government," or the "political State," etc. In these connections the word "political" is the equivalent of "class rule". "Political government" means class rule government. The social theory of Anarchy (the term is used in its strictly technical sense, as given by Anarchists themselves) presupposes government to be identical with class rule, or despotism. The theory is based upon a myth. It is not the myths of the Bible only that ethnology overthrows. It also overthrows the myths of Anarchy. Man appears on the stage of traceable or inferable history in organized society, and with government. Government was then wholly compatible with freedom. (See the address "Reform or Revolution") The social evolution and revolutions that culminated in the overthrow of the mother-right, the rise of private property, inheritance in the male line and territorial institutions, divided society into economic classes; government lost its former character of a function in co-operation, it became a means of oppression by property-holders. The building of cities being the culmination of the external development, government became "political". This "political government" means "class rule government," the "political State" means a social order reared upon the class system.

Finally a third order of connection, in which the word "political" recurs, appears in the term "political action". Here "political" means neither "appertaining to social structure," nor "class rule". At the International Socialist Congress of Zurich, 1893, Landauer, an

Anarchist of the bomb-throwing variety, demanded admission on the ground that the blowing up of capitalists was also "political action". He used the word "political" in the first of the two senses just considered. He was denied admission, and the delegate of the Socialist Labor Party contributed his vote towards the motion that kept Landauer out, and preserved for the term the technically historic meaning it had acquired. "Political action" is a purely technical expression. It means the peaceful trial of strength in social issues. As such, the term is generic. It embraces a number of things, that is, all the things necessary for its realization. It embraces primaries; conventions, or any other established method for the nomination of candidates for office in the "political," that is, the "class rule" government; campaigning, that is, agitation in favor of the principles and, of course candidates, of the party; voting (not private voting) but voting in the same place where the opponents vote; finally as a consequence, "parliamentary activity".

None of these details of "political action" has a doubtful or double meaning, except the last — "parliamentary activity."

Parliamentary activity is of two natures. One style of parliamentary activity takes place between opponents who have a common ground to stand upon. That sort of parliamentary activity is marked by "log-rolling," or "compromise". It is the parliamentary activity of free traders with protectionists, gold standard with silver standard men, pro and anti-Trust people — in short, elements who stand upon the common ground of the capitalist system. Another sort of parliamentary activity is that observed between opponents who have no common ground to stand upon. Such parliamentary activity is the only one permissible to the representatives of a party of Socialism in the parliament of a country, such as America, where feudalism is tracelessly abolished, and the two classes Capitalist and Proletarian — face each other. Such parliamentary activity does not tolerate "log-rolling". Such parliamentary activity, wherever obtainable, is, to a great extent, the continuation, upon the much more widely heard forum of parliament, of the agitation and education conducted by such a party on the forum of the stump during the campaign. Such parliamentary activity preaches and demands the revolution, the surrender of the capitalist class. Anything short of such activity by the elected candidates of a party of Socialism is "log-rolling"; "log-rolling" implies a common ground between the "log-rollers"; consequently the "log-rolling" Socialist must have shifted his ground to that of his capitalist opponent. Such a Socialist betrays the Working Class. A branch of what may be called "parliamentary activity" is the activity in executive offices. There also the principle above laid down is enforceable. Socialist incumbents may act only obedient to the principle that impossible is the attempt to represent two classes engaged in the conflict of the class war; that, consequently, they represent only one class — the Working Class.

Summing up "political action" by the revolutionary Working Class, the action means the endeavor to settle, by the peaceful method of trial of strength, the issue between the Working Class and the Capitalist Class. That issue demands the overthrow of the capitalist regimen, implies the razing to the ground of that peculiar structure of government that arose with the rising of cities from which it took its name — *political* government, class rule government. The overthrow of the capitalist regimen, in turn, means the restoration of administrative co-operation in production.

Answer to II: The discussion "As to Politics" started more than three months ago — *Daily People*, November 23, 1906. It was started with a letter from John Sandgren, California, a non-Party man, opposing political action and proposing that the S.L.P. and the S.P. both "break up camp". The same issue of *The People* contained *The People*'s answer. The principles, set up in that answer, are the principles that have been upheld throughout these more than three months.

That whatever member the S.L.P. may happen to put in charge of the editorial management of the Party's English organ may fail to voice the Party's views on this, or any other vital question that may spring up, is quite imaginable. *Un*-imaginable is that state of things under which such an S.L.P. Editor would not have been ousted long ago. The Party's constitution, together with the strict discipline that it enforces, would have suspended the Editor of *The People* within 48 hours after his first misstatement of the Party's position; and long before the discussion would have lasted three months and more, he would have been removed.

In view of this fact; in view of the further fact that not the slightest evidence of dissatisfaction has manifested itself on the part of the Party, but quite the reverse; the conclusion is justified that the position taken by *The People* in this question is the position of the S.L.P.

The word "identical" is here avoided because it is unnecessarily sweeping, although there is nothing to indicate that it would not be justified, and everything to warrant the belief that the word would fit the situation.

Answer to III: (a) What is there to conquer? Economic freedom, which involves all other freedoms.

From whom? - From the ruling class.

It does not follow that, because the *capitalist* system works out its own downfall, therefore class rule will have ceased.

It may be a question whether we are now under the capitalist system proper. Much may be said on the side of the theory that, if we are not yet under a different system, we are fast tending towards it. The downfall of capitalism from the causes indicated in the S.L.P. platform is by no means equivalent with the uprise of the Socialist Republic.

Readers of *The People* are recommended to read the booklet "Two Pages from Roman History," especially the first of the "Two Pages" in the latter third of which this very subject is handled in detail. The country is now moving into a social system to which the name "Capitalism," in its proper sense, is applying less and less. A monopoly period is now surging upward to which the designation "Plutocratic Feudalism" is the fitter term. It does not follow that, if the very Few are gathered on one side, and very Many are lumped on the other, the latter will necessarily swamp the former. They will do so only when they shall have understood their own revolutionary mission, and organized accordingly. Contrariwise—let the Working Class continue a sufficiently longer spell befuddled by the labor lieutenants of the Capitalist Class; confused by the clatter of pure and simple political Socialists on the one side, and the shrieks of pure and simple Physical Forcists, on the other; periodically swamped by the floods of misinformation with regard to things and men; and perpetually the victims of such sinister characters as the "Man of the Furred Cap" in Eugene Sue's master story "The Iron Trevet"; and let those within or in the suburbs of the Movement who are neither labor lieutenants of the Capitalist Class, nor pure and simple politicians, nor pure and simple clubbists, nor spreaders of false information, nor yet "Men of the Furred Cap," persist in the apathetic course of philosophically standing by and looking on, and fatuously expect to see things straighten up, instead of contributing emphatic share towards order — then, whatever periods of senseless (senseless because un-revolutionary and, therefore, merely riotous) upheavals may betide, the Many will sink to the depths of serfs, actual serfs of a plutocratic feudal glebe.

There will be everything to conquer — and from whom to conquer it.

Answer to III, (b) Proceeding from the belief that the conquering will be done without the country having first to go through the ordeal of Plutocratic Feudalism — proceeding from that belief, the conquering will be done by the Industrial Workers of the World, assisted, step by step, by a political party that blazons the Revolution; assisted, accordingly, by a body that expresses, in the only practical manner known, the civilized sentiment of the Industrial Workers of the World to seek a peaceful trial of strength.

What the name of that political party will be it is now too early to know. What the leading characteristics of that Party will be — *that* is knowable today. That political Party must demand the unconditional surrender of the Capitalist Class; that Party must be aware of the fact; and its every act must be in accord thereto, that the necessary evolution, which has to precede the evolutionary crisis known as "revolution," has already taken place in the womb of society in the shape of development and concentration of the means of production; consequently, that all talk about "evolution" as an excuse for bourgeois improvements, or "one thing at a time," is born either of hopeless stupidity, or of designing corruption, or of a constitutional poltroonery, from any one of which the Revolution can only expect betrayal at the critical moment; that Party must be *one* thing only to all men, *one* thing in all latitudes and longitudes of the land — no perfidy to principle under the guise of "autonomy"; that Party must have room within its camp for all the desirable social elements whose occupation excludes them from bona fide membership in the Industrial Workers of the World, and who attest their desirability, in point of sentiment and intellect, by standing unswervingly upon the class interests of the Working Class, and gladly submitting to the discipline such a Party requires; last, not least, and fundamentally to the above four features, that Party must recognize that the economic organization can no more be subject for "Neutral" treatment than the crew of a ship can be subject for "Neutral" treatment by the ship itself; that the Union, industrially organized and revolutionarily animated, is the embryo of future society, the sole constituency of the Congress of the future, the fated supplanter of "political government," hence the only available, and, withal, the all-sufficient physical power to enforce the Party's program.

The only Party that today promotes the Industrial Workers of the World program is the Socialist Labor Party. How things will shape themselves — whether the clear-headed and upright elements in the Socialist party will be able to attain control of and cleanse their own party and in that case whether that cleansed party will merge in the S.L.P., or, jointly with it, perfect a new party, under a new name; or whether those clear-headed and upright elements in the S.P. will fail within their own party, be absorbed in the S.L.P., and they, who alone impart whatever fiber and respect the S.P. today possesses and enjoys, having withdrawn and the old S.P. having inevitably collapsed in consequence, the Industrial Workers of the World will accept the S.L.P. or the newly-organized Party as its political reflex; or, as a third hypothesis, whether in any event the Industrial Workers of the World will prefer to cast its own political reflex, disentangled from all annoying reminiscences of past political conflicts — "all that, forsooth, rests on the knees of the gods."

Answer to III, (c.) and (e.): These two questions are too interdependent for separate treatment.

Since the founding of the Industrial Workers of the World, Fellow Worker Eugene V. Debs wrote a number of articles on the merits of the new organization, and the wrongfulness of the hostile posture held towards it by men of his own party, the S.P. Among these articles, two — the one originally published in the *Miner's Magazine*, October 25, 1905, and the other published in *The Worker*, July 28, 1906, both of which were reproduced in *The People* — are especially to the point. Debs ridiculed with pungent satire the "peculiar logic" that led those S.P. men to set up the theory of "boring from within" the American Federation of Labor and expect success, notwithstanding they justly reject the idea of "boring from within" the Democratic and Republican parties; and he correctly stigmatized association with the American Federation of Labor as "contamination". Debs was left unanswered. The only retort that would have turned the edge of the points he made—that retort the A-F-of-L-first-S-P-next men who dominate the S.P. did not dare to come out with. That retort was: "If you consider 'peculiar' the logic of expecting success from 'boring from within' the American Federation of Labor, and are of the conviction that association with the American Federation of Labor is 'contamination,' by what process of reason are you expecting success from 'boring from within' the S. P.?"

This retort embodies the answer to III, (c.) and (e.).

An organization is a structure. A steamer constructed for an excursion boat can not be transformed into a battleship. No amount of pruning, nursing and grafting will turn a sour apple tree into a tree that will bear oranges. The S.P. was not a scheme—though schemers may have joined it, and did. It arose obedient to a principle—the wrong principle that political action is all-sufficient, the obverse of which is the denial of the essential function of the Union in the achievement of the Social Revolution. Such a political structure can not be "bored from within". The nuisance can be abated only by its own decay which has visibly set in. The joining of, or staying in it by fresh and sound elements could have for its effect only to retard the politico-geologic and atmospheric conditions that doom the false political structure to decline and fall.

Otherwise with regard to the S.L.P. Whatever defects there may be in the Party, these defects can only be of secondary nature. They are not structural. On the fundamental issue of Unionism the Party is sound to the core. Those who would not waste their efforts should join it. By doing so, not only will they not retard, they would promote the politico-geologic and atmospheric conditions that will ripen the well-rounded, full-orbed revolutionary movement.

Should the third of the three hypotheses, considered under Answer III, (b), come to pass, then, as stated in the answer to the first Sandgren letter in this discussion, "the S.L.P. will 'break up camp' with a shout of joy if a body merging into its own ideal can be said to 'break up camp'".

Answer to III, (d.): The bulk of the answer under this head has been given under the heads of the answers to III, (b.), (c.) and (e.) — at least indirectly.

More than once has the remark been heard that it was unfortunate for the normal growth and development of the Industrial Workers of the World that there were two rival parties of Socialism in the field. Quite possibly Sandgren's position has its roots in that experience. To the obvious fact of the retarding effect upon the Industrial Workers of the World of the rivalry of these two parties probably is due his wish that they both "break up camp"; and probably hence, and not due to any conscious objection to political action, he has unwittingly flown to the extreme of the theoretical rejection of political action altogether.

However this may be, vain are all tears over facts. The only wise thing to do is to see the facts squarely in the face.

The two rival parties are in existence. Their rivalry proceeds from different conceptions regarding the function of the Union, and, inferentially, regarding the function of political action. The conception of the one, the S.L.P., tallies with that of the Industrial Workers of the World; the conception of the other, the S.P., is at variance with that of the Industrial Workers of the World. Inevitable was the experience that members of both parties should find themselves in the Industrial Workers of the World — members of the Socialist Labor Party, graduates from the Socialist Trade and Labor Alliance, entering the Industrial Workers of the World as ducks do a mill-pond; and members of the S.P., segregating into that party's component elements; one element, like ducks that had been hatched out by hens, fraternizing on and in their common element with their newly-found brothers from the S.L.P.; the other element, like hens who had hatched out ducks, cackling and fluttering and scolding, incensed at a thing that is contrary to their nature.

A comprehensive grasp of all these facts, and these confronting conditions, dictates the conclusion that the growth and full-orbed development of the Industrial Workers of the World could only be benefited, indeed, will be mightily subserved, by multiplying the "ducks" for the Industrial Workers of the World pond. Ducks are more naturally hatched by their kind; henneries are less safe. The S.L.P. is today the hatchery of revolutionists, and of the propagandists of the aims and methods of the revolution. Wisdom may be relied upon, in the fulness of time, to dictate the Industrial Workers of the

World's political expression an expression that will materialize under one or other of the three hypotheses advanced under Answer to III, (b).

-Ed. *The People*.

Supplementary

Since the closing of the discussion "As to Politics" was announced in these columns a correspondent, who prefers not to have his name published, sent in this question:

"I'm no 'pure and simple political Socialist,' as you will see; and I am no 'pure and simple physical forcist,' as you will also see. I believe with you that political action is necessary. The Labor Movement may not step down from the plane of civilized methods. If it did, none would be better suited than our capitalist masters. I hope I've set myself clear on that score. I also believe with you that the ballot is just so much paper thrown away, without the physical force to back it up, or, as you have neatly said, 'to enforce the Right that the ballot proclaims'. I've set myself clear on that score also, I hope.

"Now, what I want to know is this: Does it follow, as you seem to think, that we must have the Industrial Workers of the World, I mean an industrial Union, to supplement the ballot? I think not. I think we should concentrate our efforts, instead of dividing them. Why should we divide our efforts, and our money, and our time between a political and an economic organization? I'll watch the Letter Box."

The answer merits more thorough than off-hand treatment in the Letter-Box. Both the question and the answer will fitly supplement the discussion which closes in this issue with the answers to Rice's questions.

What our correspondent desires is to avoid a division of energy. A wise desire. Does his plan answer his desire? Evidently he fails to see that it does not. The only interpretation his plan admits of is the organizing of a military, of an armed force to back up the revolutionary ballot. The division of energy is not avoided. It is only transferred to an armed, instead of to an economic organization.

Seeing that, in either case, the evil of divided energies is incurred, and can not be escaped, the question resolves itself into this—which of the two organizations is it preferable to divide energies with, the economic or the military?

A military organization implies not one, or two, it implies a number of things. Bombs, explosives, generally, may be left out of the reckoning. They may be of incidental, but not of exclusive use by an organized force.

First of all powder is needed. The best of powder needs bullets and balls to do the business. The best of powder, bullets and balls are useless without guns. Nor are inferior guns of much avail when pitted against the up-to-date guns at the command of the capitalist class. The military organization of the revolutionary proletariat will need the most effective weapons. The question has often been asked from capitalist sources, Where will you get the money from to buy the railroads and the other capitalist plants? The question is silly. No one proposes, nor will there be any occasion, to "buy" those things. Not silly, however, but extremely pertinent, is the question, Where will the proletariat get the billions needed to purchase such a military equipment?

Suppose the billions be forthcoming. Weapons, in the hands of men unskilled in their use, are dangerous, primarily, to those who hold them. Numbers, undrilled in military evolutions, only stand in one another's way. Where and how could these numbers practice in the use of their arms, and in the military drill? Where and how could they do the two things in secret? In public, of course, it would be out of question.

Suppose, finally, that the problem of the billions were solved, and the still more insuperable problem of exercise and drill be overcome. *Suppose* the military organization of the proletariat took the field and triumphed. And then it would immediately have to dissolve. Not only will it not have been able to afford the incidental protection that the revolutionary Union could afford to the proletariat while getting ready, but all its implements, all the money that it did cost, all the tricks it will have learned, and the time consumed in learning them, will be absolutely lost. Its swords will have to be turned into pruning hooks, its guns into ploughshares; its knowledge to be unlearned.

How would things stand with the integrally organized Industrial Union?

First, its cost is trifling, positively within reach;

Secondly, every scrap of information it gathers while organizing is of permanent value;

Thirdly, it will be able to offer resistance to capitalist encroachments, and thereby to act as a breast-work for its members, while getting ready;

Fourthly, and most significant and determining of all, the day of its triumph will be the beginning of the full exercise of its functions — the administration of the productive forces of the Nation.

The fourth consideration is significant and determining. It is the consideration that Social Evolution points the finger to, dictating the course that the proletariat must take dictating its goal; dictating its methods; dictating its *means*. The proletariat, whose economic badge is poverty; the proletariat, whose badge, the first of all revolutionary classes, is economic impotence; for the benefit of that class, apparently treated so stepmotherly by Social Evolution, Social Evolution has wrought as it has wrought for none other. It has builded the smithy of capitalist industrial concentration; and, in keeping with the lofty mission of the Working Class to abolish class rule on earth, Social Evolution has gathered ready for the fashioning, not the implements of destruction, but the implements of future peace, withal the most potent weapon to clear the field of the capitalist despot — the *industrially ranked* toilers. The integrally organized Industrial Union is the weapon that Social Evolution places within the grasp of the proletariat as the means for their emancipation.

Division of energy being unavoidable, can there be any doubt what organization should divide the energies of the proletariat with their political organization — the military or the Industrial?

Syndicalism

Daily People, August 3, 1909

"*Syndicat*" is the French word for the English "Union." From that it would seem that "Syndicalism" must mean "Unionism." It does not. Due to one of those unaccountable freaks of language, "Syndicalism" has come to be understood everywhere as meaning a particular sort of "Unionism," to wit, a theory of economic organization with the revolutionary purpose of overthrowing capitalism by the specialized means of physical force.

Everybody, whose information is not below par, knows that, in order to understand an institution, a movement, or a document, the history of the country and of the times in the country of its birth must first be known. No play of Aristophanes can be properly appreciated without knowing the history of Greece; Don Quixote is a closed book, at any rate, merely a funny book, to those who do not know Spain; or, who could weigh the Civic Federation who knew nothing of American conditions? "Syndicalism," a word of French origin, reflects a thing of French birth. If these facts were kept in mind, then, on the one hand, the non-French Europeans, who denounce "Syndicalism" sweepingly, would curb their pens, and, on the other hand, the American would-be imitators of "Syndicalism" would realize that they but play the role of monkeys at the North Pole, or Polar bears under the tropics.

The point can be best understood by turning the telescope upon two typical representatives of the two seemingly opposed currents of the Movement in France—Guesde, the Anti-Syndicalist, and Lagardelle, or Herve, Pro-Syndicalists.

At Nancy, in 1907, Guesde expressed his estimate of the economic organization as a place whither men were attracted in search of immediate material and individually selfish (not therefor improper, or unnecessary) gain. The economic organization, according to him, was not and could not be a body animated with any high ideal, least of all with that loftiest of ideals, the Socialist Republic. That ideal could be pursued only by the political movement. Yet, before closing, Guesde completed his speech saying he by no means meant to deny that the hour for physical force would arrive. That hour was certain to arrive. Then the men of the party would seize the gun, and fall to. Stick a pin there.

Lagardelle, in his scholastic style, Herve, in his hammer and tongs way, interspersed with wit and satire, ridiculed the excessive expectations their opponents entertained from the political movement. That neither Lagardelle nor Herve repudiate political action appeared substantially from their being delegates to the convention of a political party. The burden of their song was, however, that the economic organization had the pre-eminent mission, and was pre-eminently called upon to gather within its fold the insurrectionary elements that would furnish the requisite physical force wherewith to knock down capitalist rule. Stick a pin, there, too.

At first blush, it would seem that the two tendencies are irreconcilable; that they are not off-shoots from a common trunk; that, consequently, one or other must be a freak affair. Not so. At this stage of maturity in the International Movement, there is no freak manifestation that does not, besides betraying intellectual weakness, generally betray also intellectual uncleanliness. The Guesde and the Lagardelle-Herve forces are too intellectually powerful and intellectually clean for either to be a freak-fraud affair, or to be even remotely tainted therewith. They are children of identical parentage: their principles will be found to resolve themselves into the identical practice.

A knowledge of French conditions makes this clear.

Herve stated in Stuttgart to the writer of this article that the factor that acts as the most powerful deterrent upon the ruling classes to push the proletariat to extremes, is the knowledge that "on the continent everyone knows how to handle a gun." The observation is pregnant with most pregnant conclusions, that bear directly upon "Syndicalism," and, not very much less directly upon the course that events dictate in other countries:

First. In a country where compulsory military service has not only made the people skillful in the handling of a gun, but has familiarized them with military tactics, an insurrectionary call to arms cannot be imagined to gather 50,000 men without the vast majority of them are readily organizable. From the militarily schooled mass the requisite military chief and lieutenants will spontaneously spring up, and be spontaneously acknowledged. The organized insurrectionary force would be on foot.

Second. In a country like France, where as yet there is no large capitalism to rank the proletariat into the battalions of an industrial insurrectionary organization, and thereby to furnish the Revolution, as an equivalent for a military force, with a mighty non-military engine of physical force, but where, on the other hand, compulsory military service has amply prepared the soil for militarily organized insurrection, and in which, moreover, national traditions lightly turn the thought to just such methods—in such a country the only real difference between the Guesde forces and the Lagardelle-Herve forces is that the latter utter the still unconscious sentiments of the former. It is a difference of importance, salutary to both. It rescues present Anti-Syndicalism from the possible danger of losing itself in the mystic mazes of what Marx called the "cretinism" (idiocy) of bourgeois parliamentarism, and it holds Syndicalism in check, lest it rush headlong, driven by premature impetuosity. It is a difference that marks the one somewhat unripe, the other somewhat too ripe. In fine, it is a difference that proves identity—the spot where both currents will and are bound eventually to merge.

Third. In all the other European countries, where, as in France, compulsory military service prepares the soil for militarily organized insurrection, but where, differently from France, temperament and traditions are other, thoughts of "Syndicalism" naturally seem wild— at present; and as naturally, will seem rational and be adopted in the ripeness of time. Present condemnation, provided the condemnation be not too sweeping, of "Syndicalism" from such quarters is imperative, even to those who may see beyond the present. Any other policy on their part would have no effect other than the harmful one of furnishing grist to the crack-brained mill of Anarchy.

Fourth. In a country like the United States, where, differently from France and other European countries, there is no compulsory military service to prepare the soil for militarily organized insurrection, but where, on the other hand and differently from everywhere else, large capitalism is in such bloom as to have ranked the proletariat into the battalions for an industrial insurrection, and thereby to have furnished the Revolution, as an equivalent for a military force, with a mighty non-military engine of physical force—in such a country Syndicalism has no place. In such a country, whosoever struts in the phraseology of Syndicalism is as ridiculous as a monkey would be in the frozen North, or a Polar bear in the wilds of the torrid zone. The social-political atmosphere makes them freak-frauds.

Fifth. Stripped of some casual expressions, "Syndicalism" is not "Industrial Unionism." Syndicalism lays hardly any stress—it cannot choose but fail to lay stress: the capitalist development in the land of its birth does not furnish it with the foundation for laying such stress—upon the *structure*, its main stress is laid upon the *function* of the economic organization—that function being, according to "Syndicalism," physical force. Industrial Unionism, on the contrary, being the product of American highly developed capitalism, lays main stress upon the *structure* of the economic organization; the *function* of the same—the overthrow of the Political State and the seizing of the reins of government as the Socialist or Industrial State— flowing, as a matter of course, from its structure.

Industrial Unionism

The Daily People Jan. 20, 1913

In these days, when the term "Industrial Unionism" is being played with fast and loose;

when, in some quarters, partly out of conviction, partly for revenue, "striking at the ballot box with an axe," theft, even murder, "sabotage," in short, is preached in its name;

when, at the National Councils of the A. F. of L., lip-service is rendered to it as a cloak under which to justify its practical denial by the advocacy and justification of scabbery, as was done at Rochester, this very year, by the Socialist Party man and International Typographical delegate Max Hayes;

when notoriety seekers strut in and thereby bedraggle its fair feathers;

when the bourgeois press, partly succumbing to the yellow streak that not a member thereof is wholly free from, partly in the interest of that confusion in which capitalist intellectuality sees the ultimate sheet-anchor of class rule, promotes, with lurid reports, "essays" and editorials, a popular misconception of the term;

at this season it is timely that the Socialist Labor Party, the organization which, more than any other, contributed in raising and finally planting, in 1905, the principle and structure of Industrialism, reassert what Industrial Unionism is, restate the problem and its import.

Capitalism is the last expression of class rule. The economic foundation of class rule is the private ownership of the necessaries for production. The social structure, or garb, of class rule is the political State—that social structure in which government is an organ separate and apart from production, with no vital function other than the maintenance of the supremacy of the ruling class.

The overthrow of class rule means the overthrow of the political State, and its substitution with the Industrial Social Order, under which the necessaries for production are collectively owned and operated by and for the people.

Goals determine methods. The goal of social evolution being the final overthrow of class rule, its methods must fit the goal.

As in nature, where optical illusions abound, and stand in the way of progress until cleared, so in society.

The fact of economic despotism by the ruling class raises, with some, the illusion that the economic organization and activity of the despotized working class is all-sufficient to remove the ills complained of.

The fact of political despotism by the ruling class raises, with others, the illusion that the political organization and activity of the despotized working class is all-sufficient to bring about redress.

The one-legged conclusion regarding economic organization and activity fatedly abuts, in the end, in pure and simple bombism, as exemplified in the A. F. of L., despite its Civic Federation and Militia of Christ affiliations, as well as by the anarcho-syndicalist so-called Chicago I.W.W.—the Bakuninism, in short, against which the genius of Marx struggled and warned.

The one-legged conclusion regarding political organization and activity as fatedly abuts, in the end, in pure and simple ballotism, as already numerously and lamentably exemplified in the Socialist Party—likewise struggled and warned against by Marx as "parliamentary idiocy."

Industrial Unionism, free from optical illusions, is clear upon the goal—the substitution of the political State with the Industrial

Government. Clearness of vision renders Industrial Unionism immune both to the Anarchist self-deceit of the "No government!" slogan, together with all the mischief that flows therefrom, and to the politician's "parliamentary idiocy" of looking to legislation for the overthrow of class rule.

The Industrial Union grasps the principle: "No government, no organization; no organization, no co-operative labor; no co-operative labor, no abundance for all without arduous toil, hence, no freedom." Hence, the Industrial Union aims at a democratically centralized government, accompanied by the democratically requisite "local self-rule."

The Industrial Union grasps the principle of the political State— central and local authorities disconnected from productive activity; and it grasps the requirement of the government of freedom—the central and local administrative authorities of the productive capabilities of the people.

The Industrial Union hearkens to the command of social evolution to cast the nation, and, with the nation, its government, in a mold different from the mold in which class rule casts nations and existing governments. While class rule casts the nation, and, with the nation, its government, in the mold of territory, Industrial Unionism casts the nation in the mold of useful occupations, and transforms the nation's government into the representations from these. Accordingly, Industrial Unionism organizes the useful occupations of the land into constituencies of future society.

In performing this all-embracing function, Industrial Unionism, the legitimate offspring of civilization, comes equipped with all the experience of the age.

Without indulging in the delusion that its progress will be a "dress parade"; and, knowing that its program carries in its fold that acute stage of all evolutionary processes known as revolution, the Industrial Union connects with the achievements of the revolutionary fathers of the country, the first to frame a constitution that denies the perpetuity of their own social system, and that, by its amendment clause, legalizes revolution. Connecting with that great achievement of the American revolution, fully aware that the revolution, which it is big with, being one that concerns the masses and that needs the masses for its execution, excludes the bare idea of conspiracy, and imperatively commands an open and above board agitational, educational and organizing activity; finally, its path lighted by the beacon tenet of Marx that none but the bona fide Union can set on foot the true political party of labor; Industrial Unionism bends its efforts to unite the working class upon the political as well as the industrial field — on the industrial field because, without the integrally organized union of the working class, the revolutionary act is impossible; on the political field, because on none other can be proclaimed the revolutionary purpose, without consciousness of which the Union is a rope of sand.

Industrial Unionism is the Socialist Republic in the making; and the goal once reached, the Industrial Union is the Socialist Republic in operation.

Accordingly, the Industrial Union is at once the battering ram with which to pound down the fortress of Capitalism, and the successor of the capitalist social structure itself.

CPSIA information can be obtained
at www.ICGtesting.com
Printed in the USA
LVHW080606020119
R14390800001B/R143908PG601761LVX3B/7/P